Contesting Cosmopolitan Moments in the Long Eighteenth Century

Edinburgh Critical Studies in Romanticism
Series Editors: Ian Duncan and Penny Fielding

Available Titles

A Feminine Enlightenment: British Women Writers and the Philosophy of Progress, 1759–1820
JoEllen DeLucia

Reinventing Liberty: Nation, Commerce and the Historical Novel from Walpole to Scott
Fiona Price

The Politics of Romanticism: The Social Contract and Literature
Zoe Beenstock

Radical Romantics: Prophets, Pirates, and the Space beyond Nation
Talissa J. Ford

Literature and Medicine in the Nineteenth-century Periodical Press: Blackwood's Edinburgh Magazine, *1817–1858*
Megan Coyer

Discovering the Footsteps of Time: Geological Travel Writing in Scotland, 1700–1820
Tom Furniss

The Dissolution of Character in Late Romanticism
Jonas Cope

Commemorating Peterloo: Violence, Resilience and Claim-making during the Romantic Era
Edited by Michael Demson and Regina Hewitt

Dialectics of Improvement: Scottish Romanticism, 1786–1831
Gerard Lee McKeever

Literary Manuscript Culture in Romantic Britain
Michelle Levy

Scottish Romanticism and Collective Memory in the British Atlantic
Kenneth McNeil

Romantic Periodicals in the Twenty-first Century: Eleven Case Studies from Blackwood's Edinburgh Magazine
Edited by Nicholas Mason and Tom Mole

Godwin and the Book: Imagining Media, 1783–1836
J. Louise McCray

Thomas De Quincey: Romanticism in Translation
Brecht de Groote

Romantic Environmental Sensibility: Nature, Class and Empire
Edited by Ve-Yin Tee

Romantic Pasts: History, Fiction and Feeling in Britain, 1790–1850
Porscha Fermanis

British Romanticism and Denmark
Cian Duffy

The Lady's Magazine (1770–1832) and the Making of Literary History
Jennie Batchelor

Mary Wollstonecraft: Cosmopolitan
Laura Kirkley

Romanticism and Consciousness, Revisited
Edited by Richard Sha and Joel Faflak

Remediating the 1820s
Edited by Jon Mee and Matthew Sangster

Romanticism and the Poetics of Orientation
Joey S. Kim

Romantic Women's Writing and Sexual Transgression
Edited by Kathryn Ready and David Sigler

Law, Equity and Romantic Writing: Seeking Justice in the Age of Revolutions
Edited by Michael Demson and Regina Hewitt

Kirkyard Romanticism: Death, Modernity and Scottish Literature in the Nineteenth Century
Sarah Sharp

Walter Scott on Monarchy: Royal Bodies and the Body Politic
Tara Ghoshal Wallace

Romanticism and Subversive Suicide: Human Rights, Existential Freedom and Biopower
Michelle Faubert

Contesting Cosmopolitan Moments in the Long Eighteenth Century
Enit Karafili Steiner

Visit our website at: www.edinburghuniversitypress.com/series/ECSR

Contesting Cosmopolitan Moments in the Long Eighteenth Century

Enit Karafili Steiner

EDINBURGH
University Press

Edinburgh University Press is one of the leading university presses in the UK. We publish academic books and journals in our selected subject areas across the humanities and social sciences, combining cutting-edge scholarship with high editorial and production values to produce academic works of lasting importance. For more information visit our website: edinburghuniversitypress.com

Edinburgh University Press Ltd
13 Infirmary Street
Edinburgh EH1 1LT

First published in hardback by Edinburgh University Press 2025

Typeset in 10.5/13pt Sabon LT Pro
by Cheshire Typesetting Ltd, Cuddington, Cheshire, and
printed and bound by CPI Group (UK) Ltd,
Croydon, CR0 4YY

A CIP record for this book is available from the British Library

ISBN 978 1 3995 2495 7 (hardback)
ISBN 978 1 3995 2496 4 (paperback)
ISBN 978 1 3995 2497 1 (webready PDF)
ISBN 978 1 3995 2498 8 (epub)

MIX
Paper | Supporting responsible forestry
FSC www.fsc.org FSC® C013604

This book is printed using paper from well-managed forests, recycling and other controlled sources

Contents

Acknowledgements

The completion of this book is a matchless opportunity to thank the people and institutions that made research and writing an enriching chapter of my life. My warmest gratitude goes to colleagues who lent precious advice at crucial moments: Martin Mühlheim, Rachel Falconer, Martine Hennard, Kevin Curran, Valérie Cossy, Kirsten Stirling and Andrew Reilly for expert note-checking. Since the early days of my employment at the University of Lausanne, the collegial and supportive spirit of the English Department, ever so often expressed in practical help, has been a reliable source of strength.

I also am indebted to Galin Tihanov for his profound knowledge in cosmopolitan philosophy and for extending cosmopolitan hospitality while I was a research fellow at the Queen Mary University of London. I will never have thanked Raphaela Hettlage enough for opening my eyes to what the future could hold. She introduced me to the prospects of the Swiss National Science Foundation, which generous grant gave the necessary impetus to this project at the take-off stage. The readers and editors at Edinburgh University Press have improved this book in more ways than I can say here; and researchers of the long eighteenth century and cosmopolitanism around the world have informed and inspired my own approach to this subject. Thinking beyond the boundaries of this book – like humans, books are no islands – makes me grateful for my former teachers Anne K. Mellor, Angela Esterhammer and Allen Reddick, whose exemplary scholarship and teaching ethos have left indelible impressions. In some ways, I continue to be their student.

A profound 'thank you' to my parents Luljeta Çakërri and Kujtim Karafili for planting in me that early association between books and friendship and for infinitely more. (Marilynne Robinson is right: 'There's so much to be grateful for, words are poor things.') Romy Nigg's loving wisdom and our little community of faith has sustained me while battling endometriosis. Thanks to them the bitter seeds of illness did not fructify.

Lea and Joshua, you give me unspeakable joy; I live, teach, write with you in mind.

Some of the material from Chapter 2 has appeared in a different form in 'Mary Wollstonecraft's "Love of Mankind" and Cosmopolitan Suffering in *Letters Written during a Short Residence in Sweden, Norway and Denmark*', *Studies in Romanticism*, vol. 58, no. 1, Spring 2019, pp. 3–26. Copyright © 2019 Trustees of Boston University. Published with permission by Johns Hopkins University Press.

A shorter version of Chapter 4 has appeared in '"Not to Abandon the Whole": Cosmopolitanism and Management in *The Travels of Mirza Abu Talib Khan* (1810)', *European Romantic Review*, vol. 29, no. 5, 2018, pp. 657–80. Reprinted by permission of the publisher Taylor & Francis.

Finally, many thanks to the National Gallery of Ireland for providing the cover image: Nathaniel Hone the Younger, Irish, 1831–1917. *A Wooded Point on the Banks of the River Nile, Egypt* 1892. Graphite and watercolour on paper. 11.9 × 19.4 cm. Bequeathed, Mrs Hone, The Artist's Widow, 1919 (Accessioned 1951). NGI.3389. Image, National Gallery of Ireland.

For all we are to each other, I dedicate this book to Jürg T. Steiner, my companion, my home.

For Jürg T. Steiner, for all this time together

All things are interwoven, and the bond that unites them is sacred, and hardly anything is alien to any other thing, for they have been ranged together and jointly ordered to form a common universe.

Marcus Aurelius, *Meditations* 59; VII.9

Introduction: What Does Cosmopolitanism Want?

> Signs are small measurable things, but interpretations are illimitable.
>
> Eliot, *Middlemarch* 40

Readers picking up this book may wonder about its title, as friends from various walks of life wondered upon learning that I was researching cosmopolitanism in eighteenth-century British literature. So frequent was the question 'what does cosmopolitanism mean?' that it became my coping strategy to prepare sentences illustrating the many faces of cosmopolitanism in everyday contexts: open-mindedness, acceptance towards foreigners, solicitude for the well-being of people from other nations and cultures, curiosity for and interest in multilingualism, world literature and arts, interfaith conversations, global human rights, sustainable travel cultures and so on. In all these attitudes lay the tendency to think and feel in inclusive terms, I'd add. There were sceptics who warily hinted that I had better choose a more recognisable word, perhaps transnational, multicultural or universal. Another warned that I was dealing with a dangerous word. As I detail in this Introduction, there are good reasons for preferring cosmopolitan instead. Sometimes glossing the Greek origins helped. The phrase 'citizen of the world' (*kosmopolitēs*) had appeal, as did those branches of ancient Greek and Roman philosophy that spoke of a common humanity which connected people of different ethnicities, places of birth or habitation, classes, religions, races and genders. And it not only connected but also endowed them with an inborn equal worth regardless of temporary, social hierarchies. The enslaved and their masters, women and men possessed the same inalienable worth. Inclusivity became tangible for my interlocutors when I stressed that cosmopolitanism, as both a philosophy and an attitude, developed to oppose the discrimination that strangers endured in ancient Athens for not being citizens of that city. Rather than emphasising someone's belonging to Athens, some Greek philosophers prioritised every person's belonging to the same worldwide community, a change of perspective that removed the barriers between long-standing citizens and newcomers. This explanation, though, did not prevent a friend from querying what a particular dialogue meant in the movie *Casablanca* (1942), when in response to the question 'What is your nationality?', the protagonist Rick quips, 'I'm a drunkard.' If cosmopolitanism meant the good things that I said it did, why then did another character declare: 'That makes Rick a citizen of the world'? An arresting question, it almost called for another book. Suffice to say that, at this point, I had the lingering suspicion that the eighteenth-century innovations of classical cosmopolitanism could shed some light on questions like this.

Such conversations came with epiphanies. I realised that, while approaching this theme as a twenty-first-century researcher, I was reflecting on three spatio-temporal moments of cosmopolitan philosophy: my own present, eighteenth-century Britain, and the ancient Greek and Roman civilisations where cosmopolitan thought and practice originated. Spanning circa 2,400 years, none of these moments is textually or intellectually straightforward. Therefore, wishing to be mindful of the long-standing sediment of principles associated with the attribute 'cosmopolitan', this book resists uncontextualised interpretations, hoping thus to allay a certain 'routinized self-satisfaction' of cosmopolitan studies (Robbins, *Perpetual War* 4). At the same time, with the increase of resignifications and the range of these studies' applicability in mind, I delineate the relevance of the long eighteenth century.

In the field of conceptual history, the long eighteenth century holds pride of place with the first mentions of 'cosmopolitanism'. In 1770, Joseph-Honoré Rémy's pamphlet *Le Cosmopolisme* proposed a distinct political philosophy. Using this French cognate in 1809, Samuel Taylor Coleridge focused on this philosophy's relationship to patriotism, an approach revisited by Thomas Carlyle in an 1828 essay of *The Edinburgh Review* (Coleridge, *Collected Works* 4: 323).[1] Carlyle seems to have been the one who ushered in the variant that prevailed in English: 'cosmopolitanism' (288). The addition of the suffix 'ism' to 'cosmopolitan' or 'cosmopolite' marked the birth of a concept. As a modifier, this suffix 'assembles and structures meanings and invests them with a specific form of temporality, a movement from the past, through the present, and into the future' that compels hermeneutic attention to 'historical and linguistic specificity' (Jordheim 315). The 'ism' performs what the adjective or noun 'cosmopolitan' cannot. It bestows the life of a concept, so that cosmopolitanism, like all concepts worth investigating, is characterised by the polysemy and definitional latitude created when concepts circulate across spatio-temporal contexts (Koselleck xxii). Hence, to research eighteenth-century cosmopolitan thought and practice is to investigate parts of the history that engendered the concept itself.

If illustrating cosmopolitan attitudes in popular culture may seem a surmountable difficulty, in cosmopolitan studies the inconclusiveness of the concept 'cosmopolitanism' has represented a stumbling block. While some begrudge the lack of a definitional centre, others counter that 'specifying cosmopolitanism positively and definitely is an uncosmopolitan thing to do', since the exclusions implemented by specification compromise the very principle of inclusivity at the core of cosmopolitan attitudes (Letteval 14; Pollock et al. 577). To remedy undecidability and eliminate doctrinising contentions, it has been suggested that the 'ism' added in the early nineteenth century be shed (Fine 451). My book, on the contrary, finds these contentions analytically and historically revealing. I take to heart the question of whether it is a cosmopolitan thing to claim that something is uncosmopolitan, therefore, undesired. This poses a question about the presence and role of critique in the cosmopolitan tradition. Considering that cosmopolitanism comes into being in its early Athenian days to neutralise Athens's xenophobia, the issue of critique demands a work of historico-philosophical precision whenever we invoke cosmopolitanism rather than impose the dismissal of the concept, its pasts and palimpsestic transmissions. Admittedly, no precision can lead us back to a pristine normative centre, and yearning for a centre of cosmopolitan norms seems even unhelpful. A better metaphor may be to think of standpoints and a cosmopolitan horizon. In this sense, this book considers how particular literary standpoints of eighteenth-century Britain respond to specific contemporary conditions, by consciously or unconsciously adapting the cosmopolitan heritage of classical predecessors. Without losing its worldwide and cross-temporal aspirations, eighteenth-century cosmopolitanism bears on investments which are bound to a specific time, place and history, so that in a double gesture its cosmopolitan values associate localised particulars with the horizon of the whole in which these particulars unfold.

My own literary approach pursues these questions: what common ground is shared collectively by human beings in a text, and how does this sharedness affect human conviviality and xenophobia (Vertovec and Cohen 1)? I call these questions cosmopolitan and not, say, universal to preserve a fertile distinctiveness. This is another way of saying that cosmopolitanism cannot be unproblematically equated with universalism or, for that matter, internationalism, transnationalism and multiculturalism. As Galin Tihanov's comparative procedure elucidates, cosmopolitanism differs from these siblings, at times even false friends. Although often used interchangeably with universalism, cosmopolitanism differs from universalism in that it 'does not obliterate but incorporates difference' (Tihanov 134). This incorporating orientation has etymological support: the Latin 'universe' meant 'turning around one, or one turn, or turned into one' (Hillman 89). The world as a universe involves centripetal movements towards a homogenising centre of 'universals, general principles', which implies a movement 'away from sensate particulars, which are the very concern of *kosmos*' and, therefore, of cosmopolitanism (Hillman 89). Neither is 'international' an unproblematic synonym for 'cosmopolitan' because, unlike the former, cosmopolitanism does not see in 'the nation and the nation state the sole embodiments and building blocks of that difference'; nor does it rest on 'a value-free descriptive framework' as transnationalism mostly does; and finally, cosmopolitanism opts for an 'interactive appreciation and assertion of otherness', privileging dialogue and engagement, unlike the potentially 'isolationist model of multiculturalism' (Tihanov 134). The existence of critique maintaining that this or that is an uncosmopolitan thing to do indicates that cosmopolitanism is not value-free but presupposes 'a shared (and accessible if not necessarily immediately transparent) human constitution that is being mobilized, or at least addressed, as the cosmopolitan project makes its case' (Tihanov 134).[2]

In this Introduction, I draw attention to cosmopolitan distinctiveness first in its ancient Greek and Roman contexts, then in some key adaptations it undergoes in the eighteenth century. I show a continuity between the modifications that cosmopolitan philosophy experiences in Greek and Roman contexts, the term's polysemy in the eighteenth century and milestones of philosophical scholarship such as Francis Hutcheson and James Moor's translation of Marcus Aurelius's *Meditations* and Elizabeth Carter's translation of Epictetus's extant work. I then explain why the notion of the 'moment', meaning both impact and a time unit, can capture the critical distinctiveness and latitude of cosmopolitan practice in eighteenth-century texts. After a brief dialogue with relevant eighteenth-century scholarship on cosmopolitanism, I provide an overview of this book's structure and a short orientation about the notion of the citizen in the early modern period and eighteenth century. The introduction, then, foregrounds salient reasons for approaching eighteenth-century cosmopolitanism as a shaping moment in the history of a tradition which was prone to modifications, adaptations and expansions from its genesis onwards.

Guiding Insights from Classical Cosmopolitanism

The literary moments examined in this book draw primarily on Stoic teaching related to cosmopolitanism. Although I benefit from Louisa Shea's indispensable *The Cynic Enlightenment*, the Cynics rarely feature in my analysis because far fewer documents of this school and of their conceptualisation of the *kosmopolitēs* survive. In contrast, the ongoing stream of editions of Stoic works and their inclusion in school and university curricula during the early modern period anticipate the relevance and appropriation of Stoic thought in the eighteenth century (Hill and Blazejak 18). We know, however, that both Cynic and Stoic cosmopolitanism maintain a worldwide shared human constitution. The Stoic Epictetus, for instance, teaches that because of this shared constitution every human being can live in a cosmopolitan way, first, by conceiving of our personal lives as being intricately related to all the lives with whom we cohabit on this planet, and second, by cultivating 'a sense of gratitude' for being constituted to partake in this planet-wide fellowship (*Discourses* 14; I.6.1).[3]

A providential cosmos, the vital enabler of life on earth, underlies Greek and Roman cosmopolitanism. In classical Greek, the word *kosmos* signifies order before signifying the world, and because order implies beauty, 'cosmos' also stands for adornment of a moral and aesthetic kind. Aesthetically, 'cosmos' translates into 'fitting order', whereas the moral evaluation implies good order, decent behaviour, as employed by Aeschylus in *Agamemnon* (458 BC). In this vein, Homer used the opposite term *kata kosmos* to convey the idea of bad, shameful arrangement. Hence, the Greek word comprehended the physical world as 'an orderly arrangement, a display of palpable things' to be 'conceived as a whole universe only because of its aesthetic and moral fittingness' (Hillman 88). It follows that from its inception cosmopolitanism combined two spaces, the world and the city (*cosmos* and *polis*). The ordered cosmos represented a constant point of reference, like a blueprint upon which humans should model their cities as communal places that were characterised by aesthetical fittingness and a sound moral order.

As we learn from Diogenes Laertius, Diogenes of Sinope (c. 412–323 BC) may have been the first to subordinate the order of the polis to that of the cosmos, when he shed his allegiance to Athens and proclaimed himself a cosmopolitan (*kosmopolitēs*), or a citizen of the cosmos. In other sources like Epictetus's lectures, assembled and published by his disciple Arrian around 108 AD, the idea originates with Socrates and not Diogenes of Sinope (*Discourses* 22; I.9.1). Cynic cosmopolitanism, derived from Diogenes, tends to negate citizenly obligations towards a human-made city, insisting that one's obligations are towards the world which is governed by natural and unimpeachable laws. Greek Stoics and their Roman successors adopted a more moderate position. They infused the Cynic tradition with more civic-mindedness, conceding to the polis the status of an 'imperfect analogue to the true 'cosmic polity' that, consequently, deserved some albeit not exclusive attention (Moles 119; Shea 86).[4] Both traditions advocated living according to nature (*eudaimonia*), but if self-sufficiency represented the most natural way of life for the Cynics, the Stoics emphasised that the very laws of the cosmos ordained each individual's duty to serve unshackled by the laws of one's own community of birth or residence. Unshackled service was the most natural way to live because, according to cosmic laws, humans were principally connected by bonds of humanity and not by bonds of convention, such as the fact that they happen to inhabit a certain city or geographical location. Consequently, to serve human beings while accepting that one cannot serve all of them equally well, is to live a cosmopolitan life, in other words, life according to nature. Although not dismissive of one's own polis, the Greek Stoics stressed that it was important not to limit service to people living there. For the Roman Stoics, although local citizenship was important, the cosmopolitan outlook remained one that opted for the service with the greatest benefits to human fellows among several options (Kleingeld and Brown). A third current that grew from and beyond the Cynic and Stoic traditions traversed the field of historiography, producing the new 'Universal History', which, differently from earlier historiography, did not record the events of disconnected places in isolation, but offered 'a view of history which was capable of giving an account of the entire new world opened up by the conquests of Alexander [the Great], of incorporating the experiences of the *barbaroi* as something less than exotic' (Mortley 1; see also Inglis and Robertson, 'Republican' 1–18). Universal History accounted for the connections that governed people's daily lives and sought to reflect on 'the international experience which they were living out', projecting a sense of unity in diversity (Mortley 1).

From the start, the question about the adequate relationship between service to the world and service to one's country was central in the debates and modifications that ensued. Noteworthily, since its early stages, the *kosmopolitēs* embodied a critical position: first, the Cynics critiqued the exclusionary demands of the (Athenian) city on citizens and outsiders, followed by the Stoics' critique of Athens's xenophobic politics but also of the Cynics' wholesale dismissal of Athens, and by the emergence of the Universal History that corrected isolated sense-making of a people's past, transfers of power and cultural practices. Apart from this critique, the philosophy nurturing Cynic and Stoic *kosmopolitēs* debated vigorously with other philosophical traditions. The political emergencies and foreign occupations, arising when the Macedonians disrupted Athenian democracy in 322 BC, stoked the urgency of philosophical debates. In Athens, where the Stoics met in that part of the agora called the painted porch (*stoa poikile*) because of its colourful murals, there were other active philosophical schools such as the Sceptics, Academics and Epicureans. Facing powerful competitors, while also winning over students from regions of the Mediterranean and Asia Minor, those meeting at the *stoa* extrapolated key consequences from the providential cosmic order that became fundamental to the three branches of their thought and praxis: ethics, logic and physics (study of nature). It was in this crucible of events and philosophical debates that emerged the figure of the *kosmopolitēs* as a 'radical' psychological portrait with ethical consequences for every aspect of human life (Richter 60). Each chapter in this book shows these consequences to be far-reaching and multifaceted.

The early history of Stoicism is also instructive because it sheds light on the inconclusiveness bemoaned by modern scholars, or the 'philosophical laxity' of cosmopolitan socio-psychology (McMurran 22). Students of classical cosmopolitanism stress the fragmentary transmission of Cynic and Stoic teaching since that allegedly first, frustratingly elliptic utterance – 'I am a cosmopolitan.' As Lisa Hill and Eden Blazejak succinctly note:

> Unlike Platonism or Aristotelianism, or even Epicureanism, Stoicism was not defined, or even dominated by a single individual. To complicate matters further, no complete works survive of any of the original Greek Stoics. Our knowledge of Greek Stoicism is therefore somewhat second-hand. (13)

Pluralistic beginnings and gaps in the 'intellectual odyssey' of Stoicism affect the line of transmission from Socrates or Diogenes to Zeno, Chrysippus, Panaetius, Posidonius, Plutarch's debates and Cicero's summaries of Stoic doctrine, the surviving writing of Seneca, the sparely available teaching of Mufonius Rufus and the lectures of his student Epictetus, Marcus Aurelius, Quintilian's absorption of the Stoic sage in his view of the good man (*vir bonus*) and appropriations of Stoic thought by early Christian theologians (Walzer 25; Rubiés 56). Fragmentation and heterogeneity linger even in the rhetorically diverse writings of Roman Stoics like Seneca, Epictetus and Marcus Aurelius, who lived within the comparatively short time span of approximately 180 years.

Theoretical latitude also results from continual processes of adaptation and innovation within the body of Stoic thought since Zeno of

Citium, who, after being tutored by the Cynic Crates, found the Stoic school in Athens around 301 BC. The figure of the cosmopolitan is particularly affected by the early Stoa's evolution. While the fragments available from Zeno's *Republic* imagine the ideal city, an allusion to Plato's *Republic*, to be exclusively populated by sages, and implicitly only these were deemed *kosmopolitēs*, his successor Chrysippus introduced an expansive innovation that called cosmopolitans all those 'who lived in the world as a universal city inhabited by rational beings regardless of their ethnic or national belongings' (Reinhardt xv).[5] Other adaptive modifications were introduced by Chrysippus's successors Diogenes of Babylon and Antipater of Tarsus in order to steel the school against the attacks of the Academics, disciples of the school founded by Plato (Reinhardt xv). In the present day, ongoing research on the early days of the Stoa continues to revise existing assumptions. Daniel Richter, for instance, provides a significant revision, demonstrating that previous research has overstated the abstract universalism of the early Stoa's political thought. This overemphasis has led to the failure of adequately contextualising 'Zeno's ideas about the unity of mankind as a response to contemporary Athenian debates over the status of "outsiders" within the *polis*' (Richter 61). At the level of doctrine, after Chrysippus, the Stoicism of the Middle Stoa undertook a modification that has since aligned Stoicism with practical philosophy. The mentorship of Panaetius of Rhodes (c. 185–110 BC) shifted the weight from idealised descriptions of the perfected philosopher to the daily life of the '*aspiring* sage' (Reinhardt xvi). Panaetius did no less than recast the Stoic *kosmopolitēs* as an apprentice and cosmopolitan living as an apprenticeship to be treated with tolerance towards one's own shortcomings. When Oliver Goldsmith calls Seneca's teaching practical philosophy, he echoes Panaetius's enduring modification. Emphasis on ongoing praxis rather than achieved sagehood loosened the grip of doctrinal fixity, opening the cosmopolitan habitus – 'the system of structured, structuring dispositions' which take shape in practice and are 'oriented towards practical functions' – to countless instances of adaptation and change (Bourdieu 52). As this book argues, British eighteenth-century literature reflects and expands on structuring dispositions that appear, at times only, loosely tethered to the figure of the citizen of the world.

Eighteenth-Century Reception and Polysemic Latitude

A more reputable word for 'looseness' is 'latitude'. To convey a sense of the challenges and innovations that latitude towards classical figures like the *kosmopolitēs* creates in texts of the long eighteenth century, I sketch here some telling complexities without aiming for an exhaustive survey.[6]

There are texts that explicitly summarise the ethical core of Stoic cosmopolitanism. A good example is Richard Cumberland's *De legibus naturae* (1672), which relates how, by viewing 'Man' not as 'absolute and unbound, but a Part of a certain Whole', the Stoics inferred the cosmopolitan disposition: 'As a Citizen of the World, and a part of the whole, Man is oblig'd to have no private Self-interest, or Advantage'; rather he 'should have no Motions nor desire any Thing, but with respect to the whole; to direct his whole Endeavour to the common Good, and to abstain from the contrary' (70, 71). Close to Cumberland's, Adam Smith's *Theory of Moral Sentiments* imparts to readers a working definition drawn from his understanding of the Stoic roots:

> Man, according to the Stoics, ought to regard himself, not as something separated and detached, but as a citizen of the world, a member of the vast commonwealth of nature. To the interest of this great community, he ought at all times to be willing that his own little interest should be sacrificed. (162)

Not always, however, is the philosophical genealogy traced as efficiently and didactically. More often than not, writers invoke the idea of world citizenship without rendering visible its belonging to Cynic or Stoic philosophy. Along with acts of implicit borrowings and reworkings, the definition varies while maintaining some affinities with the Stoic and/or Cynic *kosmopolitēs* and their transliterations. Less theoretically oriented, for instance, Percy Shelley's *Alastor* (1816) preserves the moral sense of the tradition by peremptorily declaring that those who are 'neither friends, nor lovers, nor fathers, nor citizens of the world, nor benefactors of their country' are 'morally dead' (v).

Next to texts where at least the phrase 'citizen of the world' serves as a shibboleth of sorts, many others require readers to bring pre-acquired knowledge to be able to spot a continuing line of thought. With neither recourse to the phrase nor its classical roots, Coleridge offers an alternative definition centred on 'benevolence'. Combining Smith's concept of sympathy and his exposition of Stoic cosmopolitanism mentioned above, Coleridge mounts an attack on the slave trade for destroying 'benevolence', which he defines as 'Natural Sympathy made permanent by an acquired Conviction, that the Interests of each and of all are one and the same' (*Collected Works* 2: 132). This acquired benevolence comes close to an ethical condition for cosmopolitan conviviality. Insistence on '(self-) interest', present in Cumberland, Smith and Coleridge, is the crux in the debate between those Enlightenment thinkers who maintain human beings' innate selfishness and others who capitalise on human sociability and moral sense. Often the latter view is derived from and considered to be a consequence of a well-intentioned, intelligent Creator God.

This premise governs Alexander Pope's popular *Essay on Man* (1733–34), which implicitly introduces an enduring cosmopolitan outlook to unwitting readers:

> God loves from whole to parts: but human soul
> Must rise from individual to the whole.
> Self-love but serves the virtuous mind to wake,
> As the small pebble stirs the peaceful lake;
> The centre mov'd, a circle straight succeeds,
> Another still, and still another spreads;
> Friends, parent, neighbour, first it will embrace;
> His country next; and next all human race;
> Wide and more wide, th' o'erflowings of the mind
> Take ev'ry creature in of ev'ry kind. (361–70)

A divinely ordained cosmos, shared by most Cynics and Stoics, sustains Pope's likening of the individual mind to a pebble at the centre of concentric circles of interests and affections. Despite Pope's Judaeo-Christian cosmology and lack of contextualising references to classical sources, his pebble metaphor is borrowed from the Stoic Hierocles, who makes it 'the task of a well-tempered man . . . to draw the circles together somehow towards the centre' (Ramelli lvi; see also Long and Sedley 1: 349). In the logic of *imitatio Dei*, Pope's poem democratises and ontologises this task by appointing it to the 'human soul' that 'must rise from individual to the whole'. Cosmopolitan living is the soul's calling. As we will see in Chapter 2, reliance on a providentially created soul is the launch pad for Wollstonecraft's cosmopolitanism. Popularised by Pope, Hierocles's circles are the hotly debated entry in Smith's last edition of *Theory of Moral Sentiments*, which complexly enmeshes ideas related to faith in a Christian providence with Stoic providence (Montes 51). We also encounter this providential order in Rousseau's conception of the cosmopolitan habitus, where Hierocles's circles are reinterpreted as barriers to be overcome by those 'few great cosmopolitan souls, who break through the imaginary barriers between peoples and, following the example of their sovereign creator, include the whole human race in their benevolence' (Rousseau, *Discourse on Inequality* 69). Echoing the book of Genesis, Rousseau has human souls live out their cosmopolitan potential by virtue of their being made in their Creator's image (*imago Dei*), a potential in step with Rousseau's view of Christianity as a cosmopolitan religion, in the sense that it has 'nothing exclusive in it, nothing local, nothing suited to one country rather than another' (Rousseau, *Letter* 147).

Albeit suggestive of a common denominator, these correspondences subtly involve their own complexities. Some complexities stem from the inflection of Stoic ideas by other philosophical schools as well as by individual innovations in eighteenth-century contexts. For example, recent research has delineated a stronger influence than assumed of the Stoic concept of *oikeiosis* on Smith's sympathy, which is further mingled with an understanding of the virtue of self-command that Smith borrows from a Socratic, and not a (uniquely) Stoic source (Montes 30–31). As for Rousseau, puzzling contradictions compel critics to come up with phrases like 'paradoxical cosmopolitan anti-cosmopolitanism' (Scott, 'Rousseau' 53). Similarly to Smith's sympathy, where a revitalisation of Stoic *oikeiosis* develops new facets, in Rousseau too, Stoic cosmopolitanism is so radically reinterpreted as to yield features 'peculiar' to Rousseau and dependent on his conception of human beings as essentially asocial, itself an un-Stoic premise (Scott, 'Rousseau' 54). Such break with the Stoic principle of human sociability provokes Rousseau to urge readers to '[d]istrust those cosmopolitans who go to great lengths in their books to discover duties they do not deign to fulfil around them' (*Emile* 39). As the antithesis of 'the cosmopolitan souls' cited above, the shadow of Rousseau's fickle intellectual cosmopolitan who 'loves the Tartars so as to be spared having to love his neighbours' is felt in later Romantic misgivings.

These are misgivings about the type of person who, in Amelia Opie's words, 'allowed individual suffering in her neighbourhood to pass unobserved and unrelieved', all the while philosophising about an imaginary 'unbounded love for the great family of the world' (3). Coleridge is another example of Romantic paradox. His 'On the Laws of Nations' (1810) first associates cosmopolitanism with a 'false Philosophy or mistaken Religion' that alienates the self from ties of kinship, only to later praise authentic cosmopolitanism for being 'genuine Philanthropy' and even 'the Nursling and Nurse of patriotic affection' (*Collected Works* 4: 323). Like Rousseau, who drives a wedge between cosmopolitan principle (if not lip service) and cosmopolitan action, Coleridge hastens to define the right (as opposed to erroneous) principles and effects of cosmopolitanism. Not only Coleridge but also Rousseau, with his accent on 'few cosmopolitan souls', concedes the existence of cases in which right principle agrees with praxis. Both seem more optimistic than Alexander of Aphrodisias, who believed the Stoic sage and practitioner of cosmopolitanism to be rarer than a phoenix (Celkyte 465).

If we privilege gauging family resemblances associated with eighteenth-century cosmopolitanism over the distillation of direct normative criteria, the *Encyclopédie ou Dictionnaire raisonné des* sciences, *des arts et des métiers* (1751–72) holds relevant insights. Its short entry 'Cosmopolite ou cosmopolitain' contains no fewer than four meanings and no explanations to aid readers in bringing these meanings in relation with each other:

> This name is used at times jokingly to mean a man who has no fixed domicile, or a man who is not a stranger anywhere. It comes from *κόσμος* world, and *πόλις* city.
>
> When an ancient philosopher was asked where he was from, he answered: I am cosmopolitan, that is, a citizen of the universe. I prefer, said another, my family to myself, my country to my family, and the human race to my country.[7]

The first meaning describes the jokingly critiqued vagrancy of the male traveller, a prototype given to an itinerant lifestyle reminiscent of the suspicious figure of the modern frequent flyer; the second depicts someone who does not feel foreign in any given geographical position and cultural community ('étranger nulle part'); the third and fourth meanings, conveyed anecdotally, are attributed to two anonymous philosophers: one of the two considers the universe his place of provenance, while the other values the entirety of humankind more than his own country, his family or even his own self.

The paratactic style of the entry creates a polysemy that is rendered baffling by the lack of historico-philosophical contextualisation: who are these philosophers? To which school of thought do they belong? Bafflement expands when the entry 'Cosmopolitain' is followed by the copiously glossed lemma '*cynique*', where the philosophy of Cynicism and its key figures are discussed, however, without references to the origins of the *kosmopolitēs*. Diderot, the author of this text, stresses the Cynic maxim: 'there is nothing that the sage considers strange'.[8] But he establishes no connection between this adage and the meanings listed under 'Cosmopolitain', although the maxim remains the greatest aspiration of both Cynic and Stoic cosmopolitan wisdom, memorable in Seneca's words: 'For the wise man, every place is his homeland' ('Consolation to Helvia', *Dialogues* 173; 9). Hence, 'Cosmopolitain ou cosmopolite' drifts unmoored in the history of ideas and European philosophy of the *Encyclopédie*. Readers are led to understand that the cosmopolitan can be a rootless individual but also someone capable of growing roots anywhere in the world; a person who acculturates easily (perhaps too easily if the jab means anything), a traveller, a philosopher, but also someone who reverses the circles of affections by preferring love of humankind over self-love. And the cosmopolitan could be more: the paratactic and anecdotal style, with its cumulative rather than conclusive nature, beckons further citations by sages, travellers and others. If George Eliot is right that 'Signs are small measurable things, but interpretations are illimitable' (*Middlemarch* 40), the *Encyclopédie* gives the cosmopolitan leave to be such a sign.

In fact, other qualities or traits of disposition appear scattered throughout the *Encyclopédie*. In the entry on the early seventeenth-century historiographer Joseph-Emmanuel Miniana, a citation appears in which Miniana characterises good historians as having a disposition that incites them to behave like 'citizen[s] of the world, by weighing everything' with utmost exactness and a superior love for the truth ('Valence').[9] In another anecdote, the entry 'Chantre' applauds the emperor Charlemagne for being a citizen of the world, that is, for possessing the kind of mindset that prevented him from believing that all that was good on earth could be found in his court ('Chantre').[10] The writers of the *Encyclopédie* themselves, in the preface to the third volume, apologetically declare that their work refrains from specialisation in any particular area, be it theology, literature, mathematics, jurisprudence or medical sciences, since any marked 'preference' and 'predilection' for particular domains would undermine the *Encyclopédie*'s commitment to a cosmopolitan type of erudition. In this context, the attribute 'cosmopolitan' conveys egalitarian devotion to the ambit of human knowledge production.

Several meanings propagated by the *Encyclopédie* persist later in the eighteenth century. I offer here three instances that, despite notable differences, resonate with some of the above-mentioned meanings. Onésime Henri de Loos's *Diadème des sages, ou Démonstration de la nature inférieure* (1781) resorts to parataxis to introduce its author as 'Phylantropos, Citizen of the World'. Qualifying the pseudonym Phylantropos, De Loos's citizen of the world embodies a mentality that resists the myopic propensity of human beings to be attentive to whatever is closest to them. De Loos insists that, if we want to learn about our own nature, or as Kant exhorts, dare to know (*sapere aude*), such myopic occupation is but 'a feeble resource' (vi). The citizen of the world, then, promotes an expansive outlook complemented by a desire not to restrict knowledge to one's immediate entourage but to distribute it philanthropically (out of a love for humankind) wherever such knowledge is absent. As for the *Encyclopédie*'s sense of intellectual impartiality, it resurfaces as late as 1889 in the gazette *Le Cosmopolite: Aix-les Bain la gazette* (19–21 June 1889), which, like the eponymous cosmopolitan, is independent by birth and will remain faithful to the impartiality it has adopted as its line of behaviour. Convinced that the better is wrongly denigrated as the enemy of the good, *Le Cosmopolite*'s goal, like that of Panaetius's aspiring sage, is 'always to do better'.[11]

The idea of egalitarian rather than partial commitment is maintained even in a satiric representation of the cosmopolite. In the aftermath of the July Revolution of 1830, the French daily newspaper *Figaro* of 10 December 1833 saw in the cosmopolite a somewhat mystified alternative to the revolutionary 'busingot', the young man of radical democratic beliefs). Cosmopolitan mentality and lifestyle seem able to multiply 'furiously', even to 'incarnate the universe', by belonging everywhere and partaking in singular local mores as these are practised all over the globe. The satirist calls the miraculous adaptability of the cosmopolite 'incommensurable', referring to this man who 'is everything without being nothing' ('un homme qui est tout, sans être rien'). Not aloof to political investment, the cosmopolite, however, avoids partisanship. The very raillery with which he treats all political parties is symptomatic of his poised involvement. *Figaro*'s cosmopolite has no respect for pomp and rank, giving the same treatment to the rich and the poor. While some traces of Cynic and Stoic cosmopolitanism survive here, the tide of the article turns to caricatures of Epicurean hedonism, when its cosmopolite would rather be on the lookout for occasional adultery than care for imaginative literature. An outgrowth of what *Figaro* calls 'our modern society', this cosmopolite is an indispensable chameleon, for he can insinuate himself everywhere, as situations demand: he can be a gallant dandy, a skilled dancer or a philosopher. His masculinity appears to be unstably defined because as a uniter of both sexes, he can also be androgynous. Yet there is one limit to cosmopolitan incommensurability: the cosmopolite can hardly be a woman. In the satirist's circular logic, 'une cosmopolite femelle serait par trop singulière'. As Chapters 2 and 3 in this book show, this limitation is not the uncontested representative of the long eighteenth century.

Although a work of influential learning, then, the *Encyclopédie* provided readers with varied performances of cosmopolitanism rather than a firm definitional centre. I think the *Encyclopédie* needs to be approached as an intellectual endeavour that does not passively record existing meanings but actively shapes and steers them, prising open several paths in which the cosmopolitan ethos can make its distinctive mark. The *Encyclopédie*'s meanings and performances of cosmopolitanism cultivate a family resemblance by referring to cosmopolitanism as a set of habits and convictions, a specific yet incommensurable habitus. Even in the absence of a complete exposition of constitutive behaviours and beliefs, whether the object in question is one's abode, customs, learning or partisanships, the *Encyclopédie* largely propagates the cosmopolitan habitus as a type that favours adaptability over fixity. This adaptability gestures towards another underlying resemblance: the cosmopolitan postulation that partiality to one's immediate interests (abode, customs, learning, partisanships, etc.) is not exhaustive of the human capacity to develop – Coleridge uses the word 'acquire' – negative and positive virtues, that is, avoidance of injury and promotion of welfare for self and others (*Collected Works* 2: 132).

This postulation is a response to the issue raised before, a question bequeathed to early modern philosophy by debates recorded between ancient Stoics and Epicureans: are morality, moral judgement and moral institutions natural to humanity? They are not for Epicureans and neo-Epicureans like Thomas Hobbes, Samuel Pufendorf, Bernard Mandeville and David Hume, who regard morality as an artifice, a convention contrived to check human self-interest. Self-interest is central to Cumberland's and Smith's definitions of the citizen of the world because, unlike Epicureans, the Stoics hold morality to be innate, in fact, 'a divine gift', as do their followers: Cambridge Platonists like Benjamin Whichcote, John Smith, Ralph Cudworth, the Earl of Shaftesbury and Francis Hutcheson endorse 'a special moral sense as a feature of the mind' (Haakonssen xi). It is amid the revival of this controversy that, after their rediscovery in the Renaissance, Stoic positions and cosmopolitan thought regained a place of interest for philosophers, shaping schools of Western philosophy which have come to form important aspects of our daily lives: philosophies of rights and duties, of sociability and the mind, of utilitarianism, self-ownership, hospitality, pacifism and global justice. While these have drawn the attention of scholars like Hill and Blazejak, Shea, Agnew, Forman-Barzilai and more, I dwell here on two instructive eighteenth-century milestones in the transmission of Stoic translations to highlight some intricacies that accompanied this revived interest.

The first is the 1742 translation of Marcus Aurelius's *Meditations* by Francis Hutcheson, professor of moral theology at the University of Glasgow, and James Moor, university librarian and professor of Greek at Glasgow. Hutcheson and Moor's translation reveals the difficulties of transmitting ancient philosophy to contemporary readers. For their translation, they evaluated four versions of *Meditations*: Thomas Gataker's 1697 monumental Latin translation of the original Greek of Marcus Aurelius; the translations into English by Merci Casaubon in 1634 and Jeremy Collier in 1701 (the latter was reissued in 1714 and 1726); and an edition in Greek. Hutcheson and Moor wished to introduce a fresh style to readers of English that could represent the somewhat oxymoronic 'grand simplicity' of Marcus's Greek (Moor and

Silverthorne 12). In their search for a more appealing diction, Hutcheson and Moor dealt with the type of lexical and etymological subtleties that, once pursued, could usher in nuances that opened up new avenues of sense-making.[12] If style was an all-encompassing challenge, finding English words for Stoic concepts that could convey the appropriate philosophical dimensions of the Greek was a frequent difficulty. To ground Marcus's text in Stoic philosophy, Hutcheson and Moor also provided an excerpt from Gataker's foreword ('Praeloquim') in English which they titled 'The Maxims of the Stoics' and complemented their translation with annotations. These 'Maxims' circulated even among readers who had not read the entire translation.

Hutcheson and Moor's translation, heavily influenced by Marcus Aurelius, develops a type of Stoicism that impacts Hutcheson's own philosophy of moral sense and universal happiness and is distinct from the 'Ciceronian heritage' (Montes 51). This distinctiveness goes unexplored in *Cosmopolitanism and the Enlightenment* (2023), another study that draws overwhelmingly on Cicero's understanding of Stoic cosmopolitanism even while insisting on cosmopolitanism's '*long-durée* roots in the classical and humanistic moments' (Rubiés 55).[13] Differentiation from Ciceronian Stoicism, however, merits even more attention if we heed Goldsmith's observation that Cicero took great liberties as a translator, aiming for translations not of the 'letter' but of 'the spirit' (1: 131–35).[14] Even more so in his summaries of Stoic thinkers, Cicero assumes liberty of selection and interpretation when he admits that he approached his predecessors 'not as an expositor [of their ideas], but as is my custom, drawing from their fountains when and as it seems best, using my own judgment and discretion' (*On Duties* 4; I.6).

The second milestone in the eighteenth-century history of transmission of Stoic thought and its embedded cosmopolitanism is Elizabeth Carter's 1758 translation of Epictetus's discourses and lectures from Greek into English. Ten years in the making, this magisterial translation had an astoundingly long life, remaining the standard version for readers of English until the twentieth century. Epictetus may be the most widely read Stoic, enjoying dissemination in the Islamic world through Syriac Christians, and was a beloved source in Britain for female mavericks like Mary Astell, Mary Chudleigh and Mary Wortley Montagu. But it was Carter's translation that introduced the entirety of Epictetus's surviving thought to readers of English who were untrained in the classical languages (Clarke 58–59). Classical training was assumed by two earlier Greek-Latin editions: one appeared in the sixteenth century, and the other, by the clergyman John Upton, nearly two centuries later in 1739–41.[15] Carter shaped eighteenth-century adoptions and adaptations of Stoic view not only through her translation but also through interpretations of the Stoic tradition in her forty-page introduction and many explanatory footnotes. She found laudable aspects in Epictetus's propagation of Stoic sociability, in the 'excellent rules of self-government and social behaviour', in Stoic providential cosmology and 'its noble reliance on the Aid and Protection of Heaven' (Epictetus, *Works*, trans. Carter, 31). Stoic 'perfect Resignation and Submission to the divine Will,' when subordinated to 'Christian Reflections,' could be of great value despite the rare practicability of Stoic principles (Epictetus, *Works*, trans. Carter, 31).

Carter's edition proved a powerful conveyor and influencer of eighteenth-century Stoicism, particularly among Bluestocking fellows like Catherine Talbot and Catharine Macaulay. Critics have also traced Carter's influence in works by Wollstonecraft and Jane Austen (Johns 444; Hill and Blazejak 193–96). Notwithstanding her rejection of certain Stoic tenets such as those on suicide, Carter revived and deepened an early theologised compatibility between Stoicism and the Christianity established by Church Fathers like Clement, Origen, John Chrysostom and Augustine of Hippo as well as believers of the Eastern Church (Gill xxv). It would be hasty to dub Carter's Christianising adaptations as unambiguously conservative. Hermeneutic intelligence could turn compatibility into a critique of the status quo, as did Wollstonecraft's assiduous insistence on the rational soul (grounded simultaneously in the Stoic and Christian *logos*) as the ultimate divine intention not just for men but also for women. Subordinating all gendered conventions to this divine will, Wollstonecraft made the sexless nature of the soul continuous with the sexless education of male and female citizens.

Hutcheson and Moor's translation and trailblazing philosophy of moral sense together with Carter's effort to bridge discrepancies between Epictetus's principles and those of Christianity represent two eighteenth-century facets that compete with the predominantly Ciceronian heritage, for which Cicero continues to function as the spokesperson of Stoic thought, capable even of filling gaps and completing fragments. Consequently, the eighteenth century provides a wider spectrum of theoretical resignifications of cosmopolitan values than is often assumed. Because of this rich spectrum, the literature of the long eighteenth century and the relationship it bears to the non-unified body of classical Stoicism and to recent articulations in cosmopolitan studies are worth investigating in greater detail.

How this Book Dialogues with Previous Research

Polysemic latitude does not impose an impasse; nor does it warrant a neglect of conceptual pasts and contextualised working definitions. Rather, it seems that lack of contextualisation weakens influential approaches by Kwame Anthony Appiah, Robert Fine and Ulrich Beck (Jordheim 315). Scholars of eighteenth-century and Romantic studies are right to ask for greater precision that, by staking out cosmopolitan principles and hermeneutics, avoids mentions of cosmopolitanism as mere window dressing.[16] Anne K. Mellor succinctly queries 'How much "cosmopolitanism" justifies the use of the term in relation to either literary texts or to political positions' in the long eighteenth century and now ('Embodied Cosmopolitanism' 297). This question underpins the analytical efforts of the present study.

Earlier large-scale studies like Thomas Schlereth's pioneering *Cosmopolitan Ideal in Enlightenment Thought* (1977) bypassed Mellor's concern, yet helpfully limned the shadowy contours of a resilient tradition. To Schlereth's survey of the emergence of a class of European literati and of political and economic internationalism, Mellor proposed a localised 'embodied' kind of cosmopolitan ethos potentially at work in interfaith and interracial marriage. Prior to Mellor, Karen O'Brien's *Narratives of Enlightenment: Cosmopolitan History from Voltaire to Gibbon* (1997) excavated a cosmopolitan methodology in the historiography of Hume, Gibbon, Voltaire and other Scottish historians. Like the Universal History produced under the influence of Cynic and Stoic cosmopolitanism in the Hellenistic age, some eighteenth-century historiographies understood the place of the nation in connection to the larger network of European relations. In this vein, Adriana Craciun's *British Women Writers and the French Revolution: Citizens of the World* (2005) provided contextualising details of the cosmopolitan principles nestled in the 1790s human rights movement by British women writers in response to the revolution in France. Her study was followed by two important books. Michael Scrivener's *Cosmopolitan Ideal in the Age of Revolution and Reaction, 1776–1832* (2006) revised the assumption that cosmopolitanism rested with a (vaguely defined) elite, demonstrating that calls for the equality of marginalised groups in the public sphere defied an elitist circumscription of cosmopolitanism. A few years later, Esther Wohlgemut's *Romantic Cosmopolitanism* (2009) maintained that the period's cosmopolitanism evinced attention to local realities, to the nation and patriotism (3–4).

Several other established cosmopolitan typologies in Enlightenment Europe facilitate my work. I am indebted to Pauline Kleingeld's delineation of six varieties of cosmopolitanism in late eighteenth-century Germany: moral cosmopolitanism, international federative cosmopolitanism, cosmopolitan law, cultural cosmopolitanism, market cosmopolitanism and Romantic cosmopolitanism. Additionally, Margaret C. Jacobs's appreciation of 'cosmopolitanism as a form of virtue' practised along five axes (the axes of religion, science, markets, freemasons and revolution) in early modern Europe is also an invaluable influence (3). The eighteenth century features in the title of her book *Strangers Nowhere in the World*, drawn from one of the *Encyclopédie*'s most borrowed and circulated definitions. Cosmopolitanism 'as a form of virtue' permeates the different types delineated by Kleingeld and Jacobs, creating intersections between them, some of which are discussed in the following chapters.

This book also participates in a recent debate about the efficacity of Stoic cosmopolitanism in the eighteenth century, siding with scholars who defend the shaping impact of Stoicism. To elucidate my position, I address two contrasting views by Lois Peter Agnew and Mary Helen McMurran. Agnew contends that Stoic principles are invisibly entrenched yet rarely directly cited in the writings of eighteenth-century theoreticians who made these 'ancient ideas their own in responding to modern problems' like the emergence of a public sphere through print culture, notions of civic duty, social cohesiveness and instability (2, 17). McMurran, on the contrary, surmises that eighteenth-century writers 'could not reinvest in a freightless classical source and yet did not attach new, specific content to the terms' inherited by this source (32). The processes of adaptation, meticulously traced by Agnew, contradict McMurran's dismissal. They even deliver convincing proof that the 'Stoic roots in eighteenth-century rhetorical theories . . . challenge the alignment of the categories "ancient" and "modern" in the study of eighteenth-century ideas' (Agnew 16). For example, the revitalised adoption of the Stoic *sensus communis* into Scottish common-sense theory held in tension the scientific interests of the Enlightenment and the optimistic cosmology of Stoic thought, as did the aspiration for a civically minded citizenry and an inward-looking, improvement-seeking individual. Like Agnew, Jacob Risinger comments on 'the ease with which Stoic ideas could be abstracted from their more comprehensive system' at different moments of modernity that 'helped to ensure their survival and widespread influence' (99). Therefore, I do not take McMurran's deduction as proving Stoicism's inefficacity. For McMurran, in the absence of an explicit philosophical grounding and a broad distribution 'among a range of discourses', the Stoic notion of 'the cosmopolitan was nothing, or a nobody' (32). Yet Catherine Gallagher's *Nobody's Story* (1994) is a reminder of the fertile power of nobodiness in eighteenth-century print culture which, as I argue in this book, held unprecedented potential for everybody to be citizens of the world.

Scholarly disagreement makes us ponder the factors that might have favoured the ease of appropriation and survival of Stoic cosmopolitanism. As discussed above, two important factors are the fragmentary nature of the surviving material and the ongoing innovations from the earliest days of a tradition that was not dominated by one single figure. To these, we need to add the aspiration of Stoic teachers and students to attempt to *live* and not just *teach* or *philosophise* according to nature. This emphatic difference resonates in Epictetus's irony when he tells his interlocutors that being able to read Chrysippus on their own is no proof of progress (*Discourses* 11; I.4.5–12). Mere exposure to teaching does not guarantee wisdom. Rather, as for athletes, nothing but training can testify to the (relative) success of Stoic disciples. This is to say that, in contemplative and politically active Stoics (like Seneca or Marcus Aurelius), eighteenth-century writers met with the kind of theoretical latitude that worried far less about the transmission of an airtight theoretical system than about the trainee's imperfect yet indefatigable daily enactments. Because success could only be relative and shaped by constantly changing circumstances, Marcus Aurelius admonishes himself: 'You should not hope for Plato's ideal state, but be satisfied to make even the smallest advance, and regard such an outcome as nothing contemptible' (88; IX.29).[17] Poised between striving for virtue and accepting its incompleteness, Stoic ethics had the potential to attract anyone who possessed reason (*logos*), the principle governing the Stoic cosmos and its citizens.

On the heels of work by age-shaping philosophers like Francis Hutcheson, who mined the long-standing compatibility between Christianity and Stoicism to achieve 'a fusion of the two that had lasting impact on British moral theory and ultimately rhetoric', women, people of colour, foreigners and children could lay claim to reason and, therefore, to the rights and duties associated with world-citizenship at a given place and time in human history (Agnew 2). My study focuses on the expansive adaptability mediated by alternative personhoods such as non-European strangers, the woman-mother-philosopher, the mixed-race woman teacher, the solidary child of abolitionist culture and the disenchanted decolonial diplomat. Next to the aspiring male sage, traditionally the prototypical cosmopolitan, alternative personhoods contest the range of subject positions in the spirit of Seneca's advice that '[w]hat is hardened can be softened, what is narrow can be expanded' by enlarging rather than negating its antecedent principles ('On the Tranquillity of the Mind', *Dialogues* 128; 10). The 'contesting' of this book's title is, therefore, to be understood in the sense given by Samuel Johnson's *Dictionary*: 'to emulate', to 'imitate with hope of equality, or superior excellence'.[18] By contesting to imitate or improve, eighteenth-century cosmopolitanism positioned itself in defence of animal life and ecology, of local cultural plurality, worldwide benefits of knowledge, and anti-imperialist futures.

My preference for the philosophic notion of the 'moment' over unifying masterwords such as ideal, imagination, Enlightenment or Romanticism makes possible a different kind of capaciousness that combines the sense of time, impact and influence. In Hegel's dialectic, the word 'moment' (*der/das Moment*) captures that which ceases but also continues to be preserved (sublated, *aufgehoben*). Dialectically, the 'moment' deals with contradictions without nullifying the foundations that call forth those contradictions (Balibar et al. 686). Because of this dialectical possibility, I discuss the cultural labour of these case studies as moments of imperfect cosmopolitan living which do not cancel out cosmopolitan aspirations and afterlives. These moments unfold, end and are preserved, with the potential to engender other cosmopolitan moments. The 'moment' as an analytical tool conceptualises the proliferations and afterlives of cosmopolitan living persuasively argued by Laura Kirkley's discussion of 'the good death of the cosmopolitan idea' ('Bound in Amity to All' 121). Conceptually, the 'moment' refutes a teleological understanding of a worldwide human community that grows steadily and reliably more cosmopolitan. It rather accounts for bouts of regression and progression, but also upholds the possibility for 'cosmopolitanism to come' (Derrida, *Of Hospitality* 15). Relying on this understanding of the moment provides a way to map out together classical, eighteenth-century and postmodern insights about cosmopolitan philosophy and living. It is this study's conviction that eighteenth-century articulations of cosmopolitanism echo in recent postcolonial, gender and environmental criticism, indicating persistent impacts that render the investigation of eighteenth-century contexts indispensable.

The Structure of this Book

To evidence persistence, I have selected eighteenth-century works which unfold a fuller presence when read in light of what has survived from Stoic cosmopolitanism and when put in touch with contemporary theories of alterity. Because theory does not enforce abstraction, each chapter addresses localised micro realities (foreignness, friendship, dietary habits, ambition, discrimination, disenchantment) and macro realities (revolutionary enthusiasm, industrialisation, war, illness, abuse of animal and earth life). I not only view these eighteenth-century works as being 'grounded in time and space, whatever their universalistic aspirations', but also my own understanding of cosmopolitanism as being moulded by contemporary theorists of alterity (Holton 71). To be able to hear eighteenth-century aspiring and apprenticing cosmopolitans converse with their localised realities, I must be as aware as possible of the realities that constitute my own hearing. This is a situational grounding that befits Panaetius's turn to the specific realities of a lived philosophy just as much as it acknowledges the discrepancy noted by Rousseau and others between cosmopolitan doxology and praxis.

The first two chapters of this book are concerned with the kind and extent of influence local customs are to play on worldwide values. Chapter 1 opens with Goldsmith's *Citizen of the World*, taking a cue from James Watt's remark that Goldsmith's 'appeal to the idea of the cosmopolitan, remains shadowed by a sceptical commentary on the content and meaning of this elusive term' (73).[19] I examine how *Citizen*'s impersonation exploits the elusive polysemy of the phrase 'citizen of the world' by weaving a syncretic web of knowledge from European, Persian and Confucian traditions. This syncretism opens the epistemic field of cosmopolitanism towards Eurasian expressions of knowing and living – to be further expanded in Chapter 4 – and anticipates like-minded postcolonial approaches. Goldsmith's novel mobilises syncretism in its call for justice towards animal life, a call that enlists Zoroastrian lore, Plutarch's philosophical vegetarianism and Seneca's juridical concept of *commune ius animantium* (common right of animated/living beings). Significantly, Goldsmith's text places concerns for animal life under the care of cosmopolitan citizenship, relating them to British capitalist imperialism half a century before the 1822 parliamentary 'Act to Prevent the Cruel and Improper Treatment of Cattle'. At the same time, attuned to Confucianism, Goldsmith refrains from imposing vegetarianism as a universal imperative, showing tolerance and respect for certain local mores in his cosmopolitan defence of animal life. As we will see, this position aligns the novel with a particular brand of recent ecocriticism.

The relationship between local and planetary life is the organising element in Wollstonecraft's *Short Residence in Sweden, Norway and Denmark* (1796) discussed in Chapter 2. In words reminiscent of Marcus Aurelius, Wollstonecraft gives primacy to the cultivation of 'affection for the human race', delineating as a method to achieve this goal the 'growth of each particular soil, and the gradual fruit of the ripening understanding of the nation' (*Short Residence* 198). In contribution to a recent line of research that focuses not only on Wollstonecraft's 'excavation of Stoic moral sentimentalism' but also her 'critique of its exclusions', the chapter argues that Wollstonecraft corrects the gender scepticism of Seneca's, Epictetus's and Goldsmith's male characters (Risinger 56). Like Goldsmith's *Citizen*, Wollstonecraft's narration wrestles not merely with personal melancholia, but also with social despair. To counteract despair, her narrative draws argumentative and psychic strength from the sociable ontology conveyed by the Stoic concept of *oikeiosis* that Hutcheson and other philosophers revitalised against Hobbes's and Mandeville's emphasis on a self-interested humanity. This belief distinguishes Wollstonecraft's appropriation of Stoicism from Kant's, a distinction that creates differing ramifications and concerns. Poignantly, the gender bias that Wollstonecraft challenged survives in current scholarship: the essays in *Cosmopolitanism and the Enlightenment* (2023) frequently refer to Kant, overlooking the originality of Wollstonecraft's thought even in a chapter devoted to gender.[20] Wollstonecraft follows and innovates Stoic legacy not least by enacting the meditative exercise *futurorum malorum præmeditatio* (pre-deliberating a bad future). Her innovative environmentalist critique of human technological progress shares common ground with twenty-first-century debates on 'eco-cosmopolitanism' and 'planetarity' (Heise; Spivak, *Death*).

Chapters 3 and 4 explore the alterity of personhood and cosmopolitan ethics lived and professed by a fictional mixed-race woman and an Indo-Persian Muslim traveller. Chapter 3 argues that, to meet the challenges posed by slave-labour economies, eighteenth-century literature, especially literature produced by Quaker writers and printers, performs expansions of classical cosmopolitanism that reach into children's interpretations of racialised relationships. I comparatively read texts that stage the white child's unlearning of discriminatory, hostile attitudes towards racial others. In these scenes, positive passions (*eupathéia*) like trust and friendliness supersede negative ones (*pathé*) like fear or disgust. Such acts of substitution both evoke Stoic psycho-pedagogy and radicalise Stoic aversion to slavery with abolitionist arguments pertaining to the education of children as active friends of humans of every race and provenance. Postcolonial research maintains that anti-imperialist resistance can result from the 'affective cosmopolitanism' practised in interracial friendships, as was the case in colonial India (Gandhi 17). This view acquires depth and support from the claim that eighteenth-century cosmopolitan abolitionism seized upon such a form of resistance, deploying and modifying Stoic legacy. Unlike classical Stoics, who think of slavery as an 'unnatural institution' (in contrast to Aristotle or Plato), but also, by considering it merely as an external circumstance, downplay its damaging impact on human flourishing, a dominant strand of white and black abolitionism forcefully maintains that slavery creates circumstances detrimental to human physical and moral development. This position ends up correcting what prevented Greco-Roman Stoics from articulating a socio-legal programme against slavery.

In Chapter 4, the 1810 translated travelogue of Abu Talib Khan intersects with the other chapters in several ways. The travelogue shares similar cosmopolitan positions with the other texts in relation to knowledge and history and, like them, mounts a multifaceted critique of external socio-economic circumstances. Censure, already present in classical cosmopolitanism, can and has been interpreted by decolonial scholars as harbouring the desire to 'manage' the other (Mignolo, 'Many Faces'). However, the act of translation by Charles Stewart and the very content of Abu Talib's *Travels* resist simple juxtapositions between management and cosmopolitan conviviality. Both Stewart's and Abu Talib's managerial censure is motivated by a sense of cosmopolitan duty to promote a wider dissemination of knowledge within the Eurasian paradigm of 'connected histories' (Subrahmanyam). Delineating within this paradigm an Islamic cosmopolitanism which is not the West's other, the chapter traces an opening of Western cosmopolitan thought towards Eastern and, in Abu Talib's case, specifically Muslim philosophies. The *Travels*' proverbial resolve not to despair in the face of incomplete or imperfect cosmopolitan practices reveals an agreement between Abu Talib and Epictetus which can be explained within 'the connected histories' propagated by the Eurasian spread of Epictetus's teaching.

Chapter 5 is devoted to the relationship between cosmopolitanism and imperial thinking and practice, an issue traversing all works discussed in the previous chapters. I choose Mary Shelley's *The Last Man* as a text that dissolves a symbiotic bond between cosmopolitan mentality and imperial expansion expounded as early as in Plutarch's historiography of Alexander the Great. Combining insights from Seneca, Volney and Scottish philosophers, the emphasis placed on a psychological approach to the passions correlates human psychology with the mimetic attraction of power adduced in civilisational narratives of imperial conquest like Virgil's *Aeneid*. At a politico-philosophical level, this emphasis, alluding to the Roman notion of 'just war', unmasks seemingly cosmopolitan warfare as a mere pretext for imperial aggrandisement. The novel's distrust of 'just war' is distinctly decolonial because it incrementally stages what J. E. Muñoz calls 'disidentification' with the long-standing model of empire-building couched in the trope of *translatio imperii*. The chapter stresses the dissident role of the Sibyl's prophecy in book 6 of Virgil's *Aeneid*, through which Shelley articulates polyphonic cues against the transfer of power from Constantinople to London. These cues are further fleshed out as the *translatio imperii* unravels in the throes of the global empire of the aerial plague. The plague's non-contagionist aetiology aligns the novel with the cosmopolitan side of contemporary medical debates, flagging Shelley's distance from xenophobic theories. Simultaneously, the epidemiology she develops from contemporary reports of war diseases reveals her opprobrium for projects that fail to expose and problematise the concomitance of cosmopolitanism with imperialistic warring.

A Word on Eighteenth-Century Citizens

The polysemy of the phrase 'citizen of the world' discussed above is of a piece with the philological generosity of the word 'citizen'. Across the centuries, the British history of citizenship has accumulated entangled meanings marked by elasticity towards the different discourses that marshalled the word 'citizen', be they political, philosophical, sociological, legal or economic discourses. Citizens throughout British history have been 'elite, full, and second-class citizens: local, national, supranational', protagonists of 'both theory and practice' (Heater 2). Following the French Revolution, the event credited with the invention of forms of citizenship as they currently exist in European countries including Britain, a different and more intricate legal history has come to define what citizenship means (Brubaker; Tilly; Wilson; Sredanovic). In today's Britain, the term 'citizen of the world' can denote only a moral qualification of human personhood and not a legal one. What did it denote in the long eighteenth century? In the phrase 'citizen of the world', did 'citizen' convey distinct importance or could another word, for instance 'subject', which since the early modern period had described 'a member of the community living in the same kingdom', replace 'citizen' without much loss or change of meaning (Borot)? Famously, Defoe's Crusoe calls himself king of the island and refers to the men he rescues and forces into loyalty oaths as 'my subjects'. It is safe to assume that 'my citizens' would have entailed different associations for the protagonist born a decade before the outbreak of the Civil War.

In the long eighteenth century, 'citizen' did not acquire a strictly legal sense. While Rousseau introduced himself to readers of the *Social Contract* (1762) as a 'Citizen of Geneva', highlighting both the legal and affective bond to the city of his birth, a year later, Paul-Louis de Beauclair debated against Rousseau in his *Anti-Social Contract* (1765) and referred to himself as 'A Citizen of the World' with a non-legal meaning. Hence, 'citizen' communicated not forcibly the connection between individuals and the state but primarily the involvement of individuals in civic institutions and behaviours, encompassing 'status, feeling of identity and competence; civil, political and social right; rights, duties and behaviour' (Heater 2). In this history, Scotland deserves special mention for showing unprecedented readiness to associate citizenly thinking with civic-mindedness, after King James in 1596 called upon the country to overcome its religious and clan enmities (Heater 13). Civic-mindedness is crucial for this book's understanding of citizens in general, and citizens of the world specifically.

Eighteenth-century cosmopolitan practice and critique build on what Arthur Ferguson calls the 'articulate' citizenry of the Renaissance, that is, the development of a habitus which displayed heightened keenness to seize on the opportunities of print culture and participate discursively in civil life. On the basis of a sense of duty, men and women of learning felt compelled 'to contribute to the flow of counsel upon which' they saw any good government depending (Ferguson xv). A precursor to eighteenth-century print culture and public sphere, the pamphlet literature of the Renaissance

> reflects a new sense of citizenship and new attitudes toward society and government, in particular a new willingness on the part of the educated, experienced and potentially articulate citizen to explore the problems of public concern analytically as well as critically, and even to volunteer positive suggestions for constructive policy. (Ferguson 133)

The influence of Renaissance and eighteenth-century citizenly participation survives in today's Britain, where 'citizenship' and 'subjecthood' are not juridically synonymous terms. A recent approach called 'everyday citizenship', whose objects of study are the concepts common people have of citizenship, is a branch of sociological research that has emerged from earlier views of citizenly involvement (Sredanovic). This type of research brings attention to realities where inclusive cultural and economic conceptions of citizenship can co-exist and even dominate strictly legal ones (Sredanovic).

In the eighteenth century, inclusive conceptions are furthered by the absence of uniquely state-bound understandings of the term 'citizen'. Hence, a novel like Goldsmith's *Citizen of the World* could disseminate the assumption that whoever professes to be a world citizen through participation in a specific national public sphere is also part of that nations' citizenry even if their residence in that nation is temporary. It is to Goldsmith's novel that we turn now.

Notes

1 See Coleridge's 'On the Law of Nations' in *The Friend* (1810) in *Collected Works*, vol. 4.
2 Even the anti-foundationalist stance of critics like Richard Rorty seems unable to rid itself of an implicitly shared ground, even if that be mere pragmatism (McClean 137–73).
3 Epictetus writes: 'to view each particular event in relation to the whole' (*Discourses* 14; I.6.1).
4 Louisa Shea delineates greater divergences between Cynic and Stoic traditions. See *Cynic Enlightenment*.
5 In Plato's city only one of the three classes consists of philosophers.
6 For some eighteenth-century legacies of Stoic thought and praxis see Swift 304–08.
7 'Cosmopolitain ou Cosmopolite, (*Gram. & Philosoph.*) On se sert quelquefois de ce nom en plaisantant, pour signifier *un homme qui n'a point de demeure fixe*, ou *bien un homme qui n'est étranger nulle part*. Il vient de *κόσμος*, monde, et *πόλις*, ville. Comme on demandait à un ancien philosophe d'où il était, il répondit: *Je suis Cosmopolite*, c'est-à-dire *citoyen de l'univers*. *Je préfère*, disait un autre, *ma famille à moi, ma patrie à ma famille, et le genre humain à ma patrie*.'
8 The complete maxim reads: 'Il n'y a, à proprement parler, rien d'étranger ni d'impossible à l'homme sage.'
9 'de se regarder comme citoyen du monde, de tout péser à la balance de Thémis avec la dernière exactitude, & sur-tout avec un amour dominant de la verité'.
10 'L'empereur qui voyait les objets en citoyen du monde, et qui était fort loin de croire que tout ce qui était bon sur la terre fût à sa cour.'
11 'est indépendant tel qu'il est né et il vivra avec impartialité dont il s'est fait une ligne absolue de conduite'.
12 For example, Marcus's self-admonishment to treat everyone with good will and justice 'according to the natural and social law', when translated 'according to the natural law of companionship', entails specifications of sociability vaguely present in 'social law'. I compare here Hutcheson and Moor's translation of *Meditations* III.11 with the translation proposed by Robin Hard in the 2011 Oxford World's Classics edition of *The Meditations* (Aurelius, trans. Hutcheson and Moor, 45; Aurelius, trans. Hard, 21).
13 Edited by Joan-Pau Rubiés and Neil Safier, the volume references Cicero and unspecified Stoic cosmopolitanism copiously, but mentions Marcus Aurelius only three times, Seneca twice and Epictetus once. See Rubiés's essay (55).
14 In 1758, Goldsmith reviewed a translation of the *Tusculan Disputations of Marcus Tullius Cicero*.
15 Scholars contemplate the possibility that 'the ideas behind the cosmopolitanism of the Stoa were themselves of eastern origin' (Richter 58).

References to Zeno by his contemporaries as 'the Phoenician' suggest as much.

16 Paul Stock, wary of 'the potentially imprecise generalizations of cosmopolitanism', reiterates some stereotypical shortcomings of the concept, such as the neglect of local concerns, elitism, and ongoing mobility (14).

17 Hard's translation is quoted except where otherwise stated.

18 'Contest, v.n.' in *Dictionary*; 'Emulate, v.a.' in *Dictionary*.

19 James Watt's much-needed edition of Goldsmith's *Citizen* is planned to appear in August 2024, published by Cambridge University Press.

20 Sebastiani's 'Gendered Cosmopolitanism?' is the only essay to refer, indirectly in a footnote (205), to Wollstonecraft's feminism as analysed by Barbara Taylor. Wollstonecraft appears nowhere else in this volume. Elizabeth Carter too is mentioned just once in Sebastiani's caption to Richard Samuel's painting *Characters of the Muses in the Temple of Apollo* (1778).

Chapter 1

Like Rivers Increased and Refined: Oliver Goldsmith's Citizens of the World

What is hardened can be softened, what is narrow can be expanded.
Seneca, 'On the Tranquillity of the Mind', *Dialogues* 128; 10

Oliver Goldsmith's *The Citizen of the World; or Letters from a Chinese Philosopher, Residing in London to his Friends in the East* (1762) first appeared under the title 'Letters' in the *Public Ledger or Daily Register of Commerce and Intelligence*, founded by the pioneer of children's literature John Newbery. At the time, the *Public Ledger* was London's fourth daily newspaper.[1] If the satirical pamphlet by Horace Walpole *A Letter from Xo Ho, a Chinese Philosopher at London, to his Friend Lien Chi at Pekin* (1757) spurred Goldsmith's undertaking on Newbery's invitation, the average of ten letters a month, printed between 14 January 1760 and 14 August 1761, exceeded Walpole's piece in scope and intertextual complexity, bringing unprecedented literary attention to Goldsmith (R. Taylor 98).

Perhaps the periodical and scattered appearance of the letters caused contemporary reviewers to underestimate the nature of Goldsmith's innovation to the extent that not even the author's wit and good sense could compensate for the project's unoriginality. Montesquieu's widely circulated *Lettres persanes* (1721) had already garnered praise as a trailblazing work, whereas a decade before Goldsmith another French author, Marquis d'Argens, had claimed the title *Lettres chinoises* (1751). When transferring the *Public Ledger* material into the medium of the epistolary novel, Goldsmith extended the title, by elevating to titulary prominence the phrase 'citizen of the world' that had already started to raise questions of definition, as a brief survey of the *Encyclopédie* in the Introduction showed. On the face of it, even with this new title Goldsmith's originality seems somewhat curtailed by yet another French forerunner, Louis-Charles Fougeret de Monbron's *Le Cosmopolite* (1750) – but only on the face of it. As this chapter argues, read in the polysemic context generated by the phrase 'citizen of the world', the correspondence between Lien Chi Altangi, his friend Fum Hoam and his politically persecuted son Hingpo poses different questions and suggests different answers about practical philosophy and cosmopolitan living. Another influential but contrasting precedent, *The Spectator*, had explored cosmopolitan living with a celebration of the booming commercial network of early eighteenth century London as the epitomical home of the citizen of the world, the very milieu readers encountered in the pages of the *Public Ledger* (*The Spectator* 392). Nodding to this network in the opening letter sent from Amsterdam by an unnamed merchant who introduces Lien Chi Altangi as a Chinese 'philosopher' to another London merchant, Goldsmith, however, proceeds with an epistolary exchange that insists less enthusiastically on the multicultural ties of unfettered commerce than on the practical philosophy and the duties entailed by a cosmopolitan ethos that also bears on commercial relations.

In this chapter, I suggest that we see the association of Lien Chi's letters with the appellation 'citizen of the world' as a choice that allows Goldsmith to position his novel within the indeterminacy of the eighteenth-century polysemy denoting this appellation. From this exploration ensues a type of cosmopolitanism that merges the vagrant and philosophical cosmopolitanism(s) of the *Encyclopédie* (see Introduction). Despite its far-reaching roots in Greek and Roman traditions, eighteenth-century philosophy, and by extension travelogues and novels, neither could nor did, in fact, mirror classical cosmopolitanism faithfully. The very heterogeneous and fragmentary sources the eighteenth century had inherited from antiquity made this a Quixotic undertaking. Instead of faithfulness, there are competing ideas appropriated from classical cosmopolitanism, selections and reinterpretations that contradict claims about the shift from 'singular to plural' cosmopolitanism(s) occurring for the first time in the 1980s post-Cold War era (Robbins, *Perpetual War* 9). In the most creative cases, we come across expansions of these principles, some of them more in step than others with classical cosmopolitanism. Goldsmith's distinctive cosmopolitanism participates in expansions. Like Seneca, who included insights from non-Stoic philosophy, Lien Chi interweaves European, Persian and Confucian sources of knowledge. His syncretic procedure opens the epistemic field of cosmopolitanism towards Eurasian ways of knowing and living that anticipate like-minded postcolonial approaches (Subrahmanyam; Ivanhoe; Yao; Chen). The petition of *Citizen* for justice for animal life exemplifies the workings of syncretic cosmopolitanism. Fusing Greek, Eastern and Christian theories of the transmigration of souls with Seneca's concept of *commune ius animantium* (common right of animated/living beings), Lien Chi asserts that human obligations towards animals belong to a cosmopolitan ethos.

As this chapter argues, Goldsmith's Chinese philosopher also sets limits to these obligations by not demanding the universal adoption of practical and/or philosophical vegetarianism. Lien Chi's own meat-eating diet, his approval of hunting for subsistence and his retreat from the denunciation of animal sacrifice for religious purposes inscribe such limits. The latter is probably due to the centrality of animal sacrifice in Goldsmith's understanding of Confucian cosmopolitanism. The moderate rather than universalised frame of Lien Chi's defence of animals suggests awareness on Goldsmith's part that religious rites, discussed in European colonial historiography as the Rites Controversy, constituted the bone of contention between Jesuit missionary activities in China on the one side and orders like the Franciscan and Dominican, and the Vatican itself on the other, climaxing in the expulsion of Jesuits from most Western countries from 1759 onwards. Lien Chi silently builds on the Jesuit 'accommodation method' to the extent that, for the sake of respect towards local mores, his plea retreats from universal normativism. Additionally, his cosmopolitan concern about animal life marks a deepening of the unique classical articulation in defence of animals in Seneca's 'On Mercy' (*De clementia*). At the same time, Goldsmith's ordering of this concern under the care of cosmopolitan citizenship also plays an anticipating role by predating the animal activism that ushered in the 1822 parliamentary 'Act to Prevent the Cruel and Improper Treatment of Cattle' and was later followed by similar European actions.

Before detailing the borrowings, modifications and outcomes of Goldsmith's approach, it is worth reflecting that syncretism explicitly appears in the *Citizen*'s preface. Removing himself from the responsibilities of authorship, Goldsmith nonetheless exposes his involvement as the editor, not merely translator, whose labour endowed 'with an English dress' the Chinese correspondence that readers held in their hands (*The Citizen of the World*, in *Collected Works* (hereafter *CW*) 2: xi).[2] This painstakingly crafted 'English' dress probably had to be emphasised by the 'Editor' in reaction to complaints that Goldsmith's Chinese characters possessed few Chinese features (*CW* 2: 15). The charge could not have found Goldsmith unprepared, since, while reviewing Arthur Murphy's *The Orphan of China* (1759), Goldsmith himself had jeeringly dubbed cross-ethnic impersonations as acts of 'imposture' rife with misinformation which, luckily for authors, went undetected by most readers (434). One is tempted to imagine Goldsmith's amusement had he lived to witness the travelogue of the Indo-Persian Mirza Abu Talib Khan, translated in 1810, come under similar attack in the *Quarterly Review* for not having 'more of the Oriental leaven' (review of *The Travels of Abu Taleb Khan* 89). The critical awareness of an imposture that he nonetheless undertakes transpires in Goldsmith's startling comparison of the 'Editor' to 'one of those solitary animals, that has been forced from its forest to gratify human curiosity' (*CW* 2: 15). The comparison brims with autobiographical undertones about Goldsmith's Irish heritage and his marginality in the capital of the recently formed United Kingdom. From a literary viewpoint, the preface's animal-editor beckons readers to approach the novel's Chinese impersonations as a chameleonic performance.

About twelve years after *Citizen*, the chameleon features in Goldsmith's eight-volume *History of the Earth, and Animated Nature*, where Goldsmith correlates the reptile's polychromatic shifts to the alterations of aerial conditions (7: 52). He advances a 'pointedly temporalized view of the chameleon's agency', an agency that fascinates with its cognitive and physiological sensitivity and for rendering 'visible the unseen materials of its surrounding ecology' (Camarda 53). This evaluation of the chameleon's capacity to 'undergo changes' during its negotiations with time and material environments has resonances for the ways this chapter discusses Goldsmith's Chinese performance or impersonation and this performance's inscription within a syncretic cosmopolitan tradition. What Julie Camarda writes about Goldsmith's take on the chameleon holds valuable insights for the cosmopolitan approximations in *Citizen*. Both Lien Chi's 'Chineseness' and his 'cosmopolitanness', like the chameleon, 'can occupy, suspend, and alter normative' conditions of time and space, while also having to 'accede' to limitations that arise due to unintended or unforeseeable events (Camarda 53). The chameleon's adaptive mutability, the feature behind Goldsmith's fascination, prefigures the premise of cosmopolitanism and national characters as contents to be performed rather than mirrored or expressed or, to say it with Eliot's words, as borderless interpretations rather than measurable signs (40). Speaking of performativity entails a shift from the expression of a timeless and stable set of characteristics worthy of the qualifier 'cosmopolitan' towards immeasurable creational acts of what only appears to be an already demarcated category by the sign or 'masterword' citizen of the world (Spivak, *Outside* 4). The novel's 'citizen of the world' hails an identitarian category, mobilising what Gayatri Spivak calls a 'strategic use of essentialism', an act of pretence as if there existed a signified monolithic and homogeneous group of individuals bearing a cosmopolitan essence (4). This assumed essentialisation, however, is checked by

Lien Chi's mutations, aptly observed in cognitive and mental processes that induce fluently altering positions:

> [T]hus is my whole time passed in forming conclusions which the next minute's experience may probably destroy, the present moment becomes a comment of the past, and I improve rather in humility than wisdom. (*CW* 2: 44)

Ultimately, this chapter disagrees with William Hazlitt's view of *Citizen* as a work that 'contrives to give an abstracted and somewhat perplexing view of things' (211). If abstraction means a drawing away from day-to-day realities, perplexity, as Lien Chi observes and words it, bespeaks an embodied experience rather than an abstraction. Goldsmith's impersonations come alive through mindful references to contemporaneous features of the cosmopolitan.[3] His is a merger that jettisons self-serving abstraction.

Contesting Merger

The figure of the philosopher Lien Chi combines two descriptions of cosmopolitanism that appear side by side without explanatory mediation in the *Encyclopédie*: the vagrant and the philosophical. As mentioned in the Introduction, the eighteenth century approaches the phrase and name 'citizen of the world' with suggestive philological open-endedness. Goldsmith added his own resignifications, among others, through a syncretic reworking of Stoic and Confucian principles.

In August 1760, eight months after the first letter appeared in the *Public Ledger*, the attribute 'citizen of the world' surfaced in the essay 'Reflections on National Prejudices' in the *British Magazine* for August 1760. While the essay's authorship remains contested – it has been attributed to both Tobias Smollet and Goldsmith – we can assume Goldsmith's familiarity with its content. The essay's author, a disciple of an unnamed philosopher, avoids disclosing his country of birth or provenance out of a desire to be known as a citizen of the world. Like the *Encyclopédie*'s unidentified Diogenes (or Socrates, according to Epictetus), the author refuses exclusive affiliation to 'any particular spot' or 'petty society', favouring the ecumenical 'grand society' of 'the general inhabitants of the world' (Epictetus, *Discourses* 22; I.9.1 and 'Reflections on National Prejudices' 461). This abstract and monistic definition is amply fleshed out and expanded by *Citizen*'s merger of the vagrant and philosophical cosmopolitanism(s) proposed by the *Encyclopédie*. Here, Monbron's travelogue *Le Cosmopolite, ou le citoïen du monde* (1750) with its free-wheeling male mobility is an illuminating counterexample. Two years before this entry of the *Encyclopédie* was written, Monbron's travelogue popularised this sense of rootlessness. A second edition of Monbron's book was published in London in 1753, followed eight years later by a third in London and the Netherlands. Circulated widely, it gained notoriety when pronouncement against French authorities caused Monbron's imprisonment in the Bastille in 1755.

Two insights from scholarship on Monbron's travelogue build connections to Goldsmith's novel. First, the *Cosmopolite*'s opening words seem aligned with philosophical Cynicism: 'The universe is a book of sorts. By knowing only our country, we have read merely its first page' (Monbron 3). Second, Monbron's Cynic traveller appears to have been, next to Henry Fielding's optimistic Tom Jones, a notable influence on Voltaire's *Candide*, an author Goldsmith admired and defended fervently in *Citizen*. In view of how closely Goldsmith followed the French literary scene and the fact that *Le Cosmopolite* had both a publication history and a readership in Britain, we can assume that it impacted Goldsmith's conception of his Chinese traveller for the *Public Ledger* and his distinctive appropriation of the name 'citizen of the world'. At the same time, Goldsmith departed from Monbron by merging the itinerant traveller with a philosopher who is more Stoic than Cynic. Consistently, Lien Chi contests Monbron's reduction of cosmopolitanism to a feature of locally disengaged, rootless mobility. Against reductionism, Goldsmith proposes a polyvocal epistolary exchange, different civic themes and an often satirical yet rarely sardonic tone.

Monbron's Cynicism requires the kind of scrutiny that differentiates classical Cynicism from the eighteenth-century interpretations and innovations to which *Le Cosmopolite* belongs. Shea's *The Cynic Enlightenment* (2010), to date the most cogent study of the place the eighteenth-century European Republic of Letters allowed to Diogenes and his students, identifies 'a new definition of Cynicism' in Monbron's protagonist (61). The novelty resides in the combination of new and old: Monbron explicitly models his 'citizen of the world' on the teachings of Diogenes of Sinope but also imbues him with a kind of nihilism that is Monbron's own added ingredient. For example, *Le Cosmopolite* draws on the often-cited anecdote in the eighteenth century which has Diogenes holding a lantern in broad daylight, in search of a human being among Athens's crowds. Two memorable oil paintings capture this scene: *Diogenes with the Lamp, Seeking Men in the Markets* (c. 1642) by Jacob Jordaens, and J. H. W. Tischbein's *Diogenes Looking for an Honest Man* (1780). Inspired by this anecdote, Monbron's protagonist entertains the sanguine hope of finding not just one but thousands of human beings in Britain. Once in Britain, however, the disenchanted traveller does not meet even one, concluding that not only uprightness and humanity do not exist, but that human candour and equity are nothing but masks disguising swindlers. But Monbron distorts Diogenes's gesture. If Diogenes's lantern in broad light is meant to animate his co-citizens to put a high value on human virtue by actively shaping this virtue, as his disciples aimed, Monbron gives up on humanity. As a consequence, his abandonment also negates the potential of Diogenes's legacy to teach, inspire and win over new disciples in the eighteenth century. Monbron's is an example that disproves Robbins's claim that only in the post-Cold War area, as the concept was enthusiastically appropriated by cultural studies, did cosmopolitanism 'forfeit some of its ethical prestige' (*Perpetual War* 13). This tendency already existed in the eighteenth century: neither the ethical mooring nor the normative and descriptive criterion of cosmopolitanism was as secure, definitive or singular as Robbins, among other critics, assumes (*Perpetual War* 11).

Anecdotally speaking, Monbron forfeits the instructive life of Diogenes's lantern, which, by contrast, burns bright in that of Goldsmith's Lien Chi, who departs from London convinced that 'A city like this is the soil of great virtues and great vices; the villain can soon improve here in the deepest mysteries of deceiving; and the practical philosopher can every day meet new incitements to mend his honest intentions' (*CW* 2: 404). This cautious yet welcoming attitude to the city, that space which assembles large crowds of human beings and contains varied and distinct communities, is of a piece with Lien Chi's commitment to what Ferguson calls 'articulate' citizenry. The type of the articulate citizen that starts to emerge in Renaissance culture develops and displays a habitus in men and women of learning that is marked by an acute 'willingness to analyze and to search for constructive policy' based on a sense of duty (Ferguson xv).

Monbron embraces the irreverence for which Diogenes and his disciples were (in)famously known, but in *Le Cosmopolite* there is no hint towards an appropriation of principal life choices that mark Diogenes's cosmopolitan praxis such as the renunciation not merely of wealth but also of property, the refusal of a life of comfort for one of voluntary deprivation, the readiness to learn from the least significant members of the polis and to mentor those in pursuit of a life in accordance with nature, or the disdain for the pomp of hierarchised political power and its legitimising structures. *Le Cosmopolite*'s disenchantment also lacks the sense of self-examination we encounter in Seneca, namely, the possibility that 'we live among wicked men through our own wickedness' ('On Anger', *Dialogues* 40; III.26). Diderot, who called Monbron 'a tiger on two feet', targeted such unprincipled if not predatory appropriation of

Cynicism when, in the satirical *Le Neveu de Rameau* [The Nephew of Rameau], written between 1762 and 1773, he invented the figure of the nephew, an opportunistic disillusioned Cynic, and the character of Moi, who rescues Diogenes from hijackers including Rameau's nephew and Monbron's traveller. Moi exhorts the nephew to live up to Diogenes's asceticism: 'have the courage to be a pauper' because '[i]t would be better to retire to one's garret, live on dry bread and water and discover one's real self' (qtd. in Shea 63). Ultimately, the difference between Monbron's hedonistically consumerist protagonist and Diogenes has to do with the cornerstone of their philosophical edifices: while Diogenes operates on the idea of a beautifully and morally ordered cosmos that inspires him to consider himself a cosmopolitan rather than an Athenian, Monbron, in just the second sentence of the narrative and after calling the universe a book, declares that it is a book made up of more or less equally bad pages (Monbron 3).[4]

Without emulating Diogenes's ascetic poverty (like most Stoics) and despite moments of doubt and severe dejection induced by the loss and political persecution of his family in China, Lien Chi's view of London materialises on the assumption shared by Diogenes and his Stoic successors of a morally ordained and beneficial cosmos, both the dwelling and the enabler of all life forms. The vernacular 'citizen of the world' in Goldsmith's title keeps Monbron's new kind of Cynic 'cosmopolite' at arm's length. When Goldsmith uses 'cosmopolite' – only once in *Citizen* – the word flags an awareness of and a dissociation from Monbron, providing readers with glossing directions that contradict Monbron. Lien Chi explicitly maintains that to live 'in the light of a Cosmopolite' implies finding 'as much satisfaction in scheming for the countries in which I happen to reside as for that in which I was born' (*CW* 2: 426). The satirical tone of the letter in which this definition appears should not obscure the main thrust of cosmopolitans' predisposition to benefit whichever parts of the world they can. Portraying a citizen intent upon contributing to the well-being of a cosmic family, as Seneca advises Serenus to 'make it his aim to benefit individual men and the world at large', Lien Chi takes an opposite premise to Monbron's novelty-chasing narrator, to whom 'the universe is an ongoing spectacle from which I derive amusement free of charge' (Seneca, 'On the Tranquillity of the Mind', *Dialogues* 119; 3; see also Monbron 47).[5] In fact, a critique of spectatorial consumption pulsates in Lien Chi's satire of the British craze for Chinese cultural artefacts in letters 24 and 110 – a critique close in spirit to Seneca's censure of the uninformed and decontextualised obsession with all things Hellenistic that he witnessed among his Roman contemporaries (Reinhardt xviii).

Decontextualised reductionism undergoes further censure when Lien Chi chastises travellers who cater to a superficial spectatorial taste for exoticism, for instance clothing and dress codes that remain particulars of no use to the common reader, unless the foreign traveller 'enters into the genius of those nations with whom he has conversed' (*CW* 2: 40). Goldsmith's vocabulary echoes the vocabulary developed by Adam Smith's *Theory of Moral Sentiments*, a work examined in the same number of the *Critical Review* where Goldsmith assessed *The Orphan of China*. In *Theory*, Smith describes the mechanism of sympathetic imagination. By placing ourselves in somebody else's situation, Smith writes, 'we thoroughly enter into all the passions and motives that influenced' certain observed behaviours (198). Before Smith, the same verb of proximity ('enter') had appeared in Marcus Aurelius: 'Acquire the habit . . . of entering, so far as possible, into the mind of the speaker' and '[e]nter into the ruling centre of everyone else, and let everyone else into your own' (56; VI.53 and 81; VIII.61). Unhurried engaged mindfulness is key for Marcus Aurelius, Smith and Lien Chi. After all, Smith insists, others and 'Otherness' remain unknown to us if we 'do not take time to picture out in our imagination the different circumstances' that shape their ways of being (9). This is the kind of mindfulness that Monbron's misanthropy precludes: 'I used to have no idea why I loathed human beings', an intuitive hate which, like a self-fulfilling prophecy, is validated by his travels (42).[6]

So deeply entrenched has Monbron's reinterpretation become that the twentieth-century scholarship of new cosmopolitanism has repeatedly had to push back against the reductionist equation of travel with cosmopolitan personhood. The critics Ulf Hannertz and Pnina Werbner urge us to separate the two, explaining that neither are all cosmopolitans travellers, nor are all travellers cosmopolitan (Werbner 156). This is a separation that Goldsmith establishes early in the novel by drawing a distinction between the 'philosopher' and the 'vagabond', key figures of mobility who have different driving motivations: 'a man who leaves home to mend himself and others is a philosopher, but he who goes from country to country, guided by the blind impulse of curiosity, is only a vagabond' (*CW* 2: 41).[7] If Monbron read Seneca, then he chose to disregard the latter's warning of jaded escapist wandering: 'One journey after another they embark on, one spectacle they exchange for another', without ever facing the truth that they are their own source of dissatisfaction ('On the Tranquillity of the Mind', *Dialogues* 118; 2). Epictetus even asks his audience why they journey to Olympia to see plays, thus fleeing from the inward 'spectacle to which you have been admitted' and for which no journey is needed (*Discourses* 16; I.6.25). While echoing these Stoics as he distances Lien Chi from Monbron's ennui-driven traveller, Goldsmith invokes a different cosmopolitan project by asking readers to understand Lien Chi's mobility like the travels of the Persian philosopher Zoroaster and other 'great names who endeavoured to unite the world by their travels' (*CW* 2: 41). If a feather carried hither and thither by the wind is Monbron's chosen metaphor for the detachment of the rootless 'cosmopolite', Lien Chi imagines traveller-philosophers embedded in the earth like 'rivers whose streams are not only encreased but refined, as they travel from their source' (Monbron 40; *CW* 2: 41).[8] The implicit destination of this 'not only encreased but refined' flow of bodies, knowledges and practices conjures something like an oceanic cosmopolitanism that, while grounded in the more-than-human life of the planet, also surpasses the boundaries set by the teleology of any individual river-like citizen. If we take Cynic or Stoic teaching and practice to be the source of Western cosmopolitanism, Goldsmith's metaphor implies expansion and improvement rather than nostalgic fixation on a pure originary source. A beneficial cosmological principle underlies these rivers that are nourished and enriched through the soils they come into contact with, akin to Marcus Aurelius, who desires that he like an 'olive might ripen and fall, blessing the earth that bore it and grateful to the tree that gave it growth' (*Meditations* 33; IV.48). The use of 'vivid metaphor[s] or sustained image[s]', like Lien Chi's or Marcus Aurelius', characterised Stoic rhetoric, reaching unprecedented fullness with Seneca (Reinhardt xxv). The image of both accumulating and refined rivers sustains the epistolary exchanges, the streams of letters and ideas bearing the masterword *The Citizen of the World*.

With this picture of expansive and elaborate flow in mind, an antonymic image to blinkered reductionism, I consider now the novel's advocacy for the humane treatment of animals. The geological metaphor of the ever flowing and refining watercourses captures Lien Chi's reliance on a syncretic method to tackle this theme and widen the field of his rhetoric of persuasion. Tapping into several philosophical traditions from within the eighteenth-century polysemy generated by 'cosmopolitan', Goldsmith arrives at an anthropo-critical definition in which to be 'a citizen of the world' also means being a defender of animal life.

Animals and Good Life

A former medical student, Goldsmith held an abiding interest in bodily ailments that encompassed animal suffering and disease. His 1757 review of *An Essay on the Nature, Causes, and Cure of the Contagious*

Distempers among the Horned Cattle in these Kingdoms (*CW* 1: 68–71), striking in both length and detail, prefigures the attention paid to animals in *Citizen*, which displays a wealth of animal references, some short and passing, others contextualised and polemical. Before long, readers note that animals play no decorative or digressive part in *Citizen*'s observations but are rather indicative of practical human morality towards otherness on a planet inhabited by innumerable non-human life forms.

One could do worse than broach this topic via letter 15, whose seamless navigation of such diverse belief systems as Hinduism, Christianity and ancient Greek, Roman and Zoroastrian philosophy musters cosmopolitan wisdom on behalf of animal welfare. The letter's terse commentary and concluding anecdote indict the cruelties humans inflict on animals. For cosmopolitan mindsets and affects as voiced by Lien Chi, cruelty towards animals ranges from human hypocrisy and apathy to downright torture and exploitation. The letter's indictment begins with Lien Chi's initial surprise at the 'utmost compassion for animals' among British people 'of the better sort', a designation implying both the economic and moral status of these citizens whom Lien Chi, at first blush, takes to be 'harmless friends of the whole creation' (*CW* 2: 66). In just one sentence, however, a domestic scene of men dining and 'devouring the flesh of six different animals tossed up in a fricassee' disrupts the harmonious cosmological arrangement of the first impression (*CW* 2: 66). Riveted by this disruption, Lien Chi advances a consequential relationship between dietary habits and one's being in the world, wondering: 'How can they comfort or instruct others, who can scarce feel their own existence, except from the unsavoury returns of an ill digested meal' (*CW* 2: 242). Without a question mark at the end, this statement is a possible explanation for the puzzling co-existence of human tenderness with cruelty to animals, summed up as a '[s]trange contrariety of conduct' (*CW* 2: 66). A symptom of blunted human consciousness, such paradoxical behaviour towards animals prompts Lien Chi to ethically contemplate the justice and good life owed to them.

While the relevance of debates about animal good life accrued after the industrialised animal-rearing and food-processing technologies developed to meet the food crisis in the wake of the two World Wars, the eighteenth century registered its own debates about animal life and rights within the culture of sensibility (Duncan 17). Research by Mary Ellen Bellanca and Ingrid Tague concludes that, within the anthropocentric orientation of British society, 'animal "feeling" – a conflation of physical sensation and emotion – took on unprecedented importance', raising questions about equality, morality and animal rights (Bellanca 55; Tague). The tension between anthropocentrism and 'animal feeling' is most profoundly present in the century's use of animals for the advancement of scientific research. Throughout Europe, some of the most enduring multidisciplinary insights into nerve morphology and the cognitive malleability and responsiveness of the human body have derived from vivisections, that is, dissections performed on living animals. Descartes, the researcher of animal spirits in humans, or Albert von Haller, the father of modern physiology, are two towering examples among many. The scalpel became the eerie instrument that, by laying bare animal anatomy, extracted information about the sensitivity of the nervous network running through the human body. Frogs, mice, dogs, birds came under the incisive power of vivisectionists who proved that, like the bodies of these animals, the human frame was also 'a sensible body' capable of feeling and responding to sensations, pain and pleasure (Vila 12).

The exploitation of animals for the purpose of learning met with resistance. Resistance spanned from sceptical comments like that of Lien Chi – who estimates that the knowledge gained by experimenting on animals matches neither the cost of animal suffering nor of human labour – to misgivings intimated by the same scientists experimenting on alive animals (*CW* 2: 360). For example, Bellanca traces the qualms of both Joseph Priestley and his friend the writer and educator Anna Laetitia Barbauld (Bellanca 54–57). Priestley discovered oxygen by testing the effects of different gases on living mice, while Barbauld voiced public discontent through the legalistic lamentation of a rodent in the 'The Mouse's Petition' (1773). Some twenty-three years later, S. T. Coleridge's *Watchman* commented on the poem's popularity, writing that 'thanks to Mrs Barbauld, . . . it has become universally *fashionable* to teach lessons of compassion towards animals' (*CW* 2: 313). Human 'compassion' towards animals was what deceptively impressed Goldsmith's Chinese philosopher fifteen years before Barbauld's poems and thirty-four before Coleridge's remark.

This temporal distance notwithstanding, there is common ground between Goldsmith's and Coleridge's doubts about the authenticity of human care for animals. Where Lien Chi registers a demographic factor in the pretended compassion of Britons of 'the better sort', Coleridge's ambivalence transpires in his status-based observation of mimetic morality implied by the phrase 'universally *fashionable*'. Doubt about authentic compassion reveals issues that are both decisive and disputed: what qualified as authentic sympathy? When was sympathy virtuous? How could true feeling be distinguished from mere, self-serving pretence? Few years after the *Citizen*, Goldsmith's *The Vicar of Wakefield* (1776) stepped into the midst of this debate. Margaret Anderson demonstrates that his novel consistently drew on Stoic thought and not only on eighteenth-century discourses of sensibility. The severest loss in the *Vicar* marks a crisis of virtue when, because of the manipulations of the hard-pressed Primrose family, genuine compassion dwindles into 'a self-interested project', the very shocking perversion that sets off Lien Chi's intimations about Britons' false human care for animals (Anderson 433).

The anthropocentrism in some forms of eighteenth-century sensibility should not overshadow the presence of much earlier, pre-modern models of animal rights and duties. Like Anderson, who focuses on Stoic echoes in *The Vicar*, I delineate here several classical threads that the *Citizen* interweaves to mount its plea for animal rights. Two key lines of thought reach out across the centuries from Plutarch's essays on meat-eating and Seneca's 'On Mercy', an essay in the genre of the mirror of princes (*specula principum*) in which Seneca advises the emperor Nero on the virtues of merciful leadership. 'On Mercy' prefigures Enlightenment culture's concern with violence, especially the noxious alliance of violence and power. Seneca's urging of Nero to refrain from intimidating his enemies and subjects through violent displays of power is echoed in the eighteenth century's unease with torture and 'a penal order that relied on the frequent use of gallows, gibbet, and whipping post' (Cockburn 156). It is in this piece that Seneca approaches Plutarch's position on animal rights and justice. Some precision about these positions seems necessary, given that even careful eighteenth-century research tends to represent the thought of antiquity as a monolithic precursor that indiscriminately denied to animals the possession of souls and, therefore, of rational minds (Bellanca 49). The matter is not as simple as that. The distinction and agreement between Plutarch and the Stoics illustrate this point and underpin Goldsmith's profiling of cosmopolitan animal rights.

In the eighteenth century, the authoritative advocate of animal welfare was Plutarch. To this day, he also remains the first thinker in Western philosophy to have written about the strategy of syncretism and its advantages. In his essay 'On Brotherly Love' in *Moralia*, Plutarch recorded the warring bouts among Cretans, who eventually 'made up their differences and united when outside enemies attacked; and this it was which they called "syncretism"' (313; 6).[9] Plutarch 'presents a specific example of empirical data understood in syncretic terms, that is, the unification of two distinctive cultural traditions' confronted with 'a common enemy' (Leopold 402, 404). Attuned to Plutarch's definition, the inimical factor that mobilises Lien Chi's syncretism is cruelty against animals. Plutarch also is an authoritative model because, in *Moralia*, he joins ranks with pro-vegetarians like Pythagoras and Empedocles to counter the Stoics. Goldsmith did not only read Plutarch, but also compiled *Plutarch's Lives* (1762) in an abridged text especially for young readers, explaining that, with Plutarch, he was exposing the uninitiated to an author capable of removing 'the dryness and dogmatical air of precept' and of transforming 'even precept into example' (226; 5).

Lien Chi's contempt for the meat-eating excesses of his contemporaries follows two of Plutarch's essays thematically, argumentatively and to some extent stylistically. Plutarch's argument that, by tyrannising animals, humans misjudge and abuse the purpose nature intends for them underlies the hierarchy of sentient life on earth that Lien Chi's accepts albeit in a qualified manner. Man, Lien Chi writes, 'has deviated from nature. . . . he was born to govern brute creation, but he is become their tyrant' (*CW* 2: 66). Seneca and Marcus Aurelius, too, maintain this hierarchy of governance. By this logic, uncaring behaviour towards animals is a misapplication of nature's blueprint. Lien Chi's rhetoric of indignation approaches Plutarch's dismay at seeing vegetarians being ridiculed by their meat-eating fellows: 'But it seems that we are more observant of acts contrary to convention than of those that are contrary to nature' (*Moralia* 559; 12).[10] By elevating natural law above societal conventions, Plutarch is in tune with Cynic and Stoic thought. But this agreement only accentuates Plutarch's censure of the Stoics for excluding animals from their idea of justice and, by extension, from the good life (*eudaimonia*).

The *Citizen*'s consequential association of moral corruption and human tyranny with animal-slaying and meat-eating habits has a precedent in both Plutarch and Seneca, who both identify the killing of animals as a bad seed from which human tyranny grows: 'This is the way, you may be sure, in which tyrants begin their course of bloody slaughters' (Plutarch 572; 12). In tandem with Plutarch's argument that nature has not endowed humans with the anatomy of carnivores, Lien Chi insists that no physiological need dictates meat-eating but rather human love of luxury and pleasure, even though only 'a short-lived pleasure' can be derived 'from the miseries of other creatures' (*CW* 2: 66–67). And, if Plutarch is prone to regard meat-eaters as tainted, hardened and beset with cosmic guilt by the cruelty exercised on animals and by feeding on them, Lien Chi declares that a superior relationship to the natural order arises from vegetarianism because of the 'purified and refined' sensations of those who, like the 'brahmins of the east', have 'never surfeited upon a guilty meal' (67). Goldsmith's philosopher follows Plutarch's 'philosophical vegetarianism', a term introduced by D. A. Dombrowski's seminal 1984 study to describe ancient theoretical and practical positions fostering vegetarianism as a rationally and ethically viable choice (Dombrowski; Newmyer, 'Plutarch', 41).

Like Plutarch, Lien Chi explores the outcomes of human violence on animals within belief systems that held the transmigration of souls to be the path by which nature asserts its demands on human virtue. Neither Lien Chi nor Plutarch addresses the veracity of this metaphysical path, yet both include it as a provisional hypothesis in their defence. Lien Chi is more eager to pursue this hypothesis rather than the strand of Christian theology that Goldsmith encountered in the Jesuit conjectures detailed in d'Argens's *Lettres chinoises* (2: 246–49). This strand both contradicted and upheld the codifying teachings of Thomas of Aquinas on the absence of an immortal animal soul, by claiming that animals housed the souls of evil spirits kept imprisoned until Providence meted out their final and everlasting punishment on Resurrection Day (Duncan 14; Spencer 176). That Lien Chi has no truck with views like these is evident in his statement about animals enduring punishment already in their earthly lives in the form of 'pains and hardships inflicted upon them by man, or by each other' (*CW* 2: 67). The aside 'by man, or by each other' should give us pause. By putting animal and human predators on the same plane, Lien Chi establishes a kinship between these two groups that explodes any human or animal position outside the ecological circuits, sending us back to the very issue that prompted Plutarch to indignantly ask why the Stoics left animals outside their ethics of justice.

Plutarch is right to wonder, because the Stoics are among those few classical philosophers who do not maintain that animals are soulless creatures, while nonetheless refusing to accommodate animal–human kinship in their theory of justice (Newmyer, 'Speaking' 102). Possessing a soul in Stoic thought is not the differentiating marker between humans and animals. Rather, having reason (*logos*) is that marker of difference. The pursuit and development of reason is innate to the governing principle (*hegemonikon*) of the human soul, whereas the governing principle of the animal soul is not equipped to attain comparable levels of intellectual capacity. Here, the Stoics follow Aristotle's model of man as a rational animal, a tenet parodied and reversed in Lien Chi's tale about 'the reasoning Elephant' in Letter 82 (*CW* 2: 337). Agreeing with Aristotle, Chrysippus, the third head of the Greek Stoa, argued that the chasm existing between human and animal reason makes it impossible for them to share values and interests. Therefore, no reciprocal bonds of right and duty among them are possible. Taking Chrysippus as representative of Stoic orthodoxy, Cicero's *On Duties* (*De officis*) propounds that the bonds forged by speech and reason 'reconcile men to one another, through teaching, learning, communicating, debating and making judgments, and unite them in a kind of natural fellowship. It is this that most distances us from the nature of other animals' (21; I.49). Expounding on Chrysippus's teaching, Cicero showcases the argument that animals cannot feature in the Stoic idea of justice: on the contrary, humans are entitled to employ animals to their advantage '*sine iniuria*', that is, without infringing on laws of justice (*De finibus* 116; 3.67). We also learn so much from Plutarch's censorious ventriloquising of Stoic objections: '"Of course", they [the Stoics] say, "we human beings have no compact of justice with irrational animals"' (578; 2). According to Plutarch's and Cicero's understanding of the Stoics, the conclusion resulting from this position is the Stoic rejection of considerations that would bind humans to care for animal welfare.

The *Citizen*, to sum up, endorses the Plutarchian and the Stoic (and the Judaeo-Christian) hierarchy of values, with human life embodying the highest value. At the same time, like Plutarch, Goldsmith's Chinese philosopher thematises the question of human duties towards animal life, opening up what Stoic orthodoxy had regarded as an exclusive and anthropocentric circle of justice. Goldsmith could not consistently rely on Plutarch's sparring with the Stoics on the question of animal justice because only a fragment of Plutarch's tracts was and is extant. But the pivoting phrase 'compact of justice', a precedent of the social contract theories eighteenth-century readers encountered in the writing of Hobbes and Rousseau, cannot have escaped Goldsmith. In fact, the animals of his Zoroastrian fable reclaim their rights in a court of justice. Notably, this court lends itself to being discussed as a syncretic rapprochement of metempsychosis and seventeenth-century Latitudinarian theology that also resonates with Seneca's notion of the common right of living beings (*commune ius animantium*). This notion is the expanded conceptualisation of justice that Seneca bequeathed to Stoic thought and is missing in Cicero's commentaries ('On Mercy', *Dialogues* 205; 18).

A Syncretic Approach to the Defence of Animal Life

A syncretic understanding of the world befits Lien Chi as a character created by a writer like Goldsmith, who explicitly espoused connectivity throughout his career. For example, as a reviewer, Goldsmith adjudicated Montaigne's criticism of Cicero to be a symptom of Montaigne's incapability to think 'connectedly' (*CW* 1: 131), just as he bemoaned the fact that a study titled *History and Philosophy of Earthquakes* (1755) merely offered readers disparate facts and information on wide-ranging seismological occurrences rather than 'a compilation of a connected history' (*CW* 1: 60). Whether in human or natural philosophy, Goldsmith is drawn to a method that turns references into associations, which is also the dialogic methodology at the heart of the subfield of comparative or cross-cultural philosophy (Weber 593–94). Next to Plutarch as a silent reference, Lien Chi, an adherent of Confucian teaching, explicitly widens the network of epistemic influence: he first hails Hindu Brahmins for practising vegetarianism and deserving to be called the egalitarian 'inoffensive friends of all that were born to happiness as well as you'; then engages with the theory of transmigration and Christian responses to the question of the animal soul; and, lastly, contests these with the help of Zoroastrian teaching (*CW* 2: 66).

Relying on the Zoroastrian lore produced in ancient Avestan, a language that 'has been poorly understood even by Zoroastrians themselves for more than two and a half millennia', Lien Chi tells the story of a fabulously wealthy man who vents his contempt for Brahmins, their vegetarianism and their 'holy religion' by keeping a hyperbolically sumptuous table with dishes made from the meat of a hundred different animals prepared in just as many dressings (*CW* 2: 67; Foltz 368). When death catches up with the man's intemperance, his soul is summoned to be judged by the souls of the animals killed to appease his gluttony. These investigating souls, protagonists in the metempsychotic plot of the tale, ponder the punishment by which justice would be best served. They debate to determine which animal was subjected to the worst torture and in whose body the soul of the dead man should live an appropriately miserable existence. Several propositions come before the assembly: The boar hunted and killed to flatter human vanity, the sheep whose kin is slaughtered at such a rate that, in its body, the soul of the glutton would go 'through four or five transmigrations' within a month, the daily bled and mercilessly slaughtered calf and the hen smothered in its own blood (*CW* 2: 68). The ox, finally, pitches the winning retribution. Endowed with clairvoyance, the ox foresees the birth of the dead man's disabled son whose 'decrepid [sic], feeble, sickly' body will render him 'a plague' to himself and all his kin (68), hence the proposition that the dead man's soul occupies the newborn's sick body. Elated by the 'ingenuity of his torture', the assembly follows the ox's 'advice', and the soul of the 'unmerciful tyrant' re-enters the earthly realm to endure no less than 'thirty years loaded with misery, anxiety and disease' (68). After having crossed what Pope's *Essay on Man* (1733–34) calls the thin yet 'insuperable line' between humans and animals, the thirty-year punishment closes Lien Chi's letter without the inclusion of any moralising commentary, trusting the fable to do the labour of vindicating animal justice (Pope 228).

Prior and subsequent approaches to metempsychosis resonate with Lien Chi's syncretic dabbling. A seventeenth-century deliberation popular among some Latitudinarians and Cambridge Platonists seems to be silently embedded in the attribution of the tale to Zoroastrianism, the religion of the ancient empires of Iran. Adaptations of Origen's theology of the pre-existence of the soul 'into a spiritual philosophy of the soul's eternal travels outside the human body' renewed openness to metempsychosis among European intellectuals (Yang 221, n. 27). At the end of the century, the clergyman Joseph Glanvill's *Orientalis, or An Enquiry into the Opinion of the Eastern Sages Concerning the Praexistence of the Souls* (1682) invokes the 'light' of Eastern sages to dispel 'the darkness' enveloping this issue: 'Indian Brahmans, the Persian Magi, the Agypt's Gymnosophists, the Jewish Rabbins' are called upon alongside 'some of the Graecian Philosophers, and the Christian Fathers' (26). If we draw on the *Encyclopédie*'s evaluation of Charlemagne's cosmopolitan mindset, Glanvill qualifies as a cosmopolitan theologian who, like Charlemagne, does not assume that all that is good on earth can be found in one's native traditions. In Glanvill's appeal, Goldsmith may have found the kind of syncretism where the Persian Magi, keepers of the Zoroastrian wisdom to which Lien Chi turns, converse with Greek philosophers, and the Hindu Brahmins, so greatly admired by the non-vegetarian Lien Chi. Some fifteen years after *Citizen*, J. Z. Holwell's *A Review of the Original Principles, Religious and Moral of the Ancient Bramins* (1776) identifies Brahmanism as the source of the theory of transmigration and vegetarianism, whereas in 1858, Thomas Forster, secretary to the Animals' Friend Society, an outgrowth of the pioneering Liverpool Society for the Suppression of Wanton Cruelty to Animals (1809), sees a compatibility and convergence between 'the holy doctrine of Pythagoras and the Indian School' (Forster 43). A crucial point is to acknowledge that the embrace 'of Eastern soul theory' by some British writers contrasted with frequent identifications of the East as a source of ungodly magic, fabulous excess and falsehood (Yang 122).

Adopting a cosmopolitan mindset (in the sense of the open-mindedness provided by the *Encyclopédie*), Goldsmith takes his place among those eager to learn from an enlightened East. Reliance on the doctrine of the transmigration of the souls seems to be the key link for Goldsmith's connection of the Zoroastrian belief system with the Brahmanism from which Zoroastrianism originated.[11] His choice of Zoroastrian lore complements the contemporary image of the prophet Zoroaster, especially among the French *philosophes* between the 1720s and the 1780s, as 'an advocate of humanity's agency in the exercise of moral choice between good and evil' (Sanjabi 169). The Manichean cosmology of

Zoroastrianism, a worldview governed by the contestations of forces of good and evil, transpires in the tale's polarisation of good animals and evil humans. Philosophically and historically, the tale's anathema on behalf of animal victimhood does not sit as comfortably with the Zoroastrian classification of animals into good and evil types, where the good are harmless or useful to human life and the bad are a threat. Although the fable's assumption that the Zendavesta, the holy scripture of Zoroastrianism, favours vegetarianism anticipates twentieth-century claims for Zoroastrianism being the 'original environmentalist religion', such claims must grapple with this anthropocentrically binary view of animal life as well as with long-standing Zoroastrian rituals of animal sacrifice (Foltz 370). This last point is doubly germane because, for a student of Confucius like Lien Chi, animal sacrifice performs an indispensable service in the upkeep of a healthy relationship between humans and the divine (Fan 87).

Simultaneously, the silence about religious animal sacrifice may signify the text's reticence to commit to strong animal rights that impose normative vegetarianism and prohibit any kind of sacred killing and/or eating of animal flesh. Positively put, this reticence implies a readiness to acknowledge the validity of some local conventions and particularities, a syncretism of sorts between an all-encompassing natural law and a context-sensitive law. Lien Chi's syncretism of Zoroastrianism and Confucianism represents a matter of negotiation. Zoroastrianism may be an apt choice if one seeks to defend not merely a kinship but also a non-hierarchical relationship between the souls of animals and humans. The tale of the trial would support this stance. However, as mentioned above, this type of equality seems undermined by Lien Chi's belief in a providential order where animals are subordinated to their human governors. Simultaneously, true to Confucian ethics, Lien Chi requires that humans show love towards animals by caring for them (Fan 80).

To return to the tale, what exactly does it vindicate and how does this vindication converse with Lien Chi's other prominent references to animals? The tale's primary target is the perpetration of animal suffering by human beings. Its plea for animal justice demands that humans not merely tolerate animal life but also desist from impairing it. Yet Lien Chi's animal justice seems weaker than the one embodied by the Brahmanism he praises so emphatically. No Brahmin himself, Lien Chi wittily evidences his meat-eating pleasures, during a dinner that consisted 'of an haunch of venison, a turtle and a great man', where '[t]he venison was fine, the turtle good, but the great man insupportable' (*CW* 2: 307). With its specification of vicious animal-killing to serve human vanity and gluttony and 'not to satisfy his hunger', the tale echoes Plutarch's protestation that, for humans, animal slaughtering is 'a mere appetizer' and not a matter of preservation. The anthropomorphic reasoning and emotionality of the tale's animal community borrows Plutarch's imploring rational animal: '"I do not ask to be spared in case of necessity; only spare me your arrogance! Kill me to eat, but not to please your palate!"' (Plutarch 551). Lien Chi's terse remark that the glutton eats meat 'not to satisfy his hunger' also repeats Plutarch's charge against his contemporaries, whom he accuses of having no plausible excuse for the killing: 'you who live now, what madness, what frenzy drives you to the pollution of shedding blood, you who have such a superfluity of necessities?' (Plutarch 546). It is in this logic of bare necessities that *Citizen*'s heart-wrenching story of the mendicant disabled soldier who had fought at the 1745 Battle of Flanders does not condemn the dispossessed veteran for killing a hare to avert starvation (*CW* 2: 461). Both Lien Chi and Plutarch, then, while defenders of animals, nonetheless leave room for scenarios in which it is permissible for animal life to be subordinated to interests of human survival (*CW* 2: 68; Plutarch 547). This attenuation starts to bring them closer to the Stoic conception, and, as proposed in the next section, to twenty-first-century animal rights theorists and activists who throw into relief the appropriative inter-species interdependences governing the earth's biosphere.

Stoic influence may well underlie Goldsmith's observation that, for some writers, knowledge is best used when it promotes 'practical morality' (*CW* 2: 333). And Lien Chi's tale aims to arrive at some sort of practical morality rather than to furnish readers with a treatise on animal justice, or on the transmigration of souls. The narrative, with its specific animals, the manners of and reasons for killing and the individuated vice of the dead man to be expiated in the body of his diseased son, explores the issue of justice in more tangible ways than do Lien Chi's preceding meditations on humans' perversion of their assigned role from governors into tyrants of animal life. Stylistically, Plutarch's and Lien Chi's anthropomorphism endows animals with emotions and speech, that is, the very rationality the Stoics argued animals did not possess.[12] Methodically, however, the setting of a court trial where individuated animal and human interests convene to wrestle for just inter-species relationships stages Seneca's *commune ius animantium* (the common right of living beings). *Commune ius*, a reference to shared values and community life, resonates with Lien Chi's vocabulary: the animals hold a 'tribunal' and 'assembly', and collectively deliver a verdict (*CW* 2: 68). The narrative enacts a scene of the 'compact of justice' between humans and animals for which, according to Plutarch, the Stoics found no place in their cosmopolis.

Yet, for more than one reason, Goldsmith's anecdote can be seen as operating on Seneca's 'juridically and philosophically significant expression *ius animantium*' (Tutrone 518). The *Citizen*'s tribunal of souls enjoys the ultimacy of the Senecan 'right of living beings', in that these beings derive the power to define justice from a cosmological rather than a specific cultural or conventional vantage point. Because human mores and conventions are parochial, hence subject to change over time and space, they are trumped by a cosmological or natural law which is universal and permanent. Thus, Goldsmith's text conflates Plutarchian and Senecan positions, taking advantage of the contact points between them. When upholding the superior jurisdictional power of natural law, Plutarch's argument for animal rights draws on Cynic and Stoic terminology. That meat-eaters 'are more observant of acts contrary to convention than of those that are contrary to nature' is a Cynic and Stoic approach to the relationship between natural law and local customs (Plutarch 559). In what is, to my knowledge, the most detailed and convincing reading of the passage in which Seneca mentions for the first and only time 'a form of nature-based "animal right"', Fabio Tutrone expounds that 'the uncommon expression *commune ius animantium*, with its implicit connections to the Latin juridical vocabulary, openly hints at a broad view of justice and reciprocal duties' (535). Here, Seneca adds something new to his position that the exclusive possession of *logos* creates kinship only between human bodies and souls, while animal souls, lacking *logos*, know nothing of virtue and therefore cannot partake in the human quest for virtue ('On the Happy Life', *Dialogues* 93; 9–10).

Expanded and Moderated Justice

The context of Seneca's gesture towards broader views of animal justice reveals intertextual threads that associate Goldsmith's *Citizen* with its classical predecessors. Seneca is never far away from Lien Chi's letter on the animal tribunal. He is mentioned in the previous letter next to Sir John Bolingbroke, whose *Reflexions upon Exile* openly acknowledged Seneca as a stylistic and philosophic influence. A telling point of contact between Goldsmith and Stoicism occurs in Lien Chi's espousal of Johnson's view in *Rambler* 41 on the degrees of difference rather than utter otherness that distinguish humans from animals (S. Johnson, *Yale Edition* 3: 222). If the Stoics held that the animal soul displayed lower degrees of intellect, Lien Chi, once outside the fictional universe of the fable where animals remember their past suffering, explains that animals have a less developed sense of remembrance and projection into the future. They remember what belongs to the past and anticipate future events only 'in a limited degree', while 'their whole life seems taken up in the present, regardless of the past and the future' (*CW* 2: 186). This ontological distinction potentially diminishes non-human sentient life in the eyes of the philosopher, but only until Lien Chi enviously comments that a more animal-like approach to time past, present and future would help humans in their search for happiness. Humans could learn from animals a 'method of seizing the present, unimbittered [sic] by such reflection' (*CW* 2: 187). Similarly, Seneca stresses differences in the experience of grief, recommending animals' genuine but 'short-lived' mourning as a model that teaches humans that it is 'Nature's prescription' for elegiac feelings not to be prolonged ('Consolation to Marcia', *Dialogues* 59–60; 7).

Perhaps the strongest common thread is the indictment of reprehensible human actions upon animals. Several passages in Seneca's essays suggest that he would have endorsed not only the sympathetic portrayal of animal suffering but their harshness towards humans in Lien Chi's tale. Seneca's anecdotal account of the infamous punishments of Publius Vedius Pollio indicates this much. An aide of Augustus, Pollio was known for keeping a pond with lamprey eels 'fattened' on human blood. The pond or the 'snakepit', as Seneca calls it, was a site of execution for Pollio's offenders, frequently his slaves, who were thrown in and left to be devoured by the carnivorous lampreys. Formulated under the aegis of the rights shared by all living creatures, Seneca's indictment of Pollio's cruelty is two-pronged and as emphatic as the verdict pronounced in the *Citizen*'s animal trial. In both cases, tyrants must suffer augmented retribution. In Seneca's words, Pollio 'deserved a thousand deaths whether he threw his slaves as food to lampreys he intended to eat, or whether his sole purpose in keeping lampreys was to treat them to such a diet' ('On Mercy', *Dialogues* 205; 18). The perception of Pollio's actions as a double violence committed against humans and animals alike gathers these two groups under the concept of natural law (*ius naturae*) and, like Goldsmith's anecdote, represents human and animal claims to a good life as being contiguous by virtue of both groups being beneficiaries of a 'cosmological inter-species justice' (Tutrone 542). The movement in Goldsmith's tale, from unrestrained animal slaughter for the rich man's hyperbolically sensuous banquets to the cruelty depicted in the animals' testimonies against this man, is comparable to Seneca's weighty concern with the violence committed on animals and humans, namely, the transformation of cruelty (*crudelitas*) into pleasure (*voluptas*).[13] Both Goldsmith's glutton and Seneca's Pollio are doubly castigated for being cruel and for delighting in cruelty.

Seneca's *commune ius animantium* holds relevance for other moments in Goldsmith's *Citizen*, most notably Lien Chi's appeal in letter 69 for the better treatment of sick animals. His plea elevates the topical fear of mad dogs, which inundated contemporary newspapers, escalating into perceptions of a national 'disorder peculiar to the country' (*CW* 2: 285). The first paragraphs of this letter suffice for us to grasp Lien Chi's reversal of this popular fear. A witness to scenes resembling 'the ancient Gothic custom of trying witches', a disheartened Lien Chi reports about people who close in on allegedly diseased dogs, 'teizing the devoted animal on every side' and granting him no hope for 'compassion' (*CW* 2: 287). The demonised, persecuted dogs are the true victims in his picture: the phobic frenzy of the British and not the rabies of infectious dogs constitutes the real 'national disease' spread by 'ideal calamities'. Tragically, such 'ideal', that is, imagined, terrors about mad dogs, supplant 'this devoted animal's service' in national collective memory (*CW* 2: 289). Goldsmith's weighing in on the potentially perilous conviviality between humans and animals has a precedent in Monbron's depiction of Constantinople as a capital teeming with vagrant dogs and cats to the extent that the French traveller contemptibly prophesies that the animals will soon be the city's masters (Monbron 21).[14] Their impending dominion seems appallingly plausible to the self-professed 'cosmopolite', who considers the animals to be a danger to human health. His phobic presentiment seems confirmed when, back in France, he develops a fever caused 'without doubt', he maintains, by the pestilential air of Constantinople with its disease-carrying canine and feline life (Monbron 40).[15] Lien Chi propounds the very opposite: it is not the disease issuing from mad dogs, but rather human unkindness that represents the greatest peril to the social fabric. As a sign of the ostracisation of the sick, unkindness negates the dogs' 'claim [on] the protection of man', in addition to justifying torments done to the 'faithful creature'. Lien Chi censures such collective ingratitude as a case of *iniuria* responsible for 'an ungrateful return to the trusty animal for all its services' (*CW* 2: 290). Adopted in the context of human hostility towards sick dogs, the Latin judiciary *iniuria* represents an injustice, injury and infringement of a right that Seneca's Stoicism implied as the binding obligation among sentient beings.

Not simply harking back to influential predecessors, Goldsmith's preoccupation with animal justice also anticipates recent animalist theories and activism. The disgraceful contrast between human ingratitude and animal service, drawn in the appeal for a morally responsible treatment of sick dogs, calls to mind the emphasis some animalist theorists put on the notion of respectful use. Val Plumwood's ecological position most persuasively advocates a non-dichotomous view of respect and use in animal rights studies that causes her rejection of normative veganism. Strikingly, like Lien Chi, Plumwood roots the painful instrumentalisation of animal life in 'ungrateful human desire[s]' ('Integrating' 300). Furthermore, Plumwood and Goldsmith share ground in their reluctance to impose the vegan or vegetarian imperative 'insensitively and universally, even to those peoples for whom hunting is an ecological necessity' (Plumwood, 'Integrating' 304). We encountered this necessity in Goldsmith's story of the hare-hunting veteran. Besides hegemonically favouring 'certain cultures' lands and food orientations over others', universalist normative veganism contradicts non-anthropocentric approaches by replicating anthropocentric dualism, thus reintroducing Cartesian-like exclusions: 'many ontological vegan theorists reproduce exactly the same conceptual manoeuvres to exclude plants and lower animals from moral consideration that their opponents earlier used to exclude animals' (Plumwood, 'Integrating' 304, 301). Instead of a dualistic animal–plant boundary, Plumwood advances a less polarised, more fluid understanding of animal justice that is grounded in ecological everydayness. It is an indisputable fact of ecological reality that interdependences between species make up myriads of biological cycles, yet the appropriative nature of these interdependences is largely disregarded by normative vegetarianism. The term 'appropriative' implies that predation should be seen 'in much more continuous terms' which regard all types of life (*bios*), including human bodies, as potential food (302).

We encounter a picture of ecological reality in Goldsmith's (invented) Chinese fable 'Five Animals at a Meal' (*CW* 2: 392). Developed from the observations that Goldsmith encountered in Du Halde, the fable is a snapshot of the food chain, starting with a grasshopper soon to be swallowed by a 'whangam', and moving up the chain with a serpent preying on the whangam, a bird eyeing the serpent, and a hawk aiming for the bird. Gone is the Manichean universe of Zendavesta with its victimised animals and exclusively human predators. Aptly and rather acquiescently, the fable captures a biological *oikos* that foregrounds the continuous appropriative nature of interdependences among living beings that ensure the continuance and recycling of energy in ecological communities (Plumwood, *Environmental Culture* 156). In this network of ecology, human life is one among many types that consumes other bodies and can also be consumed in return. Predatory ways of subsistence, survival and reprocessing of bio substances including flesh are no matters of mere contingency but ecological actualities and, unless we choose to abide by a hyper-separation between human and nature, predation must be accepted and integrated as a component of 'human identity' (Plumwood, *Eye* 89).[16] Lien Chi's tale offers no illustration of human bodies literally becoming food for other species. But metaphorically, this vignette depicts monetary predation in capitalist economies. The tale's ecological moral could be rendered by J. Claude Evans's lapidary statement: '*Life is appropriation*'. The context of this summary sentence matches *Citizen*'s environmental stance:

> All life, of whatever form, exists and continues to exist only because it appropriates energy in one form or another from its environment. *Life is appropriation.* Any ethical theory that does not recognise and affirm this fundamental fact is not a serious candidate for an environmental ethic. (Evans 125)

While appropriation features as a natural necessity in Goldsmith's animal ecology, it does not amount to a *carte blanche* for human predation over earth others. *Citizen*'s position on animal suffering aggravated by human ingratitude warns of such dispensation of responsibility. A crucial monition comes from Fum Hoam, Lien Chi's compatriot and closest correspondent, who ponders the destructive impact of imperial territorial expansion on ecological communities. Commenting on the Russian conquests and unification that, according to his geopolitical understanding, make this 'empire the natural enemy of the more western parts of Europe', he laments eloquently the environmental cost of Russian expansion: 'those untrodden forests, those innumerable savage animals which formerly covered the face of the country, are now removed, and colonies of mankind are planted in their room' (*CW* 2: 353). Goldsmith's source here may be Voltaire's *Essai sur les moeurs* (1760) and *Histoire de l'empire de Russie sous Pierre le Grand* (1759–63), two works rich with anecdotes that serve to capture collective psychology, the so-called national character, as required by contemporary conventions of travel narrative and historiography (Trénard 586). But in lieu of rehearsing the guiding tune of Voltaire's works, namely his eulogy of a Promethean Peter the Great, in the comparably small space of this letter and with images of both domestic and outdoor spaces, Goldsmith shifts the focus to animal displacement or extinction and the aggressive alteration of entire eco-systems for imperial purposes. In terms of scale effect, the savage animals deprived of the 'room' of their own move the critique from a national to an environmental scale implicating what are known today as green politics. With this anti-imperialist environmental mindset at the start of the letter, its last scene about the migration of swarms of locusts and torrents of ants that destroy vast agricultural territories in their unstoppable course, 'banishing men and animals', negates human control over more-than-human life. The writer confesses the formidable impact of such animal mobility only to accentuate that human mobility has been no less devastating: '[l]ike these have been the migrations of men' (*CW* 2: 354). Consequently, this negative resemblance targets a corrupted and corruptible human rationality and, by consequence, a human right to exercise control over animal life.

No isolated instance in *Citizen*, this critique involving movement between scales (individual, national and planetary) surfaces in Goldsmith's sarcastic denunciation of that migration 'of men' carried by France and Britain to Canada for the domination of the trade in animal fur. The fur trade was the primary reason for the activities of the Compagnie des Indes Occidentales (1664–74) in Canada. In 1670, the Hudson's Bay Company started to trade fur for the English. Within twenty years, the Hudson's Bay Company represented a serious contender until the French relinquished control over Canada to Britain as an outcome of the Seven Years War. The trade in animal fur represented a network of diverse and coordinated sections of labour that involved Indigenous and European people such as trappers, hunters, traders and shippers, in short, a work sector that increased towards the late eighteenth century, during the decades when *Citizen* went through more editions than in Goldsmith's lifetime (Delgado 1). In agreement with Johnson's 'Observations on the Present State of Affairs' (1756) that neither the French or the English 'can show any other right than that of power', Lien Chi contends that 'no honest man can heartily wish success to' either party (S. Johnson, *Yale Edition* 10: 186; *CW* 2: 74). Therefore, the Seven Years War is dubbed a series of 'very destructive' military conflicts of usurpation that have 'spilled much blood' across the territories of Canada (*CW* 2: 72). At first unspecified, this blood recalls the loss of human life, a justified implication in view of Lien Chi's antiwar convictions. Yet what the next step of his argument indicts is the decimation of animal and Indigenous human life.

The deeper Lien Chi delves into analysing the origins of this war, the more he foregrounds the injury done to a once balanced eco-system. Sarcastically portraying the psychology of disproportioned imperial greed, he correlates the shedding of animal blood to Britons' yen for fur, this 'object of desire' so 'indispensably necessary for the happiness of the state'; a desire which, in the eyes of the British Crown, absurdly justified the subjection of Indigenous populations in the Canadian territories (*CW* 2: 73). Critical scrutiny, here, shifts between the individual consumer scale conveyed by those who covet fur, the national scale represented by the British Crown, and the environmental scale involving the injured Canadian lands and animal and human life. Lien Chi may strike historians as courting one-sided sympathy, since he has no words to say on how North American Indigenous hunters and intertribal wars kept the fur trade with Europeans operative. Perhaps this indirectly reflects Lien Chi's stress on imperialist competition, which is corroborated by the fact that towards the mid-eighteenth century, the fur trade played 'a vital role' in British and French imperial policies, and this role exceeded the trade's 'economic value' that had dominated in earlier days (Eccles 344). On the other hand, Lien Chi's language is discriminatory when, by referring to 'the savages of Canada', he alienates the very native peoples he acknowledges as the rightful possessors of the country from 'time immemorial'. Discrimination is somewhat mitigated by the wide-ranging associations of the word 'savage' in *Citizen*, starting with the preface where the 'Editor' describes himself as 'a savage' (*CW* 2: 73); and also by his displeasure with authors who promised accounts of North America but barely went beyond parochial New York, as happened in 'North America, a Descriptive Poem' reviewed by Goldsmith in the *Monthly Review* (*CW* 1: 20). Goldsmith took this poem to task for its lack of attention to 'a country which can afford more striking originals than most others' (1: 20). Such acknowledgment notwithstanding, the ambivalence persists in Lien Chi's precolonial eco-system of Canada, a country first called 'cold, desolate, and hideous', only to be later imagined as a well-functioning ecology 'of native forests [that] produced all the necessaries of life' until thrown into irreparable disarray by British and French warring over natural resources and territories (2: 73). Not opting to Edenise precolonial North America by erasing the inimical if not lethal rivalry between human communities and animals, Lien Chi visualises Canada before the fur trade as home to native populations as well as to predatory animals like 'the prowling bear or insidious tyger' (*CW* 2: 73).[17] In this eco-system – in which, as in Plumwood's critique, humans and animals hunt for subsistence – local acts of mutual appropriation of human and animal life existed but within proportions that guaranteed each group's ecological longevity and 'might have continued to live to eternity', had it not been for the massive seizure of natural resources by European capitalists (*CW* 2: 73).

The episode, then, like Lien Chi's meat-eating habit and the novel's licensing of killing for ritualistic purposes or sheer survival, indicates *Citizen*'s acceptance of the fact that life on earth is made up of countless chains of appropriations. Therefore, a two-fold moderation must balance the demands of both human and animal good life: a moderation of absolute animal rights since universal imperatives like vegetarianism are not a viable option; and a moderation of absolute human rights over animal life to fend off exploitation. The first moderation seeks to incorporate localised mores and matters of human survival into the idea of justice, while the second moderation places ethical bounds on the (ab)use of animal life by humans. The ramifications of such double hedging of rights are extensive: the novel rejects 'the disembodied universal reason' that critics like Martha Nussbaum inconsistently link to Stoic cosmopolitanism, and instead, expanding Stoic legacy, casts cosmopolitanism not as a universal and abstract 'mode or form of reflection' but as 'an actual way of life' (Ivanhoe 33). In the next section, I examine the compatibility of Lien Chi's syncretic moderation with the novel's Confucian grounding and cosmopolitanism.

Citizen's 'small cargo of Chinese morality'

In Sino-Western history the use of animals for ritualistic purposes constitutes a critical element in the Rites Controversy that arose during Jesuit missionary contact in China and particularly in Jesuit engagement with Confucianism. Faithful to the Confucian philosophy intimated in the 'Editor's Preface' by the words 'a small cargo of Chinese morality', Lien Chi abstains from a critique of animal sacrifice in Confucian rituals. Instead, *Citizen*'s editor steers readers to appreciate borrowings from Confucianism as components that 'can help improve our understanding' without 'vitiate[ing] our taste' like the detachable artefacts of Chinoiserie, commodities circulating in Britain that were uprooted from their cultural contexts (*CW* 2: 15). Goldsmith's insertion of Confucian learning and Chinese folklore aims to spread a modest layer of this soil, a modesty deduced from the 'small' size of the 'cargo', which I think is nonetheless consequential enough for us to consider Lien Chi among the eighteenth century's 'articulate citizens' rather than a failed 'potential arbiter of taste' (Ferguson 133; Kitching 196). In lieu of successful arbitrage, Lien Chi volunteers an approach to Chinese culture that displays central features of articulate citizenry: the 'sense of citizenship' and 'willingness on the part of the educated, experienced and potentially articulate citizen to explore the problems of public concern analytically as well as critically' (Ferguson 133).

Eighteenth-century readers of the first edition of *Citizen* could learn about China and its cultural, philosophical and political past in a variety of works published since the 1580s. Most of these works assembled reports and translations by Christian missionaries in China, predominantly of the Jesuit order (Lundbaek 29). After Goldsmith's death, at the height of *Citizen's* popularity in the two revolutionary last decades of the century, during which the book went through nine posthumous London editions, more works of philosophical and Chinese history, of fictional accounts of Asian characters and themes, were published, catering to

European interest in China and its neighbouring countries (*CW* 2: xiv; Foss and Lach 179–87; Lundbaek 34–36). For instance, readers could consult two English translations of the entirety of Confucius's works, produced by Joshua Marshman in 1809 and the Protestant missionary Robert Morrison in 1812. Goldsmith's own knowledge of Confucius can be traced back to *Confucius Sinarum philosophus* (1687), perhaps the earliest and greatest work which, drawing on materials by previous China missionaries, also introduced key tenets of Confucian philosophy. Published under the patronage of Louis XIV as the joint effort of twenty-two Jesuits (helmed by Prospero Intorcetta), four Dominicans and one Franciscan, the magnificent folio provided a long introduction and paraphrased (with a noticeable Christianising tendency) the first three of the Four Books of Confucius (Lundbaek 37–38). *Confucius Sinarum philosophus* spurred abridged translations into French and English: Jean de la Brune's *La Morale de Confucius, philosophe de la Chine* (1688) was published in Amsterdam and appeared three years later in English as *The Morals of Confucius, a Chinese Philosopher who Flourished above Five Hundred Years before the Coming of Our Lord and Saviour Jesus Christ* (1691); it was followed by Louis Le Comte's *Nouveaux mémoires sur l'état présent de la Chine* (1697), Du Halde's *Description géographique de l'empire de Chine et de la Tartarie chinoise* (1734) translated into English as *A Description of the Empire of China* in 1738 and 1741 – perhaps the most influential source for eighteenth-century Sinophile philosophy in Europe – and the Marquis d'Argens's *Lettres chinoises* (1751), published one decade before Goldsmith's *Citizen* (Mungello 106; Landry-Deron).

To lesser or greater degree, all these works reproduced the 'policy of accommodation' espoused by the Jesuit order under the guidance of Matteo Ricci (1552–1610), the Italian Jesuit who founded the order's mission in China (T. Lee 2). Ricci shaped 'the 'Chinese' model for proselytising pursued by the Jesuits in China throughout the early modern period and after the rehabilitation of the Chinese rites in 1939' (Catto 74). Accommodation meant that the Jesuits evangelised while allowing the converts to participate in rituals with deep roots in Chinese mores, for example, imperial rites, ancestor worship or the worship of Confucius. Some of these rituals necessitated animal sacrifice. Under Ricci, the Jesuits estimated that, within limits, these secular rites could co-exist with Christian piety. The Jesuits' readiness to accommodate Christian teaching and worship to the localised mores of the populations they sought to evangelise, such as the Chinese, incurred the Vatican's sharp criticism. In 1715, a bull by Clement XI prohibited Christians from partaking in native rites, and this ban was confirmed by Benedict

XIV in 1742. The years from 1759 onwards saw the expulsion of Jesuits from most Western countries, with hostilities climaxing in the 1773 decree of Pope Clement XIV that abolished the order.

Ricci's method, as Thomas Lee explains, had an apologetic purpose involving refinement and conversation. Refinement meant that Confucian teaching needed to be distinguished, if not purged from Buddhist and Taoist add-ons, while conversation posited that Chinese culture could be approached in dialogue with Christianity (3). Quick to recognise that Confucianism was the backbone of Chinese moral thought, the Jesuits undertook missionary work in adaptive ways that agreed with seventeenth-century China, where religious syncretism was not just momentarily in vogue but held a secure place in the empire's intellectual tradition (T. Lee 7). In kindred spirit, when introducing Confucius to his superior general in Rome as another Seneca ('un altro Seneca'), Ricci was laying an implicitly egalitarian foundation for an inter-traditional dialogue between two great sages that responded to the syncretic propensity he encountered in China (Standaert 375). In a study of the texts composed by Ricci to familiarise the Chinese with Western culture, Nicholas Standaert concludes that 'Ricci was not only introducing Stoic thought to the Chinese, but also establishing a link between the European humanist tradition and the Confucian tradition' (376). Goldsmith's *Citizen*, albeit fictional and more covert when establishing affinities, emerges as another link in this inter-traditional dialogue. Regarding the defence of animal life, through Lien Chi's Confucian position, this dialogue implements a restraint that keeps in check the erasure of common law by the totalising conventions of universal natural law, a requirement advanced by Cynic cosmopolitanism and moderated by the Stoics.

Moderation has a comparable function in Stoicism and Confucianism. In both traditions, it mediates between abstract rules and local contexts touching on demands, duties and states of being: the demands of family members, co-citizens of the polis and of the cosmos; duties to the self and community; states of despair and hope; critique and acceptance. Ruiping Fan relates in terms resonant with Seneca and Marcus Aurelius that such mediations imply continual (self-)assessment and adjustment of one's expectations because 'To become excellent in the performance of Confucian ritual requires a long process of learning, practicing, and accumulating personal experience' (82). Compare this with Seneca's advice to Nero that, when aiming at success, he ought to 'take into account the boundaries of our human condition', or to his brother Gallio: 'it is one thing to be devoted to wisdom and another to have attained it' ('On Anger', *Dialogues* 40; III.26 and 'On the Happy Life',

Dialogues 106; 24). A cautiously moderate Seneca ranks himself with other fellow pursuers of a life in accordance with nature rather than with perfected sages. And Epictetus, conscious that his virtue will never rival Socrates', refuses to 'abandon all efforts to do my best', since 'even if I'm not too bad, that is good enough for me' (*Discourses* 9; I.3.36); similarly, Marcus Aurelius exhorts himself not 'to be disgusted, or lose heart', but 'return to the struggle and be well contented if for the most part your actions are worthier of human nature' (38; V.9). It is a struggle Lien Chi joins with humility, since 'it is easy', he admits, 'to be a deep geometrician, or a sublime astronomer, but very difficult to be a good man' (*CW* 2: 41). Referring to Quintilian's idea of *vir bonus* (good man), which Quintilian modelled upon the Stoic wise man, Lien Chi makes it an aspect of practical wisdom to appreciate the opportunities offered by daily fresh 'incitements to mend his honest intentions' (Walzer 26; *CW* 2: 404). Another piece of Confucian advice about the moderation of expectations that appears in *The Morals of Confucius* (1691) and echoes Marcus Aurelius seems to undergird Lien Chi's acceptance of this difficult task, if not struggle: 'Endeavour to imitate the Wise, and never discourage thy self, how Laborious soever it may be: If thou canst arrive at thine end, the Pleasure you will Enjoy will Recompence all thy Pains' (*Morals of Confucius* 115). Virtue, this maxim maintains, is in great part its own reward. Marcus Aurelius, to name one Stoic, agrees by asking: 'For tell me man, when you have done a good turn, what more do you want?' (92; IX.42).

My emphasis on psychological moderation stands in disagreement with those scholars who regard cosmopolitanism as an ethical orientation exclusively concerned with virtues 'pertaining to global justice, e.g. tolerance', and less with personal, embodied, localised human virtue (Chen 43). The premise of such views is that of cosmopolitanism as a unified and static tradition to be recovered and applied to the realities of postcolonial globality. With Lien Chi, Goldsmith personalises the cosmological orientation of cosmopolitanism, and both Seneca and Confucius warrant his technique. From Confucius, who 'observes that it is the duty of the learned to unite society more closely, and to persuade men to become citizens of the world', Lien Chi derives an all-embracing logic of sociability (*CW* 2: 88). Confucian hope in the persuasive work of 'the learned' finds its Western match in Seneca's self-conscious assessment as an imperfect embodiment of the sage. A mereological view on the influence that everything they do and experience has on their own individual lives and on the whole of the human race characterises the sage's everyday life and advice they give to friends and fellow citizens (Seneca, 'On Providence', *Dialogues* 6; 3). Lien Chi's river metaphor, addressed at the start of this chapter, implies that virtue does not consist in the mere accumulation of (self-)knowledge and experience but in qualitative locally effectuated improvements. That is, the refinement of these rivers and the citizens of world that they stand for needs to be consistent with a psycho-cognitive eagerness that 'enters into the genius of the nations', locations and earth others (*CW* 2: 40).

Goldsmith judges his 'cargo of Chinese morality' to be small, yet he skilfully renders this alleged smallness significant so that it exceeds the national scale, conveying more than reforms intended for British society, as the work's satirical intent has been discussed frequently (R. Taylor 99; Brooks 125). A core invitation, to use the words of the editors of the *Encyclopédie*, is that *Citizen*'s Chinese performance be read as a cosmopolitan work, whose interests and commitment exceed the national horizon. Goldsmith summoned contemporary readers to consider practices and thoughts beyond this horizon. Whoever embraced his call could benefit from the 'small cargo of Chinese morality', in itself a training of the 'ability to imagine what is not the self, to familiarize the strange and mystify the familiar' that according to Toni Morrison makes writers 'the most intellectually anarchic' of artists (15). With a little extratextual aid, readers would realise that Goldsmith's decision to focus on a philosopher who is also a married man and father to a son and daughter primes readers for the centrality of familial relationships in Chinese culture. Those seeking to learn more would find out that parental and filial duties have such salience in Confucius's teaching that love of mankind, commonly referred today in Confucian scholarship as *tianxia* (天下, all under heaven), is modelled on and across family kinships (Yao 152; Fan 85). Philip Ivanhoe convincingly argues that the Confucian cosmopolitan ideal, unlike Nussbaum's interpretation of Western cosmopolitanism, strives 'to treat strangers on the model of our family' (Ivanhoe 27). This is an outlook substantiated by the narrative of *Citizen* through the bonds forged between foreigners: the Chinese Lien Chi and the British man in black start out as strangers who meet by accident, yet by the final pages of the narrative become each other's relatives through the marriage of Lien Chi's son to the niece of the man in black. Finally, the two men choose each other as travel companions (*CW* 2: 474, 476).

Such a development between foreigners is remarkable. Although the source for the man in black was d'Argens's *Lettres chinoises*, Goldsmith appropriates what is a tertiary figure in d'Argens to weave sustained bonds between strangers primarily but not exclusively under the aegis of the Confucian ideal. The unnamed man in black stands as a sign for the unbounded possibilities of friendship for those who strive 'to treat strangers on the model of our family' (Ivanhoe 27). By no means a perfected sage himself, the man in black nonetheless contributes insights that lead the Chinese Lien Chi to rethink certain deductions and to reposition himself. The occasional corrective interventions of the man in black remind readers that the credibility of first-person narrators increases when they exert dialogic openness and willingness to question themselves and recalibrate, or as Seneca puts it, to re-'frame' their minds ('Consolation to Marcia', *Dialogues* 69; 16).

Openness towards change, dialogic self-assessment and recalibration are necessary features of *Citizen*'s cosmopolitan practical philosophy, features that are avowedly extrapolated from Confucius, whose maxim closes the narrative: 'They must often change, says Confucius, who would be constant in happiness or wisdom' (*CW* 2: 476). Walter Scott, commenting on Goldsmith's *Vicar*, applauded him for being the 'author who contrives so well to reconcile us to human nature', its vicissitudes, limits and false starts (*Biographical and Critical Notices* 178). That may be true, but it is worth revisiting the portrayal of citizens of the world as increased and refined rivers to dissociate Goldsmith's Chinese performance from the potential fatalism in Scott's assessment. Goldsmith's river-like citizens do not abandon the course. On the contrary, the daily humble mending of intentions is Lien Chi's moderate advice to fellow citizens of the world who pursue their course without giving in to illusions of self-congratulatory sagehood or fatalistic surrender. Goldsmith has Lien Chi write, report, think and rethink in the face of human and historical limitations, so that the Chinese philosopher admits the inadequacy of his hermeneutic endeavours, saying 'I am conscious, my Friend, that this is but a very confused description' of some of the cultural phenomena he encounters in Britain (*CW* 2: 411–12). The plurality of borrowings from different religious traditions to make sense of quotidian human practices and states of being (such as eating, hunting, starving, sacrificing, doubting, fearing) in changing contexts enacts cognitive concreteness, reminding us that 'syncretisms, like all cultural representations are the product of cultural input only as processed by human minds' (Martin 220). One of *Citizen*'s most valuable psycho-pedagogic insights is that cross-cultural confusions and misdirections occur as contingencies of a cosmopolitanism that is not the product of agentless abstraction, but the lived, historically bound and necessarily incomplete and imperfect enactment, or what Johnson, when discussing Stoic philosophy, calls 'the lower degrees' of an exalted ideal (S. Johnson, *Yale Edition* 2: 39).[18]

Notes

1 The *Public Ledger* debuted in 1760 and ranked fourth among the most-read newspapers and periodicals between 1730 and 1772. See Werkmeister.

2 He added two new letters (letters 121 and 122) and revised letters117 and 119. Letter 117 appeared in the fourth number of the *Bee*, and letter 119 appeared in the *British Magazine* of June 1760.

3 In this chapter, Seneca features prominently for more than one reason. Both Seneca and Goldsmith are writers invested in the epistolary mode. Most of Seneca's surviving Stoic philosophy unfolds in letters addressed to friends or family members and sometimes in conversations with imaginary interlocutors who raise the epistolary form to a favourite medium of practical philosophy and a model for Goldsmith's own figure of the 'practical philosopher' (*CW* 2: 404). Like Seneca, Goldsmith does not stake out a theoretical field of cosmopolitanism but develops features (and characters) pertaining to the cosmopolitan habitus. The psychological and psychopedagogic techniques with which their works abound are of a piece with this orientation towards the persuasion of concrete readers. Moreover, Goldsmith's syncretic, accommodative approach finds in Seneca a precursive method. Resistant to sectarian isolationism, Seneca admired, selected and deployed valuable non-Stoic ideas. So does Goldsmith take on board and combines different epistemic traditions (Reinhardt xxv). Lastly, a flair for satire as a medium of social and political critique made Seneca an influential mentor for Goldsmith, whose *Citizen* sizzles with satirical jabs that do not spare even Lien Chi. In Christopher Brooks's words, Goldsmith makes Lien Chi 'the subject and object of satire, . . . the superior form of discourse' (125). While he was composing *A History of Rome from the Earliest Times* (1769), Seneca's writing represented a source of reference for Goldsmith where knowledge of Roman history met with the satirical chastisement of key political figures, for example, in *The Pumpkinification of (the Divine) Claudius (Apocolocyntosis (divi) Claudii)*, a satire on the Roman emperor Claudius. It was also Seneca who urged his correspondents to learn from Democritus (the laughing philosopher) rather than Heraclitus (the weeping philosopher), advising that 'We must take a less serious view of all things, tolerating them in a spirit of acceptance' ('On the Tranquillity of the Mind', *Dialogues* 135; 15). However, satire and humour are not restricted to Seneca, but extend to other Stoics such as Epictetus, who taught with 'equal severity and humour' (Gellius 7).

4 'J'en ai feuilleté un assez grand nombre que j'ai trouvées presque également mauvaises.' Translations are my own unless otherwise specified.

5 'l'univers est pour moi un spectacle continu, où je prends mes récréations gratis.'

6 'Je ne savais point jadis pourquoi les hommes m'étoient odieux, l'expérience me l'a découvert.'

7 See Cresswell.

8 'je jettai la plume au vent pour savoir quel chemin je prendrais'.

9 I quote the Cherniss and Helmbold translation of *Moralia* except where otherwise stated.

10 The references are from the two tracts on meat-eating (*De esu cranium* I and II) included in volume 12 of the Loeb edition of *Moralia*, trans. Cherniss and Helmbold.
11 Duchesne-Guillemin, Stausberg and Rose discuss the European reception of Zoroastrianism.
12 According to Newmyer, Plutarch's pathos-laden rhetoric in defence of animal life is unmatched among ancient Roman or Greek philosophers ('Plutarch' 40).
13 In 'On Mercy', Seneca warns Nero of 'bloody slaughter in seeking satisfaction' because 'cruelty becomes transformed into pleasure, and it is now a source of delight to put a man to death' (*Dialogues* 210–11; 25:); see also Tutrone 541.
14 'chiens & chats seront quelques jours maître de Constantinople . . . on voit plus de chiens que d'hommes dans les rues'.
15 'sans doute par quelque esprit pestilential qui s'était glissé dans mon sang pendant mon séjour à Constantinople'.
16 Plumwood writes: 'any attempt to separate predation completely from human identity will also serve to reinforce once again the Western tradition's hyper-separation of our nature from that of animals, and its treatment of Indigenous cultures as animal-like' (*Eye* 89). See also *Eye* 84.
17 He is probably referring to a wild cat of some kind.
18 'Discourses on the Weather', *Idler*, vol. 11, 27 June 1758.

Chapter 2

Wollstonecraft's Cosmopolitanism and Planetary Suffering

In cosmopolitan studies, the publication of Immanuel Kant's *Zum ewigen Frieden: Ein philosophischer Entwurf* (1795) is often referenced for the emergence of two important insights: first, the earth as a limited space plays a central role in the notion of cosmopolitan justice; second, justice associates a cosmopolitan order with critique of imperialist abuse. References to the earth were absent in Kant's *Idea for a Universal History with a Cosmopolitan Purpose* (1784), and eleven years elapsed before his *Zum ewigen Frieden* (*Towards Perpetual Peace*) stated that every individual's right to 'present oneself to society by virtue of the right of common possession of the surface of the earth' ('Towards' 82).[1] In January 1796, ten months prior to the English publication of *Zum ewigen Frieden*, Mary Wollstonecraft published *Letters Written during A Short Residence in Sweden, Norway and Denmark* (1796), the travel memoir on her experience while journeying in Scandinavia from June to October 1795. Here, Wollstonecraft predicates her view of humankind's future upon the resources of the earth and articulates a critique of the Enlightenment faith in universal improvement. As she endorses the progress of humankind, while keenly questioning it in the name of environmental exhaustion and human suffering, Wollstonecraft ushers a moment into Enlightenment cosmopolitan philosophy in which cosmopolitanism constitutes its own inescapable critique.

This chapter discusses comparatively Kant's focus on hostility with Wollstonecraft's demand that the cultivation of 'affection for the human race' be the 'growth of each particular soil, and the gradual fruit of the ripening understanding of the nation, matured by time, not forced by an unnatural fermentation' (*Short Residence* 198). My argument is organised in three parts. The first considers the place of the nation, in particular, of vernacular literature as 'the growth of each particular soil' in the progressivist scheme that determines the future of the earth (*Short Residence* 198). Second, emphasis on vernacular literature serves the expansion of sociability and moral love, which for Wollstonecraft are the determinants of progress. Her commitment to cosmopolitan improvement depends on the kind of localism that proceeds from a planetary view of concrete and organically related singularities out of which all living matter weaves its existence. Emphasis on localism for the sake of an ever-expanding cosmopolitan orientation, I conclude, distinguishes Wollstonecraft's empathy-based from Kant's justice-based cosmopolitics. This does not signify that Wollstonecraft treats empathy as if it were unconnected or indifferent to issues of justice – as Chapter 3 shows, suffering was a primary argument in anti-slavery justice – but that she subtly incorporates these within a coactive model of thinking and feeling, modifying certain aspects of Adam Smith's sympathetic imagination.[2] Empathy, activated by Wollstonecraft's planetary understanding of the earth as an exhaustible but also recalcitrant organism, heralds a cosmopolitan critique based on suffering that confronts the exhaustion of the Enlightenment idea of progress itself, present among others in Kant's projection of a peaceful earth.[3] Throughout these claims, I remain alert to the Stoic echoes as well as modifications introduced by Wollstonecraft. These are most evident in the fruitful use she makes of the epistolary mode and in her prediction of a removed future threatened by desire, if not necessity, for progress. Her prediction silently enacts the Stoic meditative exercise that pre-deliberates a bad future (*futurorum malorum præmeditatio*), but with different emphases and outcomes.

This discussion rests on the shoulders of recent research about the influence of Stoic philosophy on Kant and, more recently, on Wollstonecraft, in spite of eighteenth-century strands of scepticism towards Stoic perfectionism or simplistic appropriations of Stoic detachment (Kleingeld, 'Moral and Political Cosmopolitanism' 15; Risinger 55–58). For the latter strand, I have in mind here Samuel Johnson's scepticism of Stoic indifference and/or detachment and Francis Greville's 'A Prayer for Indifference' (1759), which emphatically endorsed equanimity in open refusal of the fellow feeling that Hutcheson's 'moral sense' philosophy had revitalised through adaptations of Stoic thought. Rather than attack, Wollstonecraft seems prone to defend – while also reworking – Stoic philosophy. Joining forces with Catharine Macaulay, who wished to see young readers, male and female, exposed to Seneca, Epictetus and Cicero, Wollstonecraft flies in defence of Stoic principles calling for a work of recovery, because they 'deserve respect' and must be rescued from the 'unjust aspersions' and 'odious' distortions of 'bigotry and ignorance' (C. Macaulay 130; Wollstonecraft, *Works* 7: 320). Macaulay, an attentive reader of the translation of Epictetus's work by her friend Elizabeth Carter, is an important link of transmission between early eighteenth-century Stoicism and the feminist views informed by Bluestocking Stoicism and Wollstonecraft (Hill and Blazejak 200; S. Hutton 137). Lady Mary Wortley Montagu, who at the age of eighteen translated maxims by Epictetus from a Latin edition of *Enchiridion*, is an example of Stoic sympathy among women writers at the beginning of the century. Offering more detailed evidence for Risinger's claim that Wollstonecraft took for granted the early-century Stoicism promoted by the likes of Shaftesbury and Scottish philosophers 'radicalizing its cosmopolitan possibility for a new generation of writers' (25), this chapter delves into a type of eighteenth-century radicalisation proposed by Wollstonecraft that not only differs from Kant's but also can be aligned with postcolonial feminist theory.

Affinities as well as divergences between Kant's and Wollstonecraft's evocations of the earth give reason to read *A Short Residence* as a template of the planetary subjectivity that Spivak proposes against the model of global agency. Spivak coins planetarity to ward off two tendencies prevalent in the schemes and rhetoric of globalisation. The first of these is the imposition of homogenising practices, the reiterations of the same systems of exchanges, on every spot of the globe, 'that abstract ball covered in latitudes and longitudes, cut by virtual lines' (*Death* 72). Homogenisation, enabled by the very abstractness the image of the globe infuses into our relationship to the world, 'allows us to think that we can aim to control' the planet we live on (72). To counteract a relation to the earth as a manageable entity is Spivak's second motivation for inventing the concept of planetarity. Thinking of the planet as manageable represents the large scale of thinking of the other as manageable and to be managed. Planetarity counters such an ethos by positing a different relationship to alterity, and the planet itself, a relationship that cannot be resolved dialectically, but must be lived through, while alterity incessantly holds us and casts us away. A shift of recognition, then, from the globe to the planet is at work, so that we start perceiving ourselves as 'planetary subjects rather than global agents, planetary creatures rather than global entities' (*Death* 73). Spivak allots to this self-perception the ability to change our attitude to alterity: 'if we planet-feel, planet-think . . . "our other"– everything in the unbounded universe – cannot be the self-consolidating other, an other that is a neat and commensurate opposite of the self' ('World Systems' 108). This 'peculiar mindset' in which 'we must persistently educate ourselves' epitomises a cosmopolitan education that trains us into a non-oppositional relation to all that presents itself to us in the shape of otherness. This apprenticeship can also engender, as we will see through Wollstonecraft's travelogue, an exertion against the grain of the Kantian view of human 'unsociable sociability' (Kant, 'Idea' 14). For Kant, 'unsociable sociability' is an innate but beneficial evil, while Wollstonecraft would rather ascribe it to the effects of a partial civilisation. Hence, the more a human society progresses, the more a 'moral love of mankind' fosters planetary consciousness (Wollstonecraft, *Historical View* 294). For Wollstonecraft, as for Spivak, a movement towards planetarity rejects the amenability of the planet. On the contrary, planetary consciousness inhabits a deep-seated awareness of the earth as a potentially unmanageable living organism that predates and survives the individual and ultimately thwarts the *telos* of progress.

National Character, Vernacular Literature and Humankind's Progress

Wollstonecraft's reflections on national formations are closely linked to the idea of home called forth by her guest status in northern Europe. Deliberating about home anywhere on earth, Wollstonecraft sees a chasm opening between human societies that have obtained and deployed scientific knowledge and societies marked by this lack. After weeks of travelling in Scandinavia, relief spreads as she approaches Germany, for her the gateway to the scientifically developed part of Europe: 'I am now convinced [the virtues of a nation] bear an exact proportion to their scientific improvements' (*Short Residence* 173). To Wollstonecraft Europe appears fragmented, immersed in an unequal civilising process rather than the consolidated agent of civilisation in the world. However, her concluding words in *Short Residence* exude guarded satisfaction: despite dismal local circumstances such as Swedish poverty or Danish feudal slavery, 'the gigantic evils of despotism and anarchy have in a great measure vanished before the meliorating manners of Europe' (198). This final thought looks forward to 'the ideal of Europe as a harmonious system of balancing states' that Karen O'Brien considers to be the core commitment of Enlightenment cosmopolitan history (2).

With its synchronic and diachronic comparative method, its focus on the physical features of the earth as well as their impact on a people's trade, industry and political acumen, Wollstonecraft's *A Short Residence* contributes to the kind of world knowledge (*Weltkenntnis*) dubbed by Kant 'physical, moral and political geography' that anticipates his later pieces on cosmopolitan right and his version of conjectural history. As Kant glosses the utility of such study: 'The comparison of human beings with each other, and the comparison of the human today with the moral state of the human in earlier time, furnishes us with a comprehensive map of the human species' ('Announcement' 298–99). The taxonomy matters to Kant, who specifies that this kind of knowledge is not scholastic philosophy, but 'a type of cosmopolitan philosophy' (298–99) and therefore useful to the world. Utility is of paramount value to Wollstonecraft, who, with eyes set on the best service her travel account can offer to readers, draws a line between other travellers' nationalist and her own planetary orientation which she borrows and develops from the progressivist model of Scottish conjectural history. Against the nationalist orientation, she summarises the method and intention of her account in the synchronic and diachronic sense proffered by Kant: 'I do not pretend', she writes, 'to sketch a national character, but merely to note the present state of morals and manners as I trace the progress of the world's improvement' (*Short Residence* 172).

The question of national character, to which Wollstonecraft, wary of the place it held in the tradition of travel writing, returns on several occasions, reveals her efforts to represent alterity as well as the impossibility of stating anything beyond the provisional.[4] She paves a way between a wholesale cataloguing of national features – in the style of Kant's sketches in *Observations on the Feeling of the Beautiful and the Sublime* (1764) and a host of other writers – and a homogenised universal humanity.[5] She restates her distance from depictions of national character philosophically, expanding on the constructivist view of society she had defended in both *Vindications*. The argument resurfaces in *A Short Residence* in the common error of confusing the natural with the cultural character of a people:

> All are eager to give a national character; which is rarely just, because they do not discriminate the natural from the acquired difference. The natural, I believe, on due consideration, will be found to consist merely in the degree of vivacity, or thoughtfulness, pleasures, or pain, inspired by the climate, whilst the varieties which the forms of government, including religion, produce are much more numerous and unstable. (*Short Residence* 92)

Wollstonecraft relies on Hume's bipartite structure of the moral and physical factors shaping national character, while her correlation between temperament and climate echoes the climatological theories popularised by Montesquieu's *L'Esprit des lois* (1748) and further developed by some Scots, for example, Samuel Stanhope Smith, whose environmentalist sociology Wollstonecraft endorsed in the *Analytical Review* (Hume, 'National Characters' 77–92).[6] But the diminished weight ascribed to physical factors ('merely in the degree') seems mindful of Hume's rejection of climatological explanations. Nor does Wollstonecraft follow

Montesquieu in naturalising government and religion as results of climatic characteristics. Indeed, averse to linking natural or climate-induced features with forms of government, she devotes attention to the inhibiting or stimulating influence played by governments upon the abilities of their subjects. Here, in one of her most cosmopolitan minded moments, the condition of slavery illustrates her point. Arguing against the essentialist justification deployed by contemporary pro-planter and anti-abolitionist propaganda, Wollstonecraft writes: 'A people have been characterised as stupid by nature; what a paradox! because they did not consider that slaves, having no object to stimulate industry, have not their faculties sharpened by the only thing that can exercise them, self interest' (*Short Residence* 93–94). In this, Wollstonecraft differs from Hume or Kant, whose cosmopolitanism co-existed with racist views. First pronounced in Kant's *Observations on the Beautiful and the Sublime*, reiterated in his lectures on geography and anthropology in the 1780s and latent in the *Idea for a Universal History with a Cosmopolitan Purpose* (1784), these racist views are finally relinquished in *Perpetual Peace* (1795), where independently of race, every individual on earth is judged entitled to the cosmopolitan right of universal hospitality (Kleingeld, 'Kant's Changing Cosmopolitanism' 185). If Kant first legitimises the condition of slavery and white governance, because the 'Americans and Negroes cannot govern themselves', Wollstonecraft reverses the relation, condemning slavery as no condition for learning self-governance (qtd. in Kleingeld, 'Kant's Changing Cosmopolitanism' 184).

Adopting conjectural history and Stoic thought to assert every human's ability for betterment and self-governance, she critiques a version of cosmopolitanism that assumed an innate unitary European superiority based on racial features, inherent in Kant's early comments on the translatability of black skin into intellectual deficiency, or the innate passivity of Native Americans and the Hindus' intermediary potential above that of the African or Native American but inferior to the white European. 'Others', counters Wollstonecraft, 'have been brought forward as brutes, having no aptitude for the arts and sciences, only because the progress of improvement had not reached that stage which produces them' (*Short Residence* 93–94). Her work-in-progress Europe has not outgrown brutish existence, as she notes during her travels. Whatever can be said about European nations' characters is only a provisional state susceptible to revision. So, for example, she reassesses her views on French vanity and depravity in light of her Scandinavian travels, coming to wider revision of a staple of French stereotyping among British travellers (*Short Residence* 172; Hayman 7). Given that

Wollstonecraft abandoned her effort to interpret the French Revolution through the paradigm of national character as initially undertaken in her *Letter on the Present Character of the French Nation* (1793), opting eventually for the historiographic approach of *A Historical View of the French Revolution* (1794), this retrospective insight suggests her distance from a well-established tradition of racial determinism.

Despite Wollstonecraft's reluctance to perpetuate 'the factitious national characters which have been supposed permanent, though only rendered so by the permanency of ignorance', national character remains directly or obliquely addressed, for instance, in discussions of politeness, hospitality and local mores (*Short Residence* 93). But rather than conceiving of it as a justification for European imperialism, she recruits national character to account for the role of alterity within the larger scheme of humankind's progress. Alterity stands for the local singularity that becomes the 'characteristic of modernity' in conjectural history, to be reached through the sifting of innumerable details of common life (Sebastiani, 'National Character' 197). It is part and parcel of this goal to treat with silence encounters that do not transmit the experience of national alterity: 'As nothing passed at this supper to characterise the country', writes Wollstonecraft elliptically, 'I shall here close my letter' (*Short Residence* 71). At another point, the redundancy of language and the sufficiency of ocular and auditory witnessing posit the indubitable presence of such markers: 'I am persuaded that I have formed a very just opinion of the character of the Norwegians, without being able to converse with them' (113).

Communicating these characters in her travelogue runs up against cognitive barriers imposed by local singularity. More than once, Wollstonecraft's geography must speak through linguistic detours and disclaimers. Confronted with unfamiliar physical features of the earth, her language reflects on its own exhaustion, as it simultaneously seeks to perform rather than express the strangeness of local geography: 'It was too late for me to go on shore, if you will allow me to give that name to shivering rocks' (127); or, 'I hesitated to use the word country, *yet* could not find another; *still* it would sound absurd to talk of fields of rocks' (90). Significantly, the letter where Wollstonecraft rejects the permanence of national character opens with a contemplation of the unrepresentability of individuality. No medium can capture the singular, she states, her own travel memoir included:

> There is an individuality in every prospect, which remains in the memory as forcibly depicted as the particular features that have arrested our attention; *yet* we cannot find words to discriminate that individuality so as to enable a stranger to say, this is the face, that the view. (83)

In light of the unutterability of the particular, national character resembles the Derridian *supplement* or *trace* that posits a constitutive difference not simply in relation to external things, but in relation to itself. Ungraspable variety and constant mutation make national character a stranger to itself, a phantom neither present nor absent, shifting, enabled and systemised through that other Derridian concept of the *context* provided by history and geographical boundaries (*Dissemination* 7). Final ungraspability means accepting a condition of provisionality, rhetorically sustained in *A Short Residence* by the connectors 'still' and 'yet': words of lingering and waiting that prime readers to anticipate a new perspective and not settle in their ways. Like William Wordsworth and William Cowper, Wollstonecraft relies on the word 'still' in key moments. More like Cowper than like Wordsworth, her 'still' evades closure and opens up to the yet to come (Steiner, 'Mood' 35). Hence, if there is any writing of national character to be done at all, it must happen through references to the historical and geographical context calculated to temper or divert the reader's trained desire for a catalogue of national features. Wollstonecraft commits to reporting, although imperfectly, on the endless variety of particulars distilled by the consciousness of a context which she perceives as being suffused by a condition of provisionality.

But if Wollstonecraft seeks to demystify national character as a marker normalised by historical and geographical context, how do we explain the frequent commentaries on national language and literature in *A Short Residence*? Are they perforce enlisted to promote a national-minded being in the world? In other words, are these commentaries signs of an involuntary counter-movement that reinstates the mystification of the national character? An affirmative answer to this question would rest on an exclusive understanding of the nation–planet relationship. However, planetary inclusiveness lies at the core of Wollstonecraft's philosophy and the models of citizenship she endorses.

In 1789, she enthusiastically reviewed *A Discourse on the Love of Our Country* (1789) by her teacher and friend the Unitarian minister Richard Price, who in a speech commemorating the revolution of 1688 made patriotic sentiment subservient to the love of humankind. Price declared that an exclusive love of one's country suffers from short-sightedness and fails to meet the demands of a more universal, cosmopolitan love: 'We should love it [our country] ardently but not exclusively' (Price 10). Price conceives of exclusive patriotic love as owing to deficient knowledge and the cognitive and moral myopia of primary instincts:

> Our regards, according to the order of nature, begin with ourselves, and every man is charged primarily with the care of himself. Next come our families, and benefactors, and friends, and after them our country. We can

> do little for the interest of mankind at large. To this interest, however, all other interests are subordinate. The noblest principle in our nature is the regard to general justice and that good-will which embraces all the world. (9–10)

Aware that Price's text deserves far more attention than I devote to it here, I highlight two Stoic insights implicit in this passage. The first of these is the recognition that it is natural for concerns about our own immediate welfare to be those most directly impressed upon our consciousness. But, as the second insight suggests, once we revisit this seemingly self-evident fact, we end up recognising how insufficient it is to remain within this circle of care.

Both these insights bear the psycho-pedagogic stamp of the Stoics. What Price calls a primary impression of self-love and self-preservation that arises in us naturally can be grouped with the primary impressions that the Stoics acknowledge as existing, yet which they exhort their readers to further investigate rather than merely assent to. Once investigated, primary impressions often reveal themselves to be simplistic, misguided and misguiding. To counter this contingency, Epictetus insists, we have been endowed with 'the best faculty of all, the one that rules over all others, that which enables us to make right use of our impressions' (*Discourses* 4; I.1.7). For Price and the Stoics, there is a faculty (*logos*) in us waiting to be honed for the purpose of leading us to principles that lie beyond the promptings of impressions and primary instincts. It is the training of this faculty that enables us 'to view each particular event in relation to the whole' (Epictetus, *Discourses* 14; I.6.1). We may not see ourselves *ab ovo* as citizens of the universe, yet Epictetus nonetheless holds firm to the idea that we will come to this recognition if we continually study 'the organisation of the universe' (22; I.6.1). Marcus Aurelius, an ardent reader and disciple of Epictetus, commits to this training by telling himself to be alert to the fact that: 'You entered the world as a part, and you will vanish back into that which brought you to birth; or rather, you will be received back into its generative reason through a process of change' (26; IV.14). What significance could this carry for Wollstonecraft? Resilient elasticity characterises Wollstonecraft's cosmopolitan ethos, a readiness to examine what impresses itself on the mind and 'a responsibility and capacity to generate its own revisions' (Steiner, 'Mood' 29). Time and again, the narrator of *A Short Residence* argues the validity of a position only to return at a later point and reconfigure her early argument with a 'still' and 'yet'. Such reflective and context-responsive revisitations can engender the type of training recommended by Epictetus, the honing of that 'perfectible principle in our present vestment', as Wollstonecraft writes, that widens our circles of belonging (*Short Residence* 109). At one point, with Stoic optimism, Wollstonecraft advances her 'conviction' that this kind of principle 'will not be destroyed just as we begin to be sensible of improvement' (109).

Secondly, Price's model also bears resemblances to Martha Nussbaum's Stoic-inspired model of concentric circles, or *oikeiosis*, debated in *For Love of Country* (1996), a collection of essays that echoes Price's title. Here, the ego occupies the centre of several radiating circles that stand for family, community, ethnicity, the nation and the world. As mentioned in the Introduction, this metaphor appears in the teaching of the Stoic Hierocles, via Stobaeus, and was popularised by Alexander Pope's *Essay on Man* (Ramelli lvi). Echoing Hierocles, who expects 'the well-tempered man . . . to draw the circles together somehow towards the centre' (Long and Sedley 1: 349), Pope democratises this task, requiring that the 'human soul . . . rise from individual to the whole' (361–62). Like Hierocles and Pope, Price unmistakably sees that this embracing orientation of the self towards the world grows from the cultivation of understanding. Thus, to overlook the subordination of national interests to cosmopolitan love is quite natural but also the least informed disposition. Hierocles's spatial metaphor of concentric circles can account for Wollstonecraft's frequent use of 'narrow' in conjunction with a merely self-interested outlook (the narrowest circle), coupled with her attribution of heroism less to patriotic enthusiasm than to 'romantic attempts at something above our nature, and anxiety about the welfare of others' (*Short Residence* 191). These are attempts that 'Prayer for Indifference', the poem that reflects Francis Greville's inadequate understanding of Stoic detachment, desires to keep at bay. To return to Wollstonecraft, her eulogy of Price's *Love of Our Country*, a piece where 'the heart speaks to the heart', leading the reader to assent to 'obvious truths', matter-of-factly commends Price's correlation of disposition with knowledge and understanding (review of *A Discourse* 471–72). For Wollstonecraft, then, cosmopolitan love is our natural disposition towards exteriority at its most developed stage; it is both the aspiration and the outcome of our perfectibility.

Here, national language and literature enter to play a crucial but subordinated role, as suggested in Wollstonecraft's critique of the Swedes' linguistic cosmopolitanism:

> The well-bred Swedes of the capital are formed on the ancient French model, and they in general speak that language; for they have a knack at acquiring languages with tolerable fluency. This may be reckoned an advantage in some respects; but it prevents the cultivation of their own, and any considerable advance in literary pursuits. (*Short Residence* 79)

Besides tracing the neglect of vernacular languages to a hegemonic aristocratic practice that causes stagnation rather than perfectibility, Wollstonecraft's attention to vernacular literature welds freedom and cosmopolitan love. Her view differs from Carlyle's observation that contemporary cosmopolitanism had inspired a type of literature 'without any local environment' and 'not nourished by the affections which spring from a native soil' (288). Wollstonecraft seems to argue that cosmopolitanism demands and induces the proliferation of vernacular literature because the weakening of local literatures spells out a worldwide intellectual impoverishment. By so arguing, she neutralises the 'hegemonic cultural universalisation' that most insidiously threatens cosmopolitanism (Werbner 154). The comments on the Norwegians couch her cosmopolitan maturity. Lauding Norwegians for being 'the most free community', Wollstonecraft also commends the recent translations of useful German texts not least for the public discussion these have sparked (*Short Residence* 102). How, then, can her praise be reconciled with her critique of Norwegians for having 'little scientific knowledge, and still less taste for literature' (103)? This critique is softened by Wollstonecraft's stadial view of human history, because Norwegians, she estimates, 'are arriving at the epoch which precedes the introduction of the arts and sciences' (103). And in this stadial development, literary taste will grow as Norwegian local literature amply complements literature in other languages and more derivative productions like translations. Translations, in her commentary on Norwegian print culture, prepare but do not fully realise the desired level of taste for literature. In this context, another relevant nuancing pertains to freedom of press. Wollstonecraft gives her support to those who wish 'confusion' onto the European states that allied against France and 'dismembered Poland' (133). However, she finds a misapplication of freedom in the failure of the Norwegian daily press to instil cosmopolitan solidarity with the victims of the Jacobin Terror. Among these was the notable thinker and activist Olympe de Gouges. To be deaf to calls like de Gouges's *plaidoyer* for tolerant political pluralism and to drum up support for the executions of those who held different political opinions indicates for Wollstonecraft a revolutionary zeal alienated from cosmopolitan compassion. She may not call the Reign of Terror 'this monstrous mixture of all human atrocities', as de Staël does in the same year of the publication of *A Short Residence*, but she takes a stand among those to which de Staël looks forward to for an investigation of the 'causes that influenced the black proceedings of those two eventful years' (Staël, *Influence* 2).

In other words, sympathetic understanding enlarged by knowledge is the missing ingredient in Norwegian community, a lack that hampers local public enquiry and discussion: 'They love their country, but have not much public spirit' (Wollstonecraft, *Short Residence* 103). As Wollstonecraft learned from Price, 'Virtue without knowledge makes enthusiasts', while 'Liberty', the Revolution's motto, 'is the object of patriotic zeal. It is inseparable from knowledge and virtue and together with them completes the glory of a community' (Price 19). With Price's teaching in mind and refuting Thomas Cooper's *Some Information Respecting America* (1794), another eyewitness account of the Revolution in Paris that suggests 'Americans should permit you [Europeans] to be their manufacturers of literature', Wollstonecraft asserts that vernacular literature activates national resources by producing local knowledge, rather than merely consuming and recycling hegemonic productions (T. Cooper 64). Against hegemonic patronage, she insists that 'The reflection necessary to produce a certain number even of tolerable productions augments more than he is aware of the mass of knowledge in the community' (*Short Residence* 79). Cooper's advice is of a piece with his view of America as an 'infant society', an infancy which, in Wollstonecraft's view, any society must outgrow through its own continuous efforts rather than compliance with parental tutelage (T. Cooper 65). These efforts may consist in nothing more extraordinary than the recording of local practices, presumably as in the Icelandic manuscripts presented to her at the public library in Copenhagen. These local applications, Wollstonecraft concedes, may seem tedious and wearying. Yet it is 'the immense labour men will submit to, in order to transmit their ideas to posterity', imbued by 'this very delicacy of feeling and thinking [towards local practices] which probably has produced most of the performances that have benefited mankind' (*Short Residence* 176). Against the reiteration of hegemonic knowledge, Wollstonecraft pits this patient localist processing of a 'thousand little circumstances' that capture what eludes 'vulgar eyes'. Patient localism proliferates 'endless perspectives' and therefore enquiry, that most valuable Wollstonecraftian activity (80). Textually, Wollstonecraft's many references to British literary productions enlist the national literary imagination for the augmentation of cosmopolitan knowledge, or *Weltkenntnis*. This, in Wollstonecraft's philosophy, fosters the kind of moral maturity that lives and loves inclusively, as Price's cosmopolitanism would have it.

Therefore, the enlisting of national character channels a critique of local passivity and a monopolising economy of knowledge in Wollstonecraft's cosmopolitan philosophy that aligns her with Kant's commitment to *Weltkenntnis*. However, *A Short Residence* manifests foundational differences between Kant and Wollstonecraft that are rooted in their understanding of human sociability, producing a cosmopolitan critique based for Kant on justice and for Wollstonecraft on suffering. The next section elucidates the stakes of this divergence.

Sociability and Moral Love

We could start by enquiring into what motivates human beings in Wollstonecraft's and Kant's philosophy to subordinate their material and intellectual labour to the cosmopolitan good. In other words, we would be asking about the bearings human nature has on political community. Wollstonecraft's view of human nature combines an essentialist and constructivist approach. For her, the universal and foundational feature of humanity is the soul 'stamped with the heavenly image' (*Vindication of the Rights of Woman* 74). In the context of Wollstonecraft's writing, this heavenly stamp functions as a marker in the most immediate etymological sense of character or engraving (*χαρακτήρ*), an alternative to the atomised national imprints of conjectural history that nineteenth-century theories of human variegation would conflate with race (Sebastiani, 'National Character' 188).[7] In this impression of divine image is laid the innate principle of perfectibility, so that 'every being may become virtuous by the exercise of its own reason', Wollstonecraft writes in *A Vindication of the Rights of Woman* (38), demanding women's equality upon this principle.[8] The degrees and forms of rational exercise vary according to social circumstances, but the goal of reason by the logic of the soul made in the divine image is the perfection of our nature. As Natalie F. Taylor succinctly explains, such a justification of perfectibility differs fundamentally from Locke's *tabula rasa*, where reason serves only the end of self-preservation, while Wollstonecraft sees reason as 'the fulfillment of human nature' (N. F. Taylor 97). Notably, Wollstonecraft appropriates the Stoic belief in the perfection of the soul as she encountered it in Elizabeth Carter, but without voicing Carter's reservations that such a belief risked 'flattering man with false and presumptuous ideas of his own power and excellence' (Carter ii). Wollstonecraft seems confident that an ongoing, active communication between feeling and reason, often a synonym in her idiom for reflection, develops the kind of introspection that detects and discourages the self-aggrandisement feared by Carter. Stoically speaking, assenting to anyone's megalomania, including one's own, is succumbing to the potential deceit of impressions. Wollstonecraft regards the divinely given faculties of imagination and sentiments as participating in acts of reflection, for there is little 'imagination amongst people who had not acquired a habit of reflection' (*Short Residence* 73). There are critics who maintain that, in opposition to Burke, for whom passions instruct reason, Wollstonecraft sides with Godwin by giving primacy to reason without passion (Risinger 196). I doubt that such definite dichotomy applies to either Wollstonecraft or Godwin. In *Short Residence*, the word 'sentiment', which Smith made into the cornerstone of eighteenth-century moral philosophy, coalesces reason and feeling: 'that delicacy of feeling and thinking . . . characterised by the word sentiment' (73). At the same time, by making the degree of development dependent on circumstances through acts of reflection, Wollstonecraft accords greater weight to the environment, that is, to circumstances. The Stoics reduce the set of circumstances and living conditions to mere 'externals', in the sense that the latter are beyond our control and, therefore, extrinsic to our development of virtue. Hence, classical Stoics teach and practise an attitude of poise towards the 'externals', also called 'indifferents'. Wollstonecraft treats externals neither as entirely outside human control nor as irrelevant to virtuous human flourishing. For her, social virtue can remake certain circumstances in its own image and be itself whetted in the process. The synergetic expansion of feeling and thinking generates benevolence, sympathy, tenderness, and affection, all emanations of 'love which embraces all that is great and beautiful', the bequest of the heavenly stamp (*Short Residence* 99). Even if occasionally inclined to cut loose in solitariness, humans are born and intended to develop their feeling and thinking in communities. In short, for Wollstonecraft, humans are inherently and beneficially sociable beings.

Recent research has enriched the account of Wollstonecraft's indebtedness to the Scottish Enlightenment. Wollstonecraft leans on the Scots' identification of sociability, rather than self-preservation or solitariness, as the trigger factor for the birth of society (Rendall; O'Neill). The influence of Stoic philosophy on Scottish philosophy is also touched upon in the Introduction of the present book. The Stoic teachings about a providential order that affects the microcosmos of human motivations also provided Scottish philosophers with a powerful alternative to Lockean, Hobbesian or Rousseauian social contract theory, one that sees in fellow feeling, or sympathy, an adhesive constituent that impels human communities towards progress (N. Taylor 99–100). In his notes on Marcus Aurelius's meditations, Francis Hutcheson approvingly explained that the Stoic *logos*, 'the rational soul', is oriented to all moral good and is robust enough to cope with, and not be overcome by, 'sensations, lower appetites or passions' (Moor and Silverthorne xix). Cautious not to have this 'rational soul' mistaken for mere self-interest, abstract reason or, worse, cold calculation, Hutcheson gives flesh to this soul by calling it the 'heart' (Moor and Silverthorne xix). He sees a precedent for this synonymity primarily in the Stoics because they 'endevoured to make virtue eligible, from the very feelings of the heart', which is divinely equipped for this very purpose (xix).

A key passage from *A Short Residence* echoes a similar sociable ontology:

> What are these imperious sympathies? How frequently has melancholy and even misanthropy taken possession of me, when the world has disgusted me, and friends have proven unkind. I have then considered myself as a particle broken off from the grand mass of mankind; – I was alone, till some involuntary sympathetic emotion like the attraction of adhesion made me feel that I still was a part of a mighty whole, from which I could not sever myself. (70)

On the cusp of breaking loose, suddenly, the self is moved by an imaginative energy that re-tunes it into the being of humankind. This ontology of the self makes possible the planetary 'peculiar mindset' which conceives of alterity as that which 'contains us as much as it flings us away' (Spivak, *Death* 73). The narrator experiences adhesion to the whole not as a static condition but, on the contrary, as a unitary phenomenon made of movements towards severing and of movements that counter severing. 'Unitary' here means that there is no apartness between the world and this self that recognises its last living thread to be woven with the existence of humankind – not of loved ones, kin or the nation. Here, the narrator's cosmopolitan ontology is manifest. Combined with Wollstonecraft's religious sensibilities, ably demonstrated by Barbara Taylor in 'For the Love of God', this kind of reflection on the self and the planetary can be called, to use Epictetus's words, a study on the 'organisation of the universe' as 'a society' of all life forms that grow on earth, and particularly of human beings, 'who being bound to God through reason' can enter into communication with the divine. As Epictetus asks, why should someone engaged in such a study not 'call himself a citizen of the universe?' (*Discourses* 22; I.9.6).

Wollstonecraft's cosmopolitan ontology reaches even deeper into recesses that precede the mental operations associated with reasoning. By calling her attraction to the humankind 'involuntary', she recognises the often overlooked unrationalisable and incalculable processes that promote cosmopolitanism. In this premise, Wollstonecraft is closer to the Scottish philosophers she read and reviewed than to recent influential scholars such as Ulrich Beck, who grounds cosmopolitan empathy, i.e. perspective-taking, uniquely in reflection and awareness, reducing these principles to a rationalised source (*Cosmopolitan Vision* 71). In contrast, Wollstonecraft, making the Stoic observation that she is animated by a sympathetic emotion greater than her own volition – we need to take *à la lettre* Wollstonecraft's interrogation, 'what are these imperious sympathies?' – intimates the existence of what Galin Tihanov calls 'a multitude of unreflected practices' involved in cosmopolitan adjustments (133). This seems to be the premise of Scottish stadial theory too. For Hutcheson, Smith and John Millar, civilisation, that is, the development of humanity through stages marked by a change in modes of subsistence, emerges as a result of a sociability that precedes rationality and calculation. Society does not materialise through men's careful calculations for a contract that best satisfies their drive for self-preservation, but in the family, the primordial cell of human dependence and affection. Nature has placed women at the nucleus of this cell and, by entrusting them with nursing abilities, makes them the primary caretakers and agents of fellow feeling. Accordingly, in stadial theory a society becomes civilised as its men come to value and acquiesce to the sensibility and softening influence of women (O'Neill 92).

Despite fundamental agreement with the Scots, and implicitly the Stoics, *A Short Residence* implements salient differences. Wollstonecraft ratifies the active principle of human connectivity, but she also understands that stadial theory appoints to women an important yet restrictive and rather indirect role in the civilising process. Therefore, it is her enduring concern to break this linkage between gender and feeling that denies women an equally rational involvement in the civilising process. Her strategy is to carve out a position that allots moral weight to both reason and feeling by first recasting concepts such as Smith's sentiment 'into a delicacy of feeling and thinking' (*Short Residence* 102), and then splitting Smithian imagination from sympathy:

> This is not the first time I have remarked heart without sentiment: they are distinct. The former depends on the rectitude of the feelings, on truth of sympathy: these characters have more tenderness than passion; the latter has a higher source; call it imagination, genius, or what you will, it is something very different. (*Short Residence* 128)

It is this double-edged exigency that determines her image of the cosmopolitan, 'an enlightened citizen of the world, whose zeal for liberty appears to arise from the purest moral principles, and most expansive humanity' (Wollstonecraft, *Travels in the United States*).[9] I take 'expansive humanity' to reference tenderness, and 'the purest moral principles' to rise from 'the higher source' called 'imagination'. This double-edged exigency on both tenderness and imagination, or in similar words, 'feeling and thinking', motivates Wollstonecraft's investigation of traffic between these elements of human life and psyche. To the entrenched valorisation of (masculine) mind over (feminine) body in liberal political thought, Wollstonecraft responds with terse statements like 'We reason deeply when we forcibly feel' (*Short Residence* 171). Her choice of implementing this principle in the genre of travel and letter writing, as I discuss at the close of this chapter, has ramifications for the expansion that Wollstonecraft ushers into cosmopolitan philosophy and practice. But before we turn to this, let us briefly consider Kant's version of human sociability.

Kant, too, is influenced by these theories. He also believes that sociability drives men into society, but this is a sociability spiked with acrimony. Encountering the idea first in the work of Montaigne, Kant writes of man's 'unsociable sociability' (*ungesellige Geselligkeit*) in the Fourth Proposition of *Idea for a Universal History*. Unsociable sociability represents the drive of self-preservation that pulls humans both away from and towards each other. But, unlike his predecessors, Kant sees unsociable sociability as the evil out of which good may come, indeed nature's *telos*, the cosmopolitan condition itself: 'a universal *cosmopolitan condition* can come into being as the womb in which all the original predispositions of the human species developed' ('Idea' 14). 'Unsociable sociability' in Kant's thought 'serves first and foremost to explain human inventiveness and industry', the competitiveness resulting from the self-interest necessary to improve our situation (Schneewind 110). The discord and strife provoked by competitiveness, however, stimulate dormant abilities and call forth new ones, leading to improvement: 'Here the first true steps are taken from brutishness to culture, which consists, actually in, the social worth of human beings . . . to ultimately transform an agreement to society that initially had been *pathologically* coerced into a *moral* whole' (Kant, 'Idea' 7; see also Lloyd 203–06). The most valuable ability consists in man's perception of himself as possessing 'a rational nature' (Kant, 'Idea' 7): 'For this reason one should thank nature', rhapsodises Kant, 'for their quarrelsomeness, for their jealously competitive vanity, for their heartless competitive vanity, for their insatiable appetite for property and even for power!' This concoction of evil dispositions will compel humans to recognise that a cosmopolitan order more than any other reconciles self-interest with moral imperatives.

Although Wollstonecraft launches a vituperative critique of the contemporary commercial 'appetite for property',' taking to task her businessman lover Imlay and renowned theorists like Smith, she acknowledges some truth in competitiveness as inspired by the desire to improve one's situation, when writing of enslaved people as 'not [having] their faculties sharpened by the only thing that can exercise them, self-interest' (*Short Residence* 93). But Wollstonecraft does not give in to Kant's belief in individualistic abstract reasoning: fittingly, her philosophy couched in the travel epistolary reaches the reader as a dialogue with Imlay, the implicit 'you' and 'dear friend' of her letters. *A Short Residence*, as Mary Favret convincingly argues, reweaves out of the contemporary style of the sentimental heroine and philosopher a new subjectivity that incorporates 'female sensibility' and 'masculine understanding . . . feeling and reason, writer and reader in a productive enterprise' (96). Moreover, the opinions proffered in these letters, striving to render the strange as intelligible as possible, without claiming to grasp it in its final form, are provisional and await the response and challenges of the reader.

Wollstonecraft holds on to sympathy as an innate principle and the idea of self-interest as a first impetus to overcome indolence. Her travels in Scandinavia confirm an earlier conviction of hers, namely, that sympathy and self-interest undergo crucial developments as human communities exert themselves in arts and sciences; hence her foregrounding of vernacular literature, the product of local circumstances and activities. In *A Historical View of the French Revolution* (1794), she propounds: 'It was natural for men to be selfish, because they were ignorant how intimately their own comfort was connected with that of others' (96).[10] Hence, the solid recognition of the dependence of personal happiness on 'general happiness' is not the work of innate sympathy. In fact, sympathy can be bound up with 'selfish passions' by being first and foremost grounded in the self and generating only 'an extension of that family love' that culminates in patriotism, the harbinger of 'vainglory and barbarity' (96). Wollstonecraft would have probably agreed with Nancy Hirschman that 'sympathy contains an odd mixture of strong individualism and strong sociability. Sympathy translates self-reference into sociability by connecting our minds – or more accurately, our feelings and our inner lives – with those of others' (Hirschman 184). However, Wollstonecraft deems the translated self-reference of sympathy too weak to generate the cosmopolitan love exalted by Price as the *summum bonum* of human endeavour, since the impressions of sympathy are easily overwritten by stronger sensations. In Lockean logic, she writes of a crowd gaping at a public execution: here, 'sympathy is quickly effaced by curiosity' (*Short Residence* 168). Smith, too, drawing on the Stoic *oikeiosis*, believes sympathy to be active among family and kin but to lose force as the relational and spatial distance between self and others increases. This element remains understated in contemporary theory. Few recent studies on the compatibility of Smith's thought with cosmopolitanism caution against recruiting his theory of sympathy and benevolence indiscriminately in today's discourse on cosmopolitan justice (Forman-Barzilai 5). One study that does is Fonna Forman-Barzilai's book on Smith's moral theory, which responds sceptically to the faith that Amartya Sen in *The Idea of Justice* (2009) puts in Smith's sympathetic impartial spectator as a model for global justice. Forman-Barzilai refutes a seamless continuity between the Stoic concentric model and Smith's, as Martha Nussbaum would have it, since Smith recoils from the Stoics' imperative to collapse these circles in the name of universal love.

Shrewdly aware that sympathy, although an active principle, cannot reach far on its own, Wollstonecraft writes: 'It is time, that a more enlightened moral love of mankind should supplant, or *rather support* physical affections' (*Historical View* 294). A 'moral love of mankind' turns Price's cosmopolitan care into the hallmark of progress, since moral love seizes on the synergy between reason and fellow feeling to be expected from an evolving civilisation. But how does this 'more enlightened moral love of mankind' come by if 'it requires more cultivation of mind to keep awake affection, even in our own hearts' (*Short Residence* 136)? Politics, Wollstonecraft insists, is the indispensable instrument for this type of cultivation. *A Vindication of the Rights of Woman* acknowledges that 'the science of politics', mostly the domain of philosophers, 'is in its infancy' (56). Yet as it gains ground among the people, politics will supplant 'the brutal force that has governed the world so far' (56). For her politics encompass elements of the civil order and aspects of governing a people and public affairs, as Johnson glossed the word in 1755. Politics forge the citizenly public spirit, or the 'articulate' citizenry, prompting the emergence of an area where citizens can exercise civic personhood and participation (Ferguson xv). Without exercising political mindfulness, affections recede into the background of being, so that people lose sight of that grander horizon, or to resort to the Stoic's, Smith's and Price's imagery, that greatest circle enclosing all the others.

In Wollstonecraft's view, human 'exertions are, generally speaking, only for their families, which I conceive will always be the case, till politics, becoming a subject of discussion, enlarges the heart by opening the understanding' (*Short Residence* 103). The centrality of affections in the realm of politics and public politicising repudiates a compartmentalised view of society and its members in separate spheres. While Natalie F. Taylor is right to claim that 'for Wollstonecraft, human beings are not merely sociable, they are political', in light of the entrenched neglect of affections in liberal political philosophy, it is worth emphasising that Wollstonecraft's cosmopolitan philosophy conceives of the mature political subject as possessing an understanding attuned to affections (N. F. Taylor 108). This is a recognition that her feminist imagination bequeaths to political theory. This attunement, I think, never takes a firm and final form. Moving between attachment and detachment,

Wollstonecraft must revisit the correspondence between mind and affection provisionally, without letting it solidify. But training through politics, as a promoter of enquiry, shapes this correspondence by making us aware that we cannot hone an affection for humankind without enlarging our understanding, nor can an enlarged understanding afford to disregard our physical and moral attachment to humankind.

The Inhospitable Womb

These affinities and differences between Wollstonecraft and Kant come to bear on the future of cosmopolitanism in their thought. There is a common concern with different consequences in their projections: they both show an almost simultaneous interest in planetary living and in life on the earth. In *Perpetual Peace*, reflections on property, traditionally a point of antagonism, turn into a foundation for the cosmopolitan law of universal hospitality that Kant presents as:

> a right to visit, to which all human beings have a claim, to present oneself to society by virtue of the right of common possession of the surface of the earth. Since it is the surface of a sphere, they cannot scatter themselves on it without limit, but they must rather ultimately tolerate one another as neighbours, and originally no one has more of a right to be at a given place on earth than anyone else. ('Toward' 82)

We see 'unsociable sociability' raise its head in humans' tolerance coerced by lack of space on a spherical planet with limited land and waterways to share. As a result, Kant sees the shrinking distance between humans to effect familiarisation and overlapping interests on a planetary scale, so that it can 'finally bring the human species ever closer to a cosmopolitan constitution' governed by the law of universal hospitality. This law, 'a *right*' and not a philanthropic concession, requires that

> a stranger not . . . be treated in a hostile manner by another upon his arrival on the other's territory. If it can be done without causing his death, the stranger can be turned away, yet as long as the stranger behaves peacefully where he happens to be, his host may not treat him with hostility. ('Toward' 82)

Kant's repeated efforts to minimise hostility towards strangers are of one piece with the 'unsociable sociability' of *Idea*, whereas universal hospitality is the outcome of the advancement of reason as a result of man's unsociable sociability. Yet *Perpetual Peace*, unlike *Idea*, taking the habitable space of the earth as the basis for a minimal cosmopolitan ontology, extends also a critique of the contemporary excesses of unsociable sociability, in particular the imperialist practices of European states that are transformed from guests into usurpers (Lloyd 213). The right of universal hospitality, not to be confused with a right of universal settlement, offers a buffer to the many aggressive infringements witnessed in Kant's time and human history in general.

Wollstonecraft, too, extends an implicit critique predicated upon spatial confinement. But hers has a stronger organic orientation. Neither hostility nor rapaciousness or other breakouts of unsociable sociability grab her attention, but the well-being of the planet where, according to Kant, nature pursues the project of perfectibility with humans. The physical incapacity of the earth to perpetually adapt to human improvement spoils the dream of progress, hurling Wollstonecraft's imagination into a nightmarish landscape:[11]

> I anticipated the future improvement of the world, and observed how much man has still to do to obtain of the earth all it could yield. I even carried my speculations so far as to advance a million or two of years to the moment when the earth would perhaps be so perfectly cultivated, and so completely peopled, as to render it necessary to inhabit every spot; yes; these bleak shores. Imagination went still farther, and pictured the state of man when the earth could no longer support him. Whither was he to flee from universal famine? Do not smile: I really became distressed for these fellow creatures yet unborn. The images fastened on me, and the world appeared a vast prison. (*Short Residence* 131)

At least two contexts permeate this moment in Wollstonecraft's travelogue. The sort of anticipation she embarks on is as consciously evoked as the Stoic technique (*premeditatio futurorum malorum*) that visualises future evils or feared events including, most commonly, death (Colish, 'Seneca' 98). The technique or exercise, which the Stoics borrowed from Cyrenaic philosophy and which became part of the *memento mori* discourse, is prescribed for the therapeutic purpose of reducing angst about the future by envisaging feared scenarios. As we will see, Wollstonecraft does not premeditate in order to be inoculated against her fears.

The second context is eighteenth-century natural philosophy by authors like the French Comte de Buffon, the Scottish James Hutton and Jean-André Deluc, who pondered the age of the earth. Buffon and Hutton are particularly relevant for Wollstonecraft. Her peek a million or two years into the future of the earth matches Buffon's *Epochs of Nature* (1778), a conjectural history of earth's past and future ages. Taking as a starting point an incandescent earth that became habitable through continuous cooling and would lose its life-preserving abilities as the cooling entered inhospitable temperatures, Buffon estimated the age of the earth as from 75,000 years to ten million, predicting its future annihilation (Rudwick 62–68; Juengel). While critics found in Buffon's speculative calculation the novelistic vein that Kant openly confesses in his conjectural history with a cosmopolitan purpose, Wollstonecraft contemplates a bleak future with a sense of realism (Kant, 'Idea' 15).[12]

In 1785, the Scottish philosopher James Hutton, friend to Hume and Smith, presented to the Royal Society of Edinburgh his *System of the Habitable Earth with Regard to its Duration and Stability*, published as *Theory of the Earth* a year before *A Short Residence*. Hutton's insistence on soil as the vital source of subsistence and its disappearance through erosion may loom over Wollstonecraft's eschatology of a failing planet. In this context, we need to include Thomas Malthus. Wollstonecraft's apprehension of an earth 'so perfectly cultivated, and so completely peopled' reached the public two years before Malthus's *Essay on the Principle of Population* (1798).[13] But the impasse it faced suited a Buffon-like apocalypse rather than a temporarily catastrophic future in the style of Malthus or Hutton. Both Malthus and Hutton incorporate destruction into the cyclic development of the earth: after famines caused by nature's insufficiency, plagues or the sinking of soil at the sea bottom, a renewal would follow; for Malthus, through nature's self-regulating 'miraculous' powers, and for Hutton, through the heat at the deep interior of the earth that would heave up the sunken soil and create new land for humans and animals to dwell in (Rudwick 69).

Hutton, in particular, offers a contrasting transition from Stoic cosmology to Wollstonecraft's type of eco-psychological cosmopolitanism. Hutton's identification of heat harks back to the Stoic theory of conflagration or *ekpyrôsis* (ἐκπύρωσις), the intervals of all-enveloping fire that occur between endless cosmic cycles in which the elements of air, water, earth and fire re-emerge along with all animate life (Dean 265). From among the works of Stoic physical theory, I single out Seneca's *Questiones naturales*, used as a textbook in seventeenth-century universities. Written to his friend Lucilius in the aftermath of the 63 AD earthquake in Pompeii that inspired Edward Bulwer-Lytton's *The Last Days of Pompeii* (1834), the epistle channels Seneca's energies into comforting and instructing a shaken Lucilius in the face of natural disaster. Seneca's explanation of the earth as a planetary body undergoing sequences of cosmic doom and renewal reappears in Hutton's *Theory*. Seneca describes these sequences as tearing at the very belief of the permanence of any locality on earth and predicting the turmoil of forced migration, which he dismisses as an illusionary solution and which Wollstonecraft conjectures with alarm for similar reasons. Human illusion, according to Seneca, is belied by the physical properties of the earth, an organic body, which like the human body cannot afford constancy: 'I say that no lasting peace is possible for something that is capable of destroying and being destroyed', he concludes ('On Earthquakes', *Dialogues* 222; VI.2). Peace on earth, which Kant's reformulation of Stoicism predicates on the elimination of war, remains unattainable for Seneca because of the planet's inherent instability: 'Just as our own bodies suffer disorder, sustaining damage at the very moment they appear to inflict it', so the earth, both a victim and perpetrator of physical calamity, is 'subject to death' ('On Earthquakes', *Dialogues* 223; VI.3).

Invested in the coping abilities of each individual's psyche rather than the panoramic socio-psychology envisaged by Wollstonecraft, Seneca seeks to quash death's terrifying power by referring to the transcendental fundament of Stoic cosmology. For humans, death is only nature's porter to 'a better place' without 'earthquakes' or winds meeting to 'battle in a great crash of clouds' and 'conflagrations lay[ing] waste cities and regions' ('On Earthquakes', *Dialogues* 247; VI.32). In Hutton's theory, there is also comfort, in so far as the cyclic pattern adopted from Stoic physics agrees with the Christian creationist view of an intelligent design of 'provident wisdom and benevolence' (J. Hutton, *Theory* 79). By contrast, Wollstonecraft's future earth, lacking a providential blueprint of regeneration as well as transcendental references to 'a better place', is a nightmare without exit, a scenario of ultimate catastrophe: 'Whither was he to flee from universal famine?' This by no means denies Wollstonecraft's belief in transcendence. In other places, she speaks of the perfectible principle that is meant to adapt itself to 'a higher state of existence' than earthly life (*Short Residence* 109). However, while confronting planetary disaster, Wollstonecraft does not resort to the kind of quietist, if not escapist, solace in transcendence ringing through Seneca's epistle. The implication worth highlighting here is that Wollstonecraft's cosmopolitan philosophy allows such a greater space for considerations of human suffering that ultimately also leads to a different critique, a specifically Enlightenment critique.

Another crucial distinction between Seneca and Wollstonecraft lies at the level of philosophical and economical contextualisation of human suffering. If Seneca and Hutton judge the geological properties of the planet as factors of inevitable instability, Wollstonecraft zeroes in on the human factor. In Wollstonecraft's dismal vision, decay follows ripeness, and the geological despoliation results from the long-standing anthropogenic consumption of earthly resources that cannot revive or metamorphose into something sustaining and sustainable. Here, the earth evokes the womb through its maternal properties. Even if the viewer of this apocalyptic mindscape is maternal, as Rachel Seiler-Smith points out, harrowing 'speculative images "fasten" onto this nursing body, as if, in eighteenth-century nursing, they are "fastening" onto her breasts' (179).

Wollstonecraft's, however, is not the metaphorical womb (*Schoss*) of Kantian cosmopolitan history, but an all-encompassing organic womb that can no longer feed her children and must deliver them into starvation. An exacerbated variation of the cave-prison symbolism, eloquently argued by Eileen Hunt Botting, the nurturing earth-womb mutates into a fatal prison cell (175). Therefore neither the inimical disposition or unsociable sociability of Kantian humans nor Seneca's defective interplay of earthly elements causes the *huis clos* of civilisation, but rather an earth rendered inhospitable by human improvement, the self-same goal of the cherished principle of perfectibility. Wollstonecraft's analysis, then, departs from the timeless universalism of Stoic ecology as well as from the imperturbability achieved by premeditations of future evil circumstances. Instead, Wollstonecraft contemplates the impact of human agency within specific historical, philosophical and technological contexts and circumstances. This shift of attention also ends up undermining her own sanguine hope and conviction that the 'perfectible principle . . . will not be destroyed just as we begin to be sensible of improvement' (*Short Residence* 109). The persistent striving for individual and societal enlightenment surreptitiously threatens the future of enlightened human life, indeed any kind of human life. Human cohabitation on earth is put at risk by human aspirations for the better-yet-to-come. We face here the paradoxical destiny of perfectible life that must meet with its own destruction, while being driven towards betterment. This is Enlightenment against Enlightenment.

After imagining the suffering of unborn humans, the loss that cannot be mourned that is Freudian melancholia, Wollstonecraft can exit such spiralling distress by grounding her thoughts in the present as a moment of admonishment: 'Do not smile', she writes to her correspondent. To twenty-first-century readers burdened by the shared guilt of planetary exploitation, some lucky enough to belong to those not (yet) in the throes of famine that Wollstonecraft imagines, she bequeaths a different cosmopolitan ethos predicated not on justice, but on suffering from a moral love for humankind. Deborah Weiss rightly deems it Wollstonecraft's major feat 'to make female feeling generate the intellectual production that is, for her, the only way to advance society, albeit inch by inch, book by book' (221). Wollstonecraft's contribution to intellectual history is nothing less than a type of Enlightenment cosmopolitanism that commands attention not for its formulation of cosmopolitan law, but for its readiness to anticipate, see and partake in suffering. Paul Gilroy identifies this other kind of cosmopolitanism 'that was born from centring subjectivity on suffering rather than [Kantian] sovereignty or autonomy' in the Italian poet and philosopher Giacomo Leopardi, born in 1798 and deceased in 1837 (83). *A Short Residence* predates Leopardi's birth by two years. Perhaps because Wollstonecraft's medium is the travel memoir rather than a treatise of propositions for a legally regulated mobility between states, critics to this day cite Kant's *Perpetual Peace* as the moment when cosmopolitanism becomes a critique of imperial designs. However, the ethos of cosmopolitan suffering that erodes the cherished *telos* of improvement testifies to Wollstonecraft's seminal place within (post-)Enlightenment thought, displaying the ability of the Enlightenment to launch its own critique.

The critique that Wollstonecraft sees possible within the *Zeitgeist* of the European Enlightenment and the enrichment her critique bestows onto the Stoic tradition has gendered implications for the genre of travel writing. Her travelogue, addressed to an intimate correspondent in the presence of a child whose future engrosses the narrator's motherly attention, makes of the reader a witness and of the genre itself a virtue rather than a concession. One can argue that this virtue does not originate with Wollstonecraft. After all, Seneca's letters to his mother, male and female friends, pupils like young Nero, and people who claimed his affections and commitment all precede Wollstonecraft. The very survival of some of Seneca's correspondence constitutes an invaluable chapter in the enduring relevance of Stoic and cosmopolitan principles and praxis. But with respect to gender, Wollstonecraft exceeds and expands the Senecan model, which remains caught in unresolved tension between 'sexist stereotyping' and the fundamental Stoic tenet that every single human being is a recipient of *logos*, and therefore a possessor of equal worth and capabilities of development (Hill and Blazejak 200). The most recurrent gender stereotype in Seneca, and other Stoic thinkers, resonates in the phrase 'the wise man', a synonym for the sage and philosopher, and an assumption that remains materially unchallenged even by requests like those of Musonius Rufus, Epictetus's teacher, that both genders be educated equally. Seneca deepens such stereotyping when he considers Stoic philosophy to be as different from the other competitors as males are distinct from females (Hill and Blazejak 199). The superiority of masculine values over feminine ones, marshalled to argue Stoic philosophic excellence, underpins Seneca's endeavour to masculinise his female addresses as he attempts to instil in them the masculine principles of Stoic teaching and practice.

More directly than other Stoic writings, perhaps Seneca's letters to female correspondents such as his mother Helvia and friend Marcia, in which he feelingly but also firmly cautions these women to face misfortunes like exile and death with fortitude, helped foster one early modern association between Stoicism and women's virtuous resignation to the status quo (Clarke 59; Thomas, 'Instructive Moral' 144; Hill and Blazejak 25). It is the paradox of Stoicism to have been perceived at times as a philosophy of submissive acquiescence and at others as subversive to political power; the latter rings in the words of the interlocutor who interprets Epictetus's teaching as a call 'to hold kings in contempt' (*Discourses* 63; I.29.9). This is to say that resignation was not the only reappropriation of Stoic *apatheia* (imperturbability, indifference) and, eventually, not what Wollstonecraft emphatically adopted in her cosmopolitan philosophy. Mary Wortley Montagu offers an early counterexample on whose footsteps Wollstonecraft's writerly activity follows. Montagu drew on Epictetus to refute women's resignation to activities of the private sphere and to shake off the ridicule brought upon the figure of the learned woman or female sage (Montagu 1: 280). Read next to Montagu's empowering understanding of Epictetus, might the equation of Stoic teaching with resignation belong to those 'odious' and 'unjust' misrepresentations that Wollstonecraft, in agreement with Macaulay, chastised in her review of *Letters on Education* (Wollstonecraft, *Works* 7: 320)? As my reading of *A Short Residence* and Wollstonecraft's analysis of the French Revolution suggests, her ethos of cosmopolitan suffering weighs in to maximise the possibilities of Stoic sociable ontology and rhetoric, by making these not only compatible with but also engenderers of her enquiry into specific contemporary and future socio-economic conditions (*Works* 7: 320).

Generically, *A Short Residence*'s epistolary travel narrative and the triangular structure of its actors – the mother-philosopher writer, her businessman lover and the infant girl that binds them together – undermine gendered hierarchisation. The private letters bridge the conflict identified by Anne Janowitz between two forms of writerly sociability: familial pedagogy and analytical political radicalism (Janowitz 62; Vargo, 'Aikins' 84). The expanded use that Wollstonecraft makes of the Stoic epistolarity of friendship facilitates the correspondence between these two forms by merging cosmopolitan philosophy, as Kant calls the type of knowledge produced by *A Short Residence*, with the affective energies of epistolary intimacy (already present in Seneca's letters and Marcus Aurelius's *Meditations*, to name two seminal precedents). This fusion lends voice to the necessity that such contemplative critique spring from a human activity as common as travel and become exoteric, by substantiating itself in the practice of the family – the embryo of human sociability – rather than uniquely in the esoteric brotherhood of the *philosophes*.

At the same time, *A Short Residence* also radicalises potentials inherent in classical Stoicism by not merely ontologically positing or hopefully projecting the emergence of the female sage into the future, but by embodying her. Wollstonecraft – writer, mother, philosopher, traveller – is the wise woman producing and imparting knowledge to her male partner and, once her travelogue sees the light of print, to an immeasurable mixed reading public. In other words, the wise woman who couches concerns of cosmopolitan suffering in this type of personalised epistolary travelogue militates against what Valérie Cossy calls the 'kind of part-time humanity' that classical Stoicism did not challenge directly, and which acclaimed architects of the French Revolution like Jean-Jacques Rousseau not only took in their stride but even defended on the basis of gendered distinctions (Cossy). The result of this essentialist defence, as shown by Lynn Hunt's investigation of France's revolutionary pamphlets and tracts, was that 'the rights of women clearly ranked lower on the 'conceivability' scale' than those of other groups such as the racially and religiously marginalised (L. Hunt 168).

Markedly, Wollstonecraft's nightmarish anticipation of future disaster prefigures planetary cosmopolitanism, in Spivak's understanding of the term, because earth in this tale of progress proves to be ultimately unamenable. The planet responds with sterility to humankind's globalising managerial practices which have seemingly subdued and tilled it for human needs. I say 'seemingly' because the global agent that Wollstonecraft envisions at the apex of this management is a starving one, while the earth is still turning, the ultimate *pièce de resistance*. It is hard to imagine this despoiled but recalcitrantly enduring earth without hearing Spivak's admonishment that 'even a devastated planet lives a billion [years], without us' ('Reply' 247).[14] Wollstonecraft's text evinces angst, doubt and impotence, but it also offers a template for a different way of being in the world and with the planet. The narrator of her travel account remains attuned to the earth's organic life, positing herself as both a citizen and a provisional inheritor of a planet made of pluralisation: 'the endless perspectives' of concrete localities (*Short Residence* 74). It is a position which resists that of the global agent repudiated by Spivak, mentioned earlier in this chapter, derivative of the globe and the visual representations of the earth on maps and computers. Spivak's warning against the danger of such abstraction is anticipated by Wollstonecraft's only use of the word 'globe' in *A Short Residence*:

> Travellers who require that every nation should resemble their native country, had better stay at home. . . . The most essential service, I presume, that authors could render to society, would be to promote inquiry and discussion, instead of making those dogmatical assertions which only appear calculated to gird the human mind round with imaginary circles, like the paper globe which represents the one he inhabits. (93)

In her recognition, the globe is a reductive, unhelpful, if not caging metaphor. The disembodied consciousness of globalism, wrought in part by the scientific advancements that Wollstonecraft contemplates up to their toxic consequences, threatens a concrete being in the habitable space that earth is. 'No one lives' on the globe on our computers, writes Spivak (*Death* 72). The paper globe is not the structure where thousands of everyday circumstances unfold, Wollstonecraft reminds us. Rather, the globe with its girding imaginary circles stabilises into flat generalisations the provisionality of life attuned to a mutable planet, at times a vulnerable body rather than an ever-gifting cornucopia. Moreover, the globe as an imprisoning metaphor obscures the benefit of the kind of enquiry that does not shy away from pondering its own opacity and disenchantment or agonising over the soundness of its most cherished premises.

Notes

1 Thomas Beddoes reviewed *Zum ewigen Frieden* in August 1796, two months prior to the English translation.

2 See also Kirkley for a contrasting interpretation (*Mary Wollstonecraft* 9).

3 I do not address here Wollstonecraft's censoring of what she considered to be the perpetuation of women's enslavement in Muslim societies, because Wollstonecraft's eco-critique deserves a place of its own, as do her derogatory comments on Eastern enslavement from a cosmopolitan point of view. In a forthcoming essay, I tackle this issue, asking to what extent Wollstonecraft's censure of Eastern femininity, although not identical, can be compared to Abu Talib's censure of Turkish coffee-house and Indian-Persian reading cultures. For different interpretations see Zonana and Cahill.

4 John G. Hayman comments on the pressure felt by travel writers to provide an account of the characteristics of foreigners according to their national belonging (1–17).

5 Not only did national stereotypes circulate widely in print culture, but the study of national character was integral to David Hume's and Kant's early aesthetic and moral philosophy (Kant, *Observations* 58).

6 Wollstonecraft reviewed Smith's *An Essay on the Causes of the Variety of Complexion and Figure in the Human Species* in December 1788.

7 Sebastiani quotes the Scottish anatomist Robert Knox, who deploys the trope of engraving to explain racial variety: race 'stamps the man'.

8 The notion of perfectibility was debated by Godwin and Barbauld with several differences (Vargo, 'Aikins' 90).

9 The first sentence of the review disavows any incompatibility between one's national and planetary belonging, noting Brissot's double status as 'a citizen of France' and 'an enlightened citizen of the world' (37).

10 Here Wollstonecraft reiterates the selfish source of patriotism with remarkable clarity in a discussion of national heroes: 'these heroes loved their

country, because it was their country, ever showing by their conduct, that it was only a part of a narrow love of themselves' (*Historical View* 294).

11 Marked by dread and distress, the bleak vision of futurity that opens before Wollstonecraft's imaginary eye is an illustration of what Kant calls the 'terrifying sublime': 'The feeling of it is sometimes accompanied with some dread or even melancholy' (*Observations* 16).

12 Kant writes: 'it may seem that such a project could yield only a novel' ('Idea' 15).

13 Malthus transfers onto the geological processes of the earth and the survival of the human species the 'truly miraculous' powers of 'selection, combination and mutation' (77). His examples of regeneration after catastrophe range from the war-ridden fields of Flanders to the London plague of 1666 and the famines in China and Hindustan (35).

14 Spivak depicts the earth as both subjected to managerial megalomania and surviving it, albeit in despoiled shape: 'To globalize is to think a manageable world. To think of ourselves as planetary is to remember that if we live a hundred years, even a devastated planet lives a billion, without us' ('Reply' 247).

Chapter 3

Raising the Child-Friend of Abolitionism

Am I not a Friend and a Brother?

Happy Family 17

In *Blues for Mister Charlie* (1964), a tragic masterpiece written in the thick of the American Civil Rights Movement and in response to a series of murders of African American citizens, James Baldwin hoped that, while freeing the white man from the chimeras of racism was an unrealistic project, one could 'begin working toward the liberation of his children' (preface). Baldwin's was a hope with a long history and roots in the transatlantic abolitionist movement.

In view of the belated emancipation of the United States' enslaved population, two years after the abolition of slavery by British law, the American Anti-Slavery Society intensified its literary activism with a four-fold publication project: the newspaper *Human Rights*, *The Anti-Slavery Record*, *The Emancipator* and *The Slave's Friend*, a monthly magazine for young readers. Produced in a small size to fit comfortably in small hands, during its rather short lifespan of thirty-eight issues, *The Slave's Friend* (1836–38) enjoyed an impressive circulation comparable to that of the influential *Anti-Slavery Record* (Geist 27–28). Pursuing the goal of abolition among the young, the magazine informed its readers about the activities of the anti-slavery meetings and the youth it had already gained for its cause. The title, an echo of the self-representation of the worldwide Quaker community, conveyed the attitude of the largely Quaker body of writers, donors, distributers and readers of the magazine. Expanding friendship beyond racial and religious borders, the title included and exceeded these Christian Dissenters who since the mid-seventeenth century had called each other 'Friends of the Truth' or 'Friends in Truth', well before the official registration of the collective under the name 'Religious Society of Friends' in 1793 (Pullin 5).[1] Methodism was another denomination for which friendship meant a preferred human bond. In 1785, the London Methodist John Gardner founded the first 'Strangers' Friend Society', a relief scheme which, although not specifically targeting racial discrimination, conceptualised the stranger as someone in need and deserving of friendship. More such Methodist societies would follow in other cities. Quaker phraseology also left imprints on Continental abolitionism. For instance, the French abolitionist Société des Amis des Noirs (1788) hailed friendship as a binding value between blacks and whites.[2] Notably, friendship is the apex in Kant's cosmopolitan future of the earth. The pacifist argument dominating interpretations of *Perpetual Peace* has perhaps obfuscated the notion that, for all its worth, peaceful (*friedlich*) coexistence is subordinated to living in a friendly (*freundlich*) world society (Muthu 246).

Friendship and children amid racialised encounters during the transatlantic slavery are at the centre of this chapter. I first examine the surreptitious racism of what Frantz Fanon calls 'the prelogic thought of phobia' permeating white childhood in (post)colonial societies (137). The 'prelogic' of phobia is at times naturalised, at others demystified, in British literature. Secondly, in a racialised confrontation in *The Woman of Colour* (1808), I elaborate demystifying strategies that target the re-education of the white child's phobia of black skin. This novel's mixed-race female protagonist, eulogised as 'the child of humanity, the citizen of the world', shifts the discussion to cosmopolitan practices and their relationship to solidarity (*Woman of Colour* 103). In the context of black and white abolitionism, as a tutor to the white British child, this novel's female citizen of the world disproves the assumed incompatibility between cosmopolitanism and solidarity. The third section of the chapter traces solidary interpellation in conjunction with exposure to a 'cosmopolitan philosophy' tailored for child readers and in the concurrence of Quaker and Stoic thought. In the fourth section, I trace how Quaker educational xenophilic discourse draws on the Stoic technique that seeks to replace negative impressions and passions (*pathé*) with positive ones (*eupathéia*), while also expanding classical cosmopolitanism beyond the Stoic model, by not only foregrounding the woman and the child, two figures eclipsed by the classical male figure of the sage (the wise man or philosopher), but also by militating against systemic life conditions of enslavement. This strand of abolitionism, both black and white, with its insistence on environmental factors and their shaping influence on human behaviour, capacities and self-worth, both anticipates nineteenth-century naturalism and could be seen as the embryo from which grows the 'black naturalism' that Patrice Cormier-Hamilton sees at work in African American literature (110). Overall, my conclusion contradicts Srinivas Aravamudan's unsubstantiated juxtaposition between the tropicopolitan and the cosmopolitan (10). In fact, the scenes discussed here build on relations of contiguity between motherland and colonial realities (rather than metaphorised ones, as Aravamudan argues), between the white child and the racialised slave, sustaining the historicity and socio-political impact of these contiguities. The friendship between white children and racialised others is part of this history of socio-political engagement. I conclude, however, that the recovery of the figure of the cosmopolitan child-friend for white and black abolitionism, albeit emancipatory, must be savoured with alertness to Brito-centric complacencies that warrant speaking of an aspiring rather than perfected cosmopolitanism.

The magazine *The Slave's Friend* particularised the friendship that Quakers had practised and defended since the 1650. With their children's literature in general, and particularly this magazine, Quakers pushed the roots of friendship in what the new field of physio-psychology estimated to be the most malleable phase of human life: childhood.[3] The magazine strived to educate young readers about two competing views on the involvement of children in the matter of transatlantic slavery: one that considered slavery a topic unfit for children and the other that opposed insulationism. As such, the magazine writes: 'Some time ago many persons thought you [i.e. children] could not understand much about slavery, or do anything to put an end to it; and some people think so even now' ('To Juvenile Anti-Slavery Societies' 8). Change, however, has happened between 'now' and 'some time ago', with 'now' requiring a greater implication of the slavery question in the lives of children. Despite perceived resistance, *The Slave's Friend* holds the opinion that slavery need not be an unfathomable reality for children and approaches its task of enlightening young minds through a varied repertoire of strategies: poetry, heterodiegetic and homodiegetic tales, short pieces of catechism, accounts of African flora, fauna and social arrangements, commented and uncommented images, dialogues, anecdotes and songs. This broad array of genres helped sensitise young readers to two core topics of slave narratives and radical abolitionist literature: the 'violence of slavery and condemnation of racial prejudice' (P. Connolly 22). To the question of whether children should be recruited as activists, the magazine gives an unflinching 'yes', instructing children to channel activism by disseminating their knowledge of slavery, espousing solidary positions by word of mouth, distributing abolitionist literature, participating in the nationwide network of the Juvenile Anti-Slavery meetings and abstaining from slave-labour goods in favour of free-labour ones. The justice and effectiveness of activist investment nourishes the magazine's belief that abolitionist young readers will be those who deliver the fatal blow to the institution of slavery. '[N]ow I begin to fear', says a slaveholder perusing *The Slave's Friend*, 'If you make children abolitionists slavery must come to an end' ('To Juvenile Anti-Slavery Societies' 8). With an accessible style that aims to shape perception, judgement and actions, the magazine speaks to both its followers and the uninitiated. To the child asking what abolition is, it answers briskly: 'It is being good to coloured people' ('What is Abolition?' 3). In concrete terms, being good, as the title primes its readers, means being a friend. And being a friend involves refraining from hateful speech and hurtful acts towards coloured people (a recurring concern of the magazine).

This backdrop motivates the present chapter to engage with the strategies employed to shape the white child into the friend of racialised others, and particularly enslaved persons, in British abolitionist literature published before the 1833 Slavery Act.[4] Without investigating a large enough number of texts to warrant generalisation, the chapter nonetheless suggests that abolitionist activism marks the century's most explicit expansion of political awareness through children's literature, an awareness undergirded by the Rousseauian verdict that 'Those who want to treat politics and morals separately will never understand anything of either of the two' (*Emile* 235). Some of the texts discussed here reveal a more precise sense of the infiltration of children's literature by the politics of the day, thus deepening Matthew Grenby's expert survey of eighteenth-century children's literature and John Oldfield's pioneering research (Grenby 1–26; Oldfield). The chapter's combined focus on children's literature and issues of alterity also complements important studies on the figure of the stranger such as David Simpson's *Romanticism and the Question of the Stranger* (2013).

Children and the 'Prelogic' of Racial Phobia

The texts I select both convey and wrestle with the obstacles represented by exterior otherness, particularly epidermic otherness, through what cognitive sociology calls 'splitting'. The concept of 'splitting' refers to cognitive practices in which differences outweigh similarities and tend to produce closed boundaries between self and other (Zerubavel). The type of splitting investigated in this chapter results from the white child's phobic fantasy towards dark skin or skin of colour, or, to say it with Fanon, the 'epidermal racial scheme' ingrained in and by transatlantic slavery (92). In his hauntingly autobiographic analysis of the psycho-cognitive mechanism that performs the abjection of black subjectivity, Fanon's socio-genesis lays out insidious and overt preconceptions that stoke epidermalisation from early infancy. The type of psychic mechanisms revealed by Fanon resemble Stoic accounts of phobic first movements of the mind: negative feelings like fear and anger, which appropriate training can remove. This training teaches us not to assent to fear or anger, and not to treat them as self-evident truths (Colish, *Stoic Tradition* 42; Lesses 61). The long eighteenth century took note of this Stoic insight and developed empirical and philosophical accounts to explain the fear of epidermic difference. John Locke and Burke were two influential representatives.

In *Essay Concerning Human Understanding* (1690), Locke sees the confrontation of the white child with a black person as a hermeneutical crisis that triggers the child's transition from simple to complex ideas. In mildly mocking terms, Locke illustrates immature understanding with the example of 'the child [that] can demonstrate to you that a Negro is not a man, because white colour was one of the constant simple ideas of the complex idea he calls man' (465). Locke deems this crisis to be overcome once the child's experiential horizon has broadened to integrate embodiments of racial otherness within an expanding sense of personhood. In Locke's account, the white child's misreading of coloured or black skin seems partly ontological and partly conditioned by minimal empirical exposure to alterity.

Burke offers a blunt example for the purely essentialist rather than acculturated phobic response of the white child to black skin. Within his aesthetic theory of *Philosophical Inquiry into the Origin of Our Ideas of the Sublime and Beautiful* (1757), colourist fear seems both natural and universal. To drive home this point, the section 'Darkness Terrible in its Own Nature', rehearsing an anecdote that Burke encountered in his reading, tells of a white blind boy who gains his eyesight for the first time at the age of thirteen. A mixed blessing, the first experiences of visuality bring along a 'great uneasiness' that turns into 'great horror' when the boy sets eyes on a 'negro woman' (131). While Locke might have attributed the white child's negrophobic response to parochial (although not explicitly racial) socialisation, the former blind boy bursts into Burke's colourist scene as a *tabula rasa*. The consequence seems evident to Burke that

> there is no reason to think that the ill effects of black on his imagination were more owing to its connexion with any disagreeable ideas, than that the good effects of more cheerful colours were derived from their connexion with pleasuring ones. They had both probably their effects from their natural operation. (131)

Burke ascertains that because of innate blindness the child had neither time nor means by which to create habits that associated blackness with aversion. Thereby follows Burke's hypothesis that blackness or darkness of skin provokes instinctively negative human reactions or 'ill effects' that are surmounted only through experience. What is missing in Locke's and Burke's episodes is the transatlantic context of racial encounters: that is, a reckoning with the historical fact that Africans feature in sale documents as 'black cattle' and are assigned other abject labels which pervade all sense-making of reality and whose consequences could be overcome only through complex, vigorous and ongoing efforts (Krikler 414).[5] In other words, both Locke and Burke disregard the context investigated in this chapter.

The position taken by much transatlantic anti-slavery literature is closer to Fanon than to Locke or Burke, in that it assumes a phobic environment that primes children for conscious and unconscious absorptions of epidermic racial schema. There may be a silent Stoic indebtedness in this regard. For example, Seneca offers a subtly socialised explanation for phobic dispositions or first movements of the mind. Calling them 'preludes to passions', he sees first movements arise involuntarily, escaping the ordering procedures of cognition and judgement. At the same time, he cautions that we should not take these preludes to passions as being innate or ordained by nature simply because they are involuntary. On the contrary, they could be misleading, hence in disagreement with nature, and therefore must not have our consent. Seneca gives a telling illustration for the first movements resulting from habit and experience: the veteran, even after resuming 'a civilian dress', will be moved to thoughts of battle upon hearing the war trumpet ('On Anger', *Dialogues* 35; II.2). Transplanted into eighteenth-century abolitionist discourse, Seneca's and Fanon's insights on acculturated phobia justify a critical focus on children immersed in racialising ideologies. This was a focus taken by anti-slavery literature, which ever more frequently displayed a readiness to train children into not consenting to racially phobic movements of the mind. The strategy of resistance suggested in the scenes I discuss below has additional Stoic leanings that aim to steer the child away from the splitting influence of racial phobia – a response that Stoics associated with passions (*pathé*) – towards the good passions (*eupatheia*) of shared humanity. But before delving into such acts of substitution, I emphasise the type of shift that occurs if we treat children as central, rather than marginal, figures in transatlantic slavery and the societies this trade helped create and sustain.

Children appeared in diverse socio-economic constellations: they could be enslaved and freed children of colour, white children growing in slave-labouring economies and children ensconced in the more covertly racialised life of the mother country. Not only for witnessing the present but also for pointing towards futurity, children in eighteenth-century literature mediate the struggle against human enslavement left unfinished by the 1807 Slave Trade Act, before parliamentary measures outlawed slavery in British territories in 1833. Out of the political debates leading to the Slavery Abolition Act and the Reform Bill Act of 1832, and from among the children educated in the 1800s, would emerge the legislators and activists of the 1830s would emerge. Awareness of such potentiality punctuates anti-slavery writing in which children are cast as receptacles of the 'prelogic' of colourist phobia and become a focus of racial enlightenment. The nursery, while undergoing a temperate yet persistent politicisation during and after the French Revolution, markedly becomes an incubator of racial attitudes (Grenby 13–14). Within this context, characters of colour appear with greater frequency in books for children, a trend matched by references to white children growing in societies with institutionalised slave labour. Writers like Diderot, Jefferson, John Marrant, John Woolman and Granville Sharpe voice the fear that the normalising of physical and moral cruelty in slave-labour communities leads to malformations in the very children who were the marrow of the future nation: white children who witnessed inhumanity towards blacks.

The Haitian Declaration of Independence, fusing black and white abolitionism, prioritises the multitude of enslaved children waiting to be set free and restored to a state of natural freedom. Composed by the coloured French-educated freeman Lois Boisrond Tonnerre and read aloud by the former enslaved Jean-Jacques Dessalines to a crowd of supporters of independence, the Declaration culminates with a forceful address in the name of the children subjected to hereditary enslavement:

> Native citizens, men, women, girls, and children, let your gaze extend on all parts of this island: look there for your spouses, your husbands, your brothers, your sisters. Indeed! Look there for your children, your suckling infants, what have they become? . . . I shudder to say it . . . the prey of these vultures. ('Haitian Declaration' 188–91)

Vincent Brown has convincingly interpreted the Haitian Declaration as a document that enshrines 'the political importance of ancestry, mourning, and commemoration in the slaves' struggle against social alienation' (1247). Imbricated in these aspects of past, present and future communal life is also the Declaration's forward-looking gaze at the freed children and suckling infants of 1804 Haiti. For the writer of the Declaration (and notable thinkers of eighteenth-century moral and political theory), racialised slavery bequeathed a violent legacy to children on both ends of the epidermic schema with disastrous effects on the nation's afterlife.

Drawing on this recognition, Caroline Levander is among those rare scholars of nationhood who urges a perspective shift from the adult to the child-citizen, for '[t]he child is central not only to the state that was invented to govern strangers, but also to the idea of the citizen that was invented to people the state' (185). Starting with the child in lieu of the adult as the privileged real and/or textual witness of societal arrangements stresses a concern with futurity, because the resilience of the nation-state depends on its ability to reproduce itself healthily in the life of the child-citizen. Racialised enslavement in abolitionist literature is the cankerous agent marring the moral health of the child-citizens that the state both desires and needs to parent. Therefore, approaching 'questions of civic representation by way of the child rather than the adult makes explicit the primary, and often unrecognized, importance of racial formations to narratives' of nationhood (Levander 185). The absence of racial formations in seminal accounts like Benedict Anderson's model of the birth and functioning of the nation-state underscores Levander's point. In Anderson's *Imagined Communities* (1983) race is no meaning-making factor for the idea and ideal of the state, a vacuum duly lamented by African American and Latin American scholars. Thus, this chapter's focus on the child and racial socialisation revises Anderson's model, emphasising that, in the context of transatlantic slavery, the epiderma-based interpellations of nationhood compel questions about what Felipe Smith calls an 'ideology of kinship' according to which 'citizens of preferred ancestry' imagine '*out* of the nation' certain groups of people on the basis of external markings like skin, gender, and physical ability. These 'racist imaginings' are actualised 'by creating educational, economical, and political barriers to the official and unofficial avenues of national belonging' (F. Smith 5). The intersection where the child and the racial other meet is not only a place where barriers can be established or upheld but also undermined and overcome.

The novel to which I turn now is not only premised on the assumption that child-citizens are 'created and sustained through racial principles', but also dramatises *Bildung* against the racist imaginings that gave just title to human enslavement (Levander 185).

Solidary Racial *Bildung*

In *The Woman of Colour* (1808), bodies of colour confront the inimical barrier of epidermic racism but also turn this into an opportunity to perform acts of racial *Bildung* that deepen the cosmopolitan tradition. Appearing between the 1807 Slave Trade Act and 1833 Slavery Abolition Act, the novel predates by twenty-three years the female black protagonism of slave narratives like *The History of Mary Prince, a West Indian Slave* (1831). I am particularly drawn to ways in which the novel enmeshes this protagonism with questions of solidarity, racial *Bildung* and futurity, by cultivating ties with the increasingly popular genre of children's literature and by tutoring members of the generation that, in the 1830s, would declare the institution of slavery to be untenable.

The novel was published anonymously in London, and its author remains unknown, although the modern editor Dominique Lyndon entertains the 'intriguing speculation' that a mixed-race heiress called Ann Wright might be the author. In the scene that I discuss, the coloured body is doubly represented by the titular heroine Olivia Fairfield, the orphaned offspring of a white Jamaican planter and an African slave, and Dido, the slave-woman who accompanies Olivia during her journey and stay in Britain. A native human product of the slave economy and an heiress to a planter fortune, Olivia belongs to the mixed-race descendants that the Jamaican historian Lucille Mathurin Mair calls 'problem children, requiring special handling' by colonial law (85). Obligated by a clause in her late father's will that entails the estate to her marriage to a white British cousin, Olivia travels from Jamaica to London. Most letters in the novel, sent in packages by Olivia to her white governess in Jamaica, trace British imperial entanglements across the Atlantic and posit Jamaica as a location of accountability and reform. Significantly, the novel complements historiographical research on mixed-race citizens – a group that historian Kathleen Chater finds the least recorded – and how their skin colour affected their integration into white society (163).

The Woman of Colour's biracial protagonist enjoys a privileged socio-economic position, while also articulating the horizontal form of solidarity that Aimé Césaire considers to be a political intervention of *négritude*. Césaire finds *négritude* active in the 'common response to the situation of submission to colonialism and racism', articulated from diverse intersectional existences where gender, class, race, religion, and other factors of human life meet (Diagne; see also Mair 97). Olivia's privilege is confirmed by the historical fact that only a minority of the offspring issuing from relationships between white men and enslaved women were manumitted by their fathers, educated as free children and provided with some sort of legal provision – all advantages displayed in Olivia's sociability, eloquence and freedom to make economic choices.[6] She is among those few who can claim a dual heritage, with British belonging being assured by blood, education and inheritance. Yet this privilege co-exists with a besieged black subjectivity in the heart of a metropole that is guilty of racism, and embarrassed and divided by it. For her besieged social body, solidarity means a conscious effort that goes against personal privilege and interest, the type of political solidarity that Césaire argues does not forcibly rest on shared socio-economic situations, but on a 'common response' to colonial and racist subjugation (Diagne). Within the hiatus separating the 1807 Act and the 1833 Slavery Act, solidarity matters greatly because, as historians remind us, the abolition of the transatlantic slave trade and of slavery in the leading slave-based economy of the world was anything but an inevitable event. On the contrary, even after this achievement, the British model received little European or American support (C. Brown 23).[7] The scene I select from *The Woman of Colour* siphons dissatisfaction with the half-way solution provided by the 1807 Act and asserts cosmopolitan solidarity as the way forward.

In this scene, Olivia's white nephew comes running, appalled by an attempt by Dido (Olivia's black servant) to kiss him: '[T]hat nasty black woman has been kissing me, and dirtying my face all over', he exclaims (*Woman of Colour* 78). When the rest of the family takes the 'nasty black woman' to be Olivia, the boy replies: 'I don't mean her, but one much dirtier – so very dirty, you can't think, mamma! – Nasty woman, to dirty my face' (78). This moment has been compared to an incident of epidermalisation recounted by Fanon, highlighting the contrast between Olivia's instructive activism and Fanon's ineffable paralysis.[8] The children in *The Woman of Colour* and in Fanon's incident display, to put it in Locke's words, the child's simple understanding of the human, but that is not all they display.

The child in *The Woman of Colour* literalises the long-standing element of social phobia, popularised in Aesop's fable about washing the Ethiopian white, more commonly circulated in the eighteenth century as 'washing the Blackamoor white' (Wheeler 9). In 1807, a year prior to the publication of *The Woman of Colour*, William Godwin adapted Aesop's tales 'for the use of children' in his volume *Fables, Ancient and Modern* (145). Here Godwin recounts the story of 'a very foolish woman' who, finding her newly hired black footman pleasing in everything but skin colour, attempts to wash him with the man's permission but despite his explanation that he was born to black parents 'many thousand miles off under a burning sun' (146). Showing compassion for the 'poor' black footman who endures half a day's scrubbing, the narrator chastises the white woman's frantic mysophobia, ascribing it, as Locke had, to her narrow understanding, and particularly her unschooled knowledge of geography: she 'had never heard of anything further than London, and she thought that was the end of the world' (146). A map or globe, adds the narrator with firm faith in the enlightening power of natural history, would have taught her that black skin is just as natural as white skin. The tale's greater picture leads its young readership to think of the uneducated woman as an anomaly within an otherwise prejudice-free London neighbourhood. The *Woman of Colour* handles things more critically and limns a different picture of the imperial capital.

In this other London, the threat of epidermic discrimination lurks everywhere. Far from being purged with a map and a globe, epidermalisation is spread among children and adults. This other London is at best *hostipital*, to use Derrida's coinage ('Hostipitality' 364). Oppressed by the psychic power of the metropole's racial profiling, Olivia's epistolarity discloses fear and self-doubt. Her experience can be described as what W. E. B. Du Bois, in *The Souls of Black Folk* (1903), calls the 'peculiar sensation' of the 'double consciousness' that the self develops when one's soul is measured 'by the tape of a world that looks on in amused contempt and pity' (364). The very same outspoken protagonist who symbolically rallies with Jamaica's enslaved people is haunted and diminished by the fear of repulsing her future white husband: '[M]y person', meaning appearance or complexion, 'may disgust him!' (*Woman of Colour* 53). The narrative justifies this anticipated fear, making Jamaican racism and London racism co-extensive, when Olivia's husband confesses to a friend: 'I started back with a momentary feeling nearly allied to disgust for I beheld a skin approaching to the hue of a negro's, in the woman whom my father introduced to me as my intended wife!' (102). Among her white British relatives, the mixed-race woman dramatises the psychic burden grafted onto the black body so poignantly captured in Du Bois's plain question: 'How does it feel to be a problem?' (363). The mysophobic white child thrusts open the covert reality of Olivia's skin being a problem.

The child's openness is met with openness and with Stoic self-composure. Against erroneous phobic movements of the mind, or 'preludes to passions', Olivia rebukes all adult attempt to silence the boy. Then, putting a handkerchief in his hand and compelling him to observe and experiment with her own skin, she literalises the dirt implied in metaphorical whitewashing only to disprove it. Not only does literalisation discredit myths that feed discrimination, but it also summons the child-subject, the recipient of racial slurs and metaphors, from the margins of cultural spectatorship to the epicentre of the event. Using the logic and idiom of British empiricism, the mixed-race woman demands that the white child 'prove the truth' of coloured skin with her handkerchief (*Woman of Colour* 79). In this experiment the child learns what Robert Boyle, Fellow of the Royal Society, had concluded in *Experiments and Considerations Touching Colours* (1664): that the difference between white and black skin is skin-deep and the result neither of climatic conditions nor of divine curse: 'the Seat of that Colour seems to be but the thin Epiderme, the outward Skin' (164–65). Underneath this superficial layer of difference, Boyle confirms, there is the commonality of human flesh. The same argument is advanced by *The Slave's Friend* in cognitive and tangible terms: 'They [the enslaved] have eyes, and ears, and fingers and would learn if they were permitted to' ('The Deaf, and Dumb, and Blind' 4). This is also Olivia's constructivist verdict, similar in its attention to environmental causes to what we previously encountered in Wollstonecraft. If 'black naturalism' adds the impact of racially motivated disadvantage to the naturalistic 'idea that one's social and physical environment can drastically affect one's nature and potential for surviving and succeeding in this word', *The Woman of Colour*, Wollstonecraft and *The Slave's Friend* stress the reality that exclusion from education inscribes social inferiority onto enslaved people and people of colour at large (Cormier-Hamilton 110). So, too, Josiah Wedgwood's cameo 'Am I Not a Man and a Brother?' (1787), in which Saidiya Hartman's trenchant account unilaterally perceives 'the defeated posture' of the pet slave, aims for a black naturalistic verisimilitude that visualises the forceful subjection chaining down the potential for survival and success of the individual (169); that debasing, imposed fettering – physical, economical, spiritual – is the initiator and propagator of the exploitative environments of transatlantic enslavement. The mental association of unfreedom with chains, impressed on readers by Rousseau's pithy prose 'Man is *born free and everywhere he is in chains*', receives visual concretisation.

The Woman of Colour's black naturalism rests on monogenetic arguments which, against polygenetic strategies of splitting, hold on to a shared humanity through the same divine agency of creation. The physical proximity of the child sitting on her lap, prefiguring the maternal receptacle, resembles that of William Blake's poem 'Little Black Boy' (1789), in which the mother takes the black child 'on her lap' and kisses him, explaining through a Christian creationist metaphor that God has clothed humans with clouds, some black, some white, to cover their souls until the time comes when all clouds disappear (Blake 16).

The insertion of this emblematic face-to-face scene, in which a child is the subject of anti-racist teaching, concurs with the rise of anti-slavery sentiment in the children's literature of the late eighteenth century that I discuss in the next section. However, there is a significant reversal in this concurrence; while children's literature mostly assumed a knowledgeable adult audience teaching the young, the scene of childhood from *The Woman of Colour* posits a double audience: the white child and the adults witnessing the scene. In view of this audience that includes and rebukes the adult, thereby mounting a critique of systemic racism, this scene of instruction has something in common with the interludes of anti-colonialist *philosophes* like Diderot, that is, interludes of political catechism (Aravamudan 293).

I believe that cosmopolitan solidarity is the hallmark of the racial political catechism I discuss here. Solidarity with enslaved populations is a major tenet of this type of political catechism and its cosmopolitan ethos, although traditionally solidarity goes against the inclusive principle of cosmopolitanism. Solidarity stands opposite to cosmopolitanism when particular ethnic, national or religious affiliations take precedence over one's commitment to worldwide human fellowship. While they both prize care and moral responsibility, solidarity attends to obligations towards a community with which one is affiliated, whereas cosmopolitanism correlates community demands with obligations to the worldwide human community, including, when necessary, disregarding one's partiality for one's community (Derpmann 304–06). However, this incompatibility can be overcome, and solidarity turns cosmopolitan when it motivates people to engage in 'redistributive arrangements' of justice 'drastically different from those that would maximize their own self-interest' (Pensky 168). We see this occur in *The Woman of Colour* and abolitionist literature.

The notions of self-interest and solidarity co-exist from the early days of abolitionist opposition in the seventeenth century and throughout the eighteenth century. Self-interest appears first as religious fear of divine retribution for the sins committed in slave labour and second in relation to financial benefit. Christopher Leslie Brown notes that '[o]ften activists took up the issue of slavery less because they cared about Africans than because they regretted its impact on society, on the empire, on public morals, or on the collective sense of self' (26). This prudential solidarity in abolitionist discourse cultivates white affiliations and the moral health of white communities. The infringement of prudential solidarity was dangerous enough for planters, who felt vilified and threatened by anti-slavery attitudes that tore at the fabric of white unity. Cynric R. Williams's anti-abolitionist novel *Hamel, the Obea Man* (1827) goes so far as to expostulate that the erosion of white solidarity instigated by abolitionists represents the Achilles heel of plantocratic economy and conviviality. However, the self-interest lodged in this strand of abolitionism, with its hushing of the evils wrought by slavery on enslaved individuals, was distinct from cosmopolitan solidarity. As for financial self-interest, related arguments resurface at key moments and muddle the history of British transatlantic abolitionism. The strategies that brought the abolitionist bill to fruition in the House of Commons and the House of Lords in 1806 shed light on the relationship between abolitionist action and economic profit. As David Beck Ryden demonstrates, 'the humanitarian argument' based on solidarity with African slaves successfully dominated debates in the House of Commons. By contrast, in the House of Lords, which had refuted earlier bills that argued against the injustice of the slave trade, the argument of financial self-interest carried the day when Lord Grenville defended the bill by urging the Lords '[t]o abolish the importation of Slaves from the Coast of Africa, not for humanity, or upon considerations of justice, but upon the ground of policy, and to prevent the ruin of those islands' (Ryden 181–83).[9] Fiscal prudence was the antidote to the greatest possible ruin, and in this line of argument, ruin was of the monetary rather than moral kind.

Solidarity also mattered in the daily practice of transatlantic slavery. The planter class anxiously sought to uphold the appearance of white unison in front of the enslaved population, while eroding solidarity among slaves through a system of negative incentives like the infliction of pain, execution or postmortem violence, and positive ones such as the promotion of a few selected slaves as skilled labourers or companions as well as recipients of material gifts and privileges (Ryden 133–35). *The Woman of Colour* is sensitive to the upkeeping of white solidarity, for it evinces knowledge of a pro-planter discourse that expects Olivia's loyalty to her planter father and to the slave economy that metamorphoses mixed-race offspring like her into covetable individuals in the metropole (Steiner, 'Lessons' 56). Olivia, the product of plantocratic benevolence, must align herself with her white parentage, since to break ranks with the interests of the planter class is to kill the very income source empowering mixed-race heirs and heiresses. As Mair's research shows, breaking ranks with white power was not a viable option for most biracial women in plantocratic Jamaica, who lived with the bitterness of double resentment:

> If the mulatto nursed a resentment against the white society that would never fully accept her, she bore an even greater resentment against the black ancestry which made her unacceptable. If, on the one hand, she could exploit her command of white male attention, on the other, she could exercise the

extreme of prejudice and discrimination against her black kin. In a crisis, she could be relied on to throw her lot in with the white interest, which always promised promotion, which accommodated, albeit uneasily, the brown skin, as long as it wore its mask. (97)

Diverging from this sobering tableau, *The Woman of Colour*'s solidarity is cosmopolitan because it subordinates Olivia's self-promotion via 'white interest' to the interests of the black Jamaican community. Of course, the novel enriches the spectrum of eighteenth-century human subjectivity, but I think it is cosmopolitan solidarity and the racial *Bildung* of the white child by a person of colour that renders its biracial representations progressive. This is worth underscoring because there has been an enduring inclination to regard biraciality as a guaranteed challenge to conservative ideology. Yet belief in the automatic salvific powers of biraciality crumbles under the weight of historical evidence. To Mair's conclusion we can add the pro-slavery ideology propagated, for instance, by the South Carolina Quaker planter Zephaniah Kingsley that defended both slavery and miscegenation.[10] Therefore, the novel's biraciality becomes markedly cosmopolitan and emancipatory when the 'feelings of humanity' and Christian principles impel the protagonist to reject 'this disgraceful traffic' and 'be anxious for the emancipation of my more immediate *brethren*' (*Woman of Colour* 81). While she does not negate her white lineage, Olivia's kinship to Jamaica's enslaved is the 'more immediate' one. This voluntary closeness refutes epidermal chimeras and abandons the historically prudent choice for Jamaican mixed-race individuals and, motivated by a principle of human equality, sheds white solidarity.

Finally, the novel intervenes to expose the ideological whiteness of Enlightenment brotherhood for enabling the institution of transatlantic slavery. It also argues that a colour-sensitive opening of this brotherhood and sisterhood requires the kind of solidarity that outstrips the dominion of fear and self-interest. This opening speaks against Aravamudan's under-theorised and unhistoricised cosmopolitan subject in a century that kept imbuing the name (*nom*), as the *Encyclopédie* calls it, with new associations. Read in the light of solidarity in Jamaica's plantocracy and its relation to cosmopolitan practice, *The Woman of Colour* 'tropicalizes Enlightenment cosmopolitanism', requesting its radical fulfilment rather than annulment (Steiner, 'Lessons' 49). The white child may not yet grasp how sturdily and extensively this solidarity could undermine white self-interest by weighing against imperial profit in slave labour. Despite this temporary limitation, the novel implies, children can be impressed with a fear-free experience of the racialised body that substitutes for their fear of being threatened or soiled by it and primes them for more conscious acts of solidarity. This strategy of substitution conforms with the Stoic advice that we 'put aside this inclination to take offence and vent hatred' and replace it with positive passions like pity, understanding and benign dispositions (Epictetus, *Discourses* 42; I.18). Informed by an enlarged view of the world and reformed through such acts of substitution, the white xenophobic child can grow into the future citizen of cosmopolitan solidarity. Some strands of children's literature dramatise this formative and reformative performance, opting for exposure to alterity and, more explicitly, for friendship between the child and enslaved persons of colour.

Drawing the Child to 'Cosmopolitan Philosophy'

Children's literature of the eighteenth century increasingly exposed young readerships to imperial realities at a time when such exposure was necessary on ethical and pragmatist grounds. The sheer fact that, by the mid-1760s, the British Empire already predominantly consisted of people of non-European descent imposed the induction of white children into colonial socio-economic structures and unprecedented preparation to navigate, in James Vernon's words, a growing 'society of strangers' (31). Troy Bickham has recently proposed that the literature of the second half of the eighteenth century reflects a print market interpellating white children as inheritors of the largest imperial system that Britain became between the Seven Years War and Victoria's reign. Bickham surveys literature and games that aimed to familiarise children with colonial processes and duties, as well as with encounters with alterity. As I focus on strategies of interpretation and persuasion in several children's books that thematise transatlantic slavery in the colonial matrix, I bear in mind Bickham's finding that 'the connections between empire and childhood in pre-Victorian Britain remain underexplored' (659). The works discussed below show that, with children being prefigured as future citizens and inheritors of amassed territorial, human and financial capital, a certain type of children's literature trained a cosmopolitan-minded citizenship which fused political and moral cultivation.

The type of exposure that children received in the second half of the eighteenth century through storytelling and a wealth of geography books and travel writing fits Kant's label of the field of 'cosmopolitan philosophy' invoked in Chapter 2 (Kant, 'Announcement' 298–99). Acknowledging that this acculturation did not consistently rid itself of Brito-centric values, I turn to the children's book *Little Truths Better than Great Fables* (1787) to demonstrate the fluidity of topics and interconnectedness of knowledge at both the local and the planetary scale that are triggered by the child's queries and commentaries (Darton 63–70). Written by the Quaker William Darton, *Little Truths* abandons third-person narration, a widespread device in children's books, and opts for the dialogic form seen in *The Woman of Colour*. Handed down by Plato and later adapted into Christian catechism, the Socratic dialogue between the sage and someone of lesser wisdom is the foundational ancestor of the dialogue between adults and children from which Diderot seems to draw the alternative of *catéchisme politique et morale* (Bushnell 59). In comparison with the interlocutors of the classical model, the child in Darton's book plays a more shaping role, while the adult, unlike Socrates, does not assume feigned ignorance.

Dominated by the adult's reactions to the child's prompting, a conversation of six to seven pages in *Little Truths* moves seamlessly from descriptions of pelicans in the wilderness to travel accounts of pelicans living on the Cape of Good Hope. Silently refuting Christian iconography, the child's intervention debunks the myth that pelicans kill themselves to feed their young. This in turn leads towards the custom of Native Americans to craft bags and tobacco pouches with pelican skin, which takes the conversation to tobacco smoking among Britons and to remarks on a portrait of Sir Walter Raleigh smoking a presumably anachronistic pipe. Then Sir Walter Raleigh is contrasted with a paragon of abstinence, Omia, the Pacific Islander who accompanied James Cook on his second voyage back to Britain in 1774 and refused snuff. This discussion about the wise Omia ushers in the topic of skin colour. A consumer of print culture, the child remembers having seen 'a print of Omia, which looked as if he was a black man: where did he come from?' (Darton 68).[11] This could refer to representations in newspapers, perhaps Francisco Bartollozzi's *Omai, a Native of Ulaietea* (1774), or the 1777 engraving by James Caldwal, or Joshua Reynolds's portrait *Omai* (1775–76). The adult, in *Little Truths*, corrects the child's categorisation by saying that Omia has copper skin and 'very black' hair. When introduced to Omia's country, the South Seas, a location the child cannot visualise without a map, the child pulls the conversation back to skin colour: 'But what makes some people black and where do they come from?' he wants to know (Darton 68).

For the first time in Darton's volume, the African continent is mentioned and skin colour is its calling card: '[T]he natives of the South and South-West Coasts of Africa are all black', explains the adult (68–69). This division deviates from the distinction made on the basis of skin colour between North and Sub-Saharan Africans. The East and the West Indies appear as other zones of hot weather inhabited by dark-skinned populations. *Little Truths* offers a climatic explanation for blackness, an approach popularised by Montesquieu's *The Spirit of Laws* (1748), the work that most famously considered human constitution, customs and laws to be shaped by the physical environments that humans inhabited. Strikingly, *Little Truths* is so fluid that skin fails to be a racial feature but is rather a phenomenon of biological adaptability: if white children were sent to live in hot regions, their skin would blacken 'in degree'. Vice versa, if 'natives of any of these warm countries dwell in England, they frequently become whiter and whiter' (Darton 69). Two ramifications appear here: first, qualifiers like 'in degree' and 'frequently' neither assume nor covet scientific certainty, accounting for whiteness and blackness to appear in many shades. Second, the child emerges as the most mobile agent between whiteness and blackness. With the white child moving south and turning black and the black child moving north and turning white, the riddle behind white, black or brown skins seems to be a binding sameness: human skin's ability to adapt to sunlight. This sameness confirms the (Biblically inspired) theory of monogenesis that strengthened anti-slavery claims against polygenetic splitting.

Slavery is not far from the inquisitive child reader of *Little Truths*. With a rapid succession of questions, the child addresses the geo-ethnic backdrop of black enslavement, of which the book assumes children are aware and, therefore, must be given essential tools to make sense of it:

> *Why do they call some black people Negroes*? From Negroland, the name of a large tract of country, on the borders of River Niger, in Africa. *But why are they called slaves*? On account of being made so by great numbers of people, who go from England, Holland, and France, and encourage the strong and wicked people on the land to make war, and steal away inland natives, whom the Europeans purchase by hundreds, and carry to America and the West India islands, where these poor creatures must work as long as they live! And, not contented while enslaving the parents, they retain their children's children in perpetual slavery. (Darton 69–70)

The etymology disavows the epidermic origin of the Portuguese 'Negro', replacing it with a geographical origin related to the river Niger (unless the etymology for Niger here leads to the Latin *niger*). *Little Truths* gives remarkable details about the constructivist process of 'being made' a slave. The Europeans, initiators of the slave trade, incite intertribal warfare to secure war prisoners, whom Africans sell to European slave merchants. Elsewhere in the text, the slaves' desecrated Sundays, their brutal transportation across the Atlantic where human bodies are thrown together with elephant teeth, and their relentless work in European colonies culminate in the grim future borne out by their children's condemnation to inheritable enslavement. The fixity of enslaved children starkly contrasts with the previous mobility of white and black children migrating north and south and adapting to new environments on planet Earth. If mobility is associated with natural processes of skin adaptation, the imprisoning of children of African descent in an inescapable state of inherited slavery is not just man-made, unnatural and profane, but also rife with desperate acts of revenge and suicide, both of which are alluded to in the text. In a nutshell, the cosmopolitan philosophy of *Little Truths* does not spare the white child from a confrontation with the horrific realities of transatlantic slavery.

The depiction of the forceful separation of African families, textually rendered by the profusion of dashes, the punctuation mark that Lawrence Sterne's *Sentimental Journey* made famous not least in connection with the unfathomable harm of the transatlantic slave trade, aims to 'affect the human mind' of the young listener or reader (*Sentimental Journey* 127). *Little Truths*' account of the transatlantic slave trade causes the child's momentary dissociation from his national imagined community – '*I did not think there had been any people in England so wicked as to do those things . . . And why do they do them*?' – followed by an enquiry into dissenting agents within this imagined community who, against 'an evil desire of gain' and in solidarity with the enslaved, act for their liberation from bondage: '*There, are many good people in England, why do they not strive to stop such cruelties*?' (Darton 71, 72). In politicised vocabulary, the adult apprises the child of endeavours 'to abolish a trade so big with numberless evils' (72). The influence of abolitionist ethics is present in the description of the Middle Passage derived *verbatim* from *Considerations on the Keeping of Negroes, Second Part* (1762), written two decades earlier by the American Quaker preacher John Woolman (280). However, politicisation does not reach so far as to expose state policies and complicities. There is no mention of the Royal African Company, established in 1660 and operational from 1752 to 1821 under the name of the African Company of Merchants, nor of anti-slavery societies and/or activist topics like the boycott of imperial produce. Woolman's Christian critique of consumerism, in which 'every degree of luxury is connected with evil', is only abstractly evoked and not mobilised to reveal the brutal human exploitation for the making of imperial goods, such as the chocolate consumed during this scene of *Little Truths* (Woolman 56). Solidarity of this kind remains unattempted in *Little Truths*, which conceives of the child more as a repository of broadly cosmopolitan ideas than as the cosmopolitan activist of *The Slave's Friend*. Such reticence leaves behind the weight of a disturbing silence if we consider that around this time, to bypass and accelerate parliamentary reform, outspoken abolitionists like the pamphleteer William Fox and the poet William Cowper were pleading for the boycott of slave-labour produce as a localised form of defiance. Boycotting citizens brought to prominence in the mainland the realities of production occurring in the geographical peripheries of empire (Sussman 42).[12]

In the mediated experience of the child reader, the cosmopolitan education about the brutality of the Middle Passage could be compounded by a connection to de-humanisation. The much read and circulated *Newtonian System of Philosophy* by 'Tom Telescope' (1761) draws a wedge between brute animals and enslaved Africans, rejecting the brutalisation of the black body for enslaving and exploiting ends. The lumping of Africans with brute animals is maintained by pro-slavery discourse. For example, the pro-slavery *Hamel* perversely has a self-interested conniving abolitionist refer to the enslaved as 'the more brute beasts whom are preached up as the best part of humanity' (Williams 141). In *The Newtonian System of Philosophy*, the category 'animals' is 'naturally divided into Men and Brutes', while 'Men' are of four different kinds (101). Skin colour offers the most visible structuring element: white (most Europeans and some Asians), tawny (Africans by the Mediterranean Sea), black (Africans on the coast of Guinea) *and* red (Americans). While operating within deeply problematic eighteenth-century racialist paradigms (by Linnaeus, Buffon, Kant and later Blumenbach), this didactic moment rests nonetheless on a cosmopolitan principle as it deems diversity not to be a source of confusion (*kata cosmos*) but an element of order, even moral order in the sense of the Greek *cosmos*, by which providential care guarantees each and every person's irreducible human dignity (Telescope 91). This is a dignity trampled upon by the inhumanity of the un-Christian slave trade that provokes malformations of human sensibility because, the text insists, only a deformed sensibility can lead a human being to be affected by the instinct of motherhood in dogs and other pets, without having 'the least compunction of mind' when tearing a man from his wife and children for having committed 'no other crime' than having black skin (134). Only a deformed human sensibility can excuse the buying and selling of humans 'like so many horses' (134).

From the perspective of cosmopolitan philosophy, something more abject than the animalisation of black people and acts offensive to 'humanity and tenderness' combine in the psycho-genesis of the slave-owner who has compassion for horses and dogs because they afford him pleasure, 'fancy or self-love', 'but to other creatures that afford him none, he is absolutely insensible' (Telescope 133). These 'other' creatures include the 'poor children shivering at his gate' in the heart of empire as well as the enslaved black people brutalised in its tropical outgrowth. Both the topic of hunger and the topic of de-humanisation that reduces the enslaved to a status below animals, specifically horses, resurface with gut-wrenching details in the childhood episodes of the *Narrative of the Life of Frederic Douglass* (1845). The-less-than-animal (black) child, re-humanised and defended by white anti-slavery authors like Darton and black abolitionists like the fugitive slave Douglass, delineates the long emancipatory distance that black humanity must cover to gain inalienable equality in the context of the transatlantic slave trade.

Training the Child-Friend

The solidary friendship hailed between the white child and the black enslaved person stands juxtaposed and in response to the abject demotion discussed in the previous section. A scene from *The Happy Family or, Winter Evenings' Employment* (1801), to which I turn now, works out hermeneutics of inclusion through an emphasis on friendship with the powerless and exploited (16). The book, illustrated by Thomas Bewick and openly indebted to the work of the abolitionist Hannah More, consists largely of stories on religio-moral topics (like intemperance, sincerity and the employment of time) told by an older boy to two younger children over the course of seven evenings.[13] While six out of the seven are stories that interpret the evening's topic, the second evening has no pre-announced topic and instead features a conversation between the older boy, the eight-year-old Edward and six-year-old Eliza. With no adult present, the older boy promptly summons the other two children (and the implied children reading the book) to contemplate the picture of the kneeling, enchained slave that Josiah Wedgwood created for the seal of the Society for the Purpose of Effecting the Abolition of the Slave Trade in 1787.

In step with the society's belief in the emotive effectiveness of iconography, the older boy asks his peers to contemplate the image before he begins to depict the fate of the enslaved man represented there. A misunderstanding occurs when six-year-old Eliza denigrates the suffering slave. Captivated by his chains, she misreads his distress: 'Lo! What a disagreeable black looking creature! I never saw anything so frightful and all hung about with chains, I declare: I dare say he fancies himself my Lord Mayor or some such fine man' (*Happy Family* 17). Startled by black skin, the girl also mistakes the chains for an absurdly heavy attire, failing to respond with the empathy that the older boy solicits. Her misreading has a vaguely parodic parentage with the richly dressed and adorned black servants, signifiers of status symbols in aristocratic portraits that Aravamudan categorises as white petting of Africans (29).[14] The decision to include this image in *The Happy Family* bespeaks the anxiety stirred by the awareness that visual culture is necessarily part of children's hermeneutic archives. The misreading, on the other hand, accentuates the vulnerability of a young audience to visual representations and visuality's potential to trigger the unpredictable and incommensurable. Once the little girl's misreading disavows the transparency of visual representation, the older boy delves into the hermeneutics of epidermalisation and transatlantic enslavement. What ensues is a moment of moral catechism that is markedly politicised by the modified emblematic image that represented abolitionist interests on the floor of the British Parliament.

The older boy counters the misinterpretation of his six-year-old friend by contextualising the flagrantly decontextualised figure of the kneeling slave through a network of human relations. The little girl is taught to see the enchained slave not as a hypothetical black man but rather as someone real, someone with a history, a lamented husband and father, or even someone who may 'by this time, be loaded with chains' and 'dragged from his country, his connections, his friends' (*Happy Family* 17). Imbuing the white child's conception of the racialised human with intimacy, the dramatisation of the man's enslavement attempts to overcome the 'dialectic of abstraction', the hallmark of a modern 'society of strangers' (Vernon 29). If such fleshing-out still has vagueness about it, the little girl is taught to contextualise the black man in the daily concreteness of exploited persons brought to public awareness in reports on the activities of the free-labour colony led by the Sierra Leone Company (*Happy Family* 17–18).[15] The children in *The Happy Family* learn about the infrastructure, i.e. the daily workings of the transatlantic slave trade, and its superstructure, to which the political and activist dealings of the Sierra Leone Company belongs.

The third leg of this exposure involves an increase of immediacy, when, striving to reform the young (mis)reader, the older boy conjures an inversion of positions: what if 'your brother' is wrenched from the comforts of the very fireplace around which these evening scenes are set and violently shipped away in chains, only to find himself scorned by some girl in Africa saying: 'Lo! What a disagreeable *red and white* looking creature! –how frightful!' (*Happy Family* 18). Indirectly, adults reading *The Happy Family* to their children by a fireplace would be reminded of William Cowper's *The Task* (1785) and its anti-slavery indictment. A similar, albeit milder, strategy of inversion occurs in

Edward and George (1818), also a production of the Darton family. Here, upon marvelling at the black skin of a passer-by, a little white girl must face the relative (ab)normality of white skin: 'If you were to go to Africa, Jane, the children there would be as much surprised at your white skin, as you were at the black skin of the man who just now passed' (*Edward and George* 75). The inverted supposition achieves the conversion of these young (mis)readers from abjection to confession of guilt and finally physical intimacy with the black enslaved person: 'I wish I could take these ugly chains, tear them link from link and could raise him up from his knees', proclaims the young and recently converted abolitionist of *The Happy Family*, imagining the enchained man no longer crouched down but standing (18). Finally, to erase any trace of phobia, she concludes, 'I would kiss him' (18).

Inverted scenarios are elements of political catechism that bring uprooting and racism home, imaginatively rendering Africa, the British hearth and its colonies not merely interchangeable but also co-extensive. If Rousseau in *Discourse on Political Economy* was right to say that cosmopolitan duty relied on unrealistic expectations, because 'the sentiment of humanity evaporates and weakens as it extends itself across the globe' (17) – and Smith's conceptualisation of the concentric circles of sympathy would side with Rousseau – the counterfactual method of inversing subject positions collapses the distance between Britons, African homes and the enslaved in colonies. This collapse serves to stimulate sentiments of humanity by conjuring a difference that makes the homely uncanny, heftily so in a book titled *The Happy Family* (Rousseau, *Discourse on Political Economy* 40). Rhetorically, the counterfactual inversion aims to activate the sort of training that Hierocles expects of citizens of the world: to surmount the distance between the self and those living in remote places (Long and Sedley 1: 349).

By the early nineteenth century, the tactic of inversion drew strength from at least two distinguished practitioners: Benjamin Franklin and Denis Diderot. Speaking directly to the abolitionist question in Congress in an incisive parody published in 1790, Franklin ventriloquised a North African Muslim slave trader arguing in favour of the enslavement of Christians by the Algerian state for the same reasons reiterated by American pro-slavery lobbyists. As for Diderot, in the *Supplément au voyage de Bougainville* (1796) he advanced an anti-imperialist counter-history in which Tahitians rejected the arrogant civilising enterprise of the Europeans, delegitimising the latter's claims to territories that did not belong to any of the contemporary powers or empires. The strategy of inversion in children's literature reads like a home edition of these influential anti-imperialist and anti-slavery political precursors.

Ultimately, such a strategy seeks to instil and reshape the children's prelogical phobic disposition from distrust of alterity towards friendliness, a claim that takes us back to the Stoic psycho-pedagogy of substitution underscored by the recurrence of the word 'friend' in abolitionist literature and practice. These texts do not thematise fear merely as a psychological response and offer ways to cope with it. They are premised on a sociological approach to human cognition, which goes beyond Samuel Johnson's Stoically inspired analysis of fear as a reaction that when 'discovered to be groundless, it is to be eradicated like other false opinions, and antipathies are generally superable by a single effort' (*Yale Edition* 4: 309). In these texts, racialised fear is not innate but acculturated. The confrontation of the phobic and abject fantasies of the white child, the de-mystification of epidermic alterity, the humanisation and contextualisation of alterity through cosmopolitan philosophy, references to the infra- and superstructure of transatlantic slavery and lastly the inversion of situations like the one seen in *The Woman of Colour* and abolitionist children's literature collaborate to enact not only the unlearning of the child's phobic and inimical impressions or preludes to passions, but also their replacement with positive ones, just as Stoic teaching proposed. It may come as a surprise to find such an educational precedent in Stoicism, which, as discussed in the Introduction, became popular in the eighteenth century for promoting the absence of the passions and feelings and the pursuit of indifference (*apatheia*). As Marcia L Colish insists, and as Wollstonecraft also did in her own way, this is a misconceived, truncated understanding of Stoic passions: *apatheia* differs from *anaesthesia*, the state of no feeling at all (*Stoic Tradition* 42). Contrastingly, *apatheia* holds on to good emotions, that is, 'rational passions, consistent with the duties and relationships that flow from *logos*'. It follows that the goal of *apatheia* is not the evacuation of emotive responsiveness, but the replacement of passions conducive to negative dispositions and inimical attitudes with *eupatheia*, or good passions, like 'sympathy, benevolence, mercy, and the joys of sober friendship' (42). Such substitution, far more than an emotionally vacuous self, is consistent with the hospitable disposition of the Stoic cosmopolitan.

In certain strands of abolitionist literature, psychic and emotional hospitability takes the more accessible shape of friendship. *The Happy Family* is a good starting point with which to argue this claim, for it deploys Wedgwood's emblematic kneeling slave with relevant modifications. The illustrator Thomas Bewick has the enslaved man pose an interrogation denoted by the question mark that was often absent in reproductions of the image. The question mark was even replaced by a full stop in the evidence document delivered before a select committee of the House of Commons for the abolition of the slave trade in 1790–91. Bewick's image asks its immediate audience – the children appearing in the book and those reading it – to take a moral stand by answering 'yes' or 'no'. Second, this enslaved man asks 'Am I not a Friend and a Brother?', rather than 'Am I not a Man and a Brother', favouring the social category of 'friend' in lieu of the ontological 'man', and thus paraphrasing the slave's humanity in terms of human kinship (brother) and amical mutuality (friend). The reformulation taps into Biblical principles – 'A friend loves at all times; and a brother is born for adversity' (New International Version, Proverbs 17.17) – signalling a crescendo of intimacy that is not predicated on blood ties, because the friend who offers practical help in times of hardship can grow into a brother and a sister (Proverbs 17.17). In Biblical wisdom literature, concrete help starts with speaking on behalf of those muted by hardship 'in the cause of all such as are appointed to destruction' (King James Version, Proverbs 31.8), hence the admonishment: 'open your mouth, judge righteously, and plead the cause of the poor and needy' (Proverbs 31.8). The New Testament complements this principle of activism in an idiom that both anticipates Smith's mechanism of sympathetic imagination and acquires specific poignancy in the abolitionist context by centring on the (physical) state of bondage: 'Remember them that are in bonds, as bound with them; and them which suffer adversity, as being yourselves also in the body' (Hebrews 13.3). As Biblical scholars emphasise, 'remember', a verb often associated with God's interventions to assist humans in distress, goes beyond just recalling or being aware of something, compelling those who remember to commit to thoughtful and helpful acts (Enns and Longman 647). We can read Bewick's adaptation as one such act that radicalises the rehumanising intention of Wedgwood's cameo by invoking tighter and more palpable affective ties between young readers and the enslaved person.

The priority given to 'friend' rather than 'man' bolsters *The Happy Family*'s frequent invocations of friendship, starting with the anonymous author, who seeks young readers' proximity by introducing herself or himself with the moniker 'a Friend of Youth' at the end of the preface as well as the last paragraph of the book. Replicating this type of sociability, the older boy hails his younger peers and interlocutors in the book and his readership at large, referring to them as 'my little brothers, sisters, and friends' (*Happy Family* 16). To posit the racial other as a friend and a brother deepens the premise of social affections espoused by Scottish philosophers like Francis Hutcheson, who repurposed Stoic principles to counter contractarians like Hobbes, Mandeville and Locke. Some versions of the abolitionist discourse more than others register the bitter fact that Locke's emphasis on property as the value protected by the social contract had spectacularly failed enslaved persons, who had been transformed to chattel property. The very idea of property, decried in Rousseau's *Social Contract*, lay at the genesis of the enchainment of human beings. The pivotal subject positions for Locke were humans as an ontological category, and not friends or brothers, let alone sisters.

I propose that we read this insistence on friendship – friendship between authors and their young readers, between the characters as well as between all these and the enslaved black community – as a branch of the religiously sustained notion of friendship in the Quaker tradition. When transplanted in seventeenth-century colonies, Quaker friendship did not immediately include abolitionism. Rather the reciprocal liberty to which American Quakerism later subscribed was modelled upon, if not demanded by, the Indigenous peoples in Lenape regions who fiercely opposed enslavement (Soderlund 16). Yet Aristotle's word for friendly love, *phileô*, which Marcus Aurelius, writing 'Love the human race. Follow God', reverently recruits for the psychology of the citizen of the world, lives in the name given to William Penn's Quaker colony in present-day Philadelphia, which became the capital of Quaker abolitionism and of the free labour produce movement (*Meditations* 63; VII.31; Nussbaum, *Cosmopolitan Tradition* 84). In the name of *phileô*, the Quaker London Yearly Committee spoke to fellow Friends against the slave trade in 1727: '[the] importing of Negroes from their native country and relations by Friends is not a commendable nor allowed practice . . . and that practice is censured by this meeting' (qtd. in Reese 75). After thirty years of apparent inactivity, the Quaker Meeting for Sufferings appointed a sub-committee to oversee the anti-slave-trade work and publications of Quaker networks in Britain and the colonies. This was the first anti-slavery structure in Britain. The Abolitionist Society founded in London in 1787 grew out of this sub-committee's influence and transatlantic network. Nine of the twelve members of the London committee of the Society for the Abolition of the Slave Trade were Friends. One milestone of this increasingly resourceful and active group was the first abolitionist petition presented to Parliament by the Quaker London Meeting for Sufferings in 1783.

The culture of friendship cultivated by Quakers lent itself to cosmopolitan solidarity. Naomi Pullin's study of Quaker female friendship within and outside the body of the Society of Friends argues that Quakers adopted a Christian notion of friendship that 'opened an expansive sense of identity that was no longer confined to local communities or biological families but enabled members to imagine themselves as part of a larger world of godly people' (Pullin 5). I think that by writing 'imagine themselves' Pullin underscores the possibility of long-distance friendships that draw closer to the self those in distant geographical and affective circles. However, Pullin juxtaposes Quaker friendship with the classical notion of the highest friendship (*amicitia perfecta*), which required the equal social and intellectual status of friends (169). She rightly emphasises the Quakers building on a type of friendship modelled by Christ. Indeed, in the Gospels, Christ's followers are endowed with a new status: 'I no longer call you servants, because a servant does not know his master's business. Instead, I have called you friends, for everything that I learned from my Father I have made known to you' (John 15.15). Here, a principally egalitarian friendship substitutes for an unambiguously hierarchical servanthood. However, some refinement is needed regarding Pullin's wholesale dismissal of classical friendship.

Her analysis isolates Christian friendship at the expense of Stoic friendship, which is a strand in the web of congruencies and synergies between Christian and Stoic teaching already developed by early Church Fathers and revitalised in more recent memory by both the Puritan movement and, relevantly for this chapter, the Quakers (Ayres 55; Cochran). Scholars of Greco-Roman Stoicism argue that friendship is the glue that holds together the members of the ideal worldwide polis (R. Weiss, 194–98). A crucial inclusive impetus came from Seneca, who shifted Stoic friendship from friends who are fully accomplished sages to friends who have not achieved this perfected state and are at different stages of their development. Thus Pullin overlooks the fact that Christ's emphasis on friendship is congruent with friendship's pride of place in the Stoic art of living as an index of social virtue (Colish, *Stoic Tradition* 41; Lesses 58).[16] For instance, this communal aspect endows Stoic friends with capacities to assist each other as mentors, counsellors and 'guides in virtue' (Colish, *Stoic Tradition* 41). Pullin's study confirms the presence of such capacities in Quaker friendships but misses their classical (and not purely Christian) parentage. Also she convincingly demonstrates how the 'highly mobile and literate nature of the movement' explains the permeation of written culture, including children's literature, with Quaker values, and 'a shared religious bond [that] could solidify friendships' between Friends living long distances apart across the globe, thus overcoming the very obstacle to empathy that preoccupies Smith and Rousseau (Pullin 154).

William Penn's much read and republished address 'Advice to his Children, Relating to their Civil and Religious Conduct' (1699) bespeaks the centrality of children (and the child reader) in Quaker communities as well as the influence of Stoic thought on Quakerism. Penn delineates synergies between Christian and Stoic views of human dignity on which a non-hierarchical concept of friendship could grow. In 'Of Gentile Divinity' (1699), Penn looks up to Zeno, the founder of the Stoa, then to Zeno's Greek and Roman disciples for valorising the principle according to which every human being is possessed of capabilities implanted by an intelligent, incorruptible and benevolent divine source. In 'Primitive Christianity Revived' (1696), Penn held that the Gentiles, even in the absence of Christ or Christian teaching, had not been devoid of divine revelation. The Stoics especially appear among those Gentiles who had recognised and obediently followed the truth of divine instruction in their practical efforts to live in agreement with nature (or *eudaimonia*, literally, good spirit). Neither did Penn find fault with the incompleteness of Stoic teaching or praxis, which like Christian life itself, assuming the immortality of the soul, was a persevering work in progress to be perfected only in the 'world without end' ('Primitive Christianity Revived', in Penn 5: 281). Nigel Smith takes the presence of Stoic writings, particularly of Epictetus, in the books held in Quaker home libraries and circulated among Friends, to be expressive of a profile shared by 'seeking perfectionists' that discerned 'an ancient Greek prefiguration of Christian perfection' (62). Smith's observation is backed by Penn's references to Church Fathers like Justin Martyr, Origen and Clemens Alexandrius, who did not lessen the reputation of Christianity by bearing great respect to these Gentile philosophers that defended Christian truths, so to speak, *avant la lettre*. Of the five influential philosophers Penn mentions next to Plato and Plutarch, three are Stoics: Seneca, Epictetus and Marcus Aurelius ('Primitive Christianity Revived', in Penn 5: 303). 'Advice to his Children' establishes the contiguity between the Stoic art of living (*instituto vitae*) and Christian life, providing a list of summary attributes that convey the idea of the divine entity revealed in the cosmos and captured by the Stoic *logos*. In Penn's view, Pythagoras spoke of the 'Great Light and Salt of Ages', Zeno of 'the Maker and Father of all', Timaeus of the 'unbegotten principle, and Author of all Light, Seneca and Epictetus of 'a Domestick God, or God within' ('Advice', in Penn 5: 472). For Penn, as children of this one 'Maker and Father of all', all humans carry the 'God within' that guarantees their distinct dignity.

Penn is appreciative of the cosmology that motivated the Stoics to maintain the human dignity of the slave, insisting that no external circumstance, however degrading, can rob enslaved persons of their innate humanity and the *logos* they possess. Human dignity is a typological feature of the human soul and, therefore, inalienable in the etymological sense: untransferable. The ameliorationist abolitionism of the long eighteenth century fits the classical Stoic ethos by demanding masters to treat slaves kindly without challenging the masters' ownership of the enslaved population. The most radical strand of British white and black abolitionism, however, argues that ownership of the body is also inalienable and therefore amelioration is only defensible as a temporary intervention and not an endpoint. So *The Slave's Friend*, demanding semantic rigour, admonishes its readers: 'Do not ever say *slave-owner*, but *slave-holder*. No man *owns* a man' ('Slave Holder' 2). This strand was sensitive to living and labour conditions such as access to literacy, economic and spiritual capital, self-governance and, not least, cultural history. Out of this contextualising interest, a naturalistic view germinated, for which total control over another human's body and soul, and all the infrastructure and superstructure that go with it, create circumstances detrimental to human life and development.

This naturalistic position corrected the Stoic view that humans cannot be alienated from their innate humanity by such external factors as circumstances and living conditions. Most of the texts discussed here put Stoic substitution at the service of this new activist solicitation. The active citizenship advocated by Roman Stoicism that had inspired the Puritans and Dissenters registered powerfully with the Quakers, who found a strengthened call for concrete assistance of downtrodden sufferers in Christ's teaching: 'I tell you, whatever you did for one of the least of these brothers and sisters of mine, you did for me' (Matthew 25.40). Quaker abolitionists like Benezet made concrete efforts to do well by dispossessed and belittled persons by building schools for freed children of colour. In *Excursions of North America* (1806), some twenty years after Benezet's death, Priscilla Wakefield evaluated his tutoring among youth of colour as the vocation of a 'friend of humanity' (20). Crucially, the friend of humanity embodied by Benezet corrects the Stoic aloofness to externals, living by the conviction that externals can affect human dignity and even starve one's innate capabilities to pursue the good life intended for human dignity.

Philosophers like Martha Nussbaum deplore the fact that such recognition is rare in classical Stoicism, and underwent notable modification only in Cicero's dispensation that externals can determine the degree of the good life (*eudaimonia*) in book V of *De finibus* (Nussbaum, *Cosmic Tradition* 72). I consider the transatlantic abolitionist activism, and particularly Quaker activism, to be a milestone in the modifications brought to the Stoic cosmopolitan tradition; a modification that springs from the embarrassed position of the Stoic sage, who simultaneously posits detachment from externals and a personal investment in education and training that is at odds with the status quo of socio-economic circumstances. Nussbaum helpfully pinpoints this paradox:

> [The Stoics] are forced to admit that something politics can deliver or fail to deliver is of such great importance that it makes sense to be passionate about. Or if they don't make this concession, they have difficulty explaining their own zeal for the broad dissemination of philosophical teaching. (*Cosmic Tradition* 82)

Many commentators emphasise the non-hierarchical friendship arising between Stoic thinkers of starkly different social backgrounds. Presumably only an emperor adhering to the universal dignity of human life could admire a formerly enslaved sage as genuinely as Marcus Aurelius admired Epictetus. I also think it is worth remembering at this point the dialogue in which Seneca staunchly corrects an interlocutor who calls the slave 'a slave' ('*Servus est*'): 'No, he is a human being' ('*Immo homo est*') is Seneca's amendment (qtd. in Nussbaum, *Cosmic Tradition* 37). Seneca's intervention to reform the vocabulary of his contemporaries by teaching them to foreground the humanity and not the status of enslaved persons resonates with Wedgwood's succinct pseudo-interrogative or semi-interrogative line: 'Am I not a Man and a Brother'. However, despite this acknowledgement of the reformatory potential of Stoicism, the systemic paradox outlined by Nussbaum remains.

The Quaker tradition, spurred by contiguous views between Christian and Stoic life, rose beyond the limits of this paradox by disseminating and actualising egalitarian convictions among adults and children; and these convictions lent a further activist profile to the cosmopolitan tradition inherited by classical cosmopolitanism. The body of writers, illustrators, subscribers and donors, many of them Quakers, who backed the production and circulation of *The Slave's Friend* emphasise the importance of literacy among enslaved people, runaway slaves or emancipated black people. Wakefield, despite her Brito-centrism, which I address shortly, traces the continuity between the activism of Benezet and Woolman. As she notes, the equation of the emancipation of enslaved persons with 'the cause of humanity' and the appropriation of pragmatic skills like reading and writing enable black populations to 'participate with the other races of mankind' in a cosmopolitan network of knowledge (21, 22).

This participation reached a remarkable height with the publication of *The Interesting Narrative of the Life of Olaudah Equiano* (1789), an autobiography that explicitly rested on the formative influence of Benezet's abolitionism. In its paratext, letters and reviews, the phrase 'friends of humanity' shows an indebtedness to the Quakers, while being extended to any person desiring the abolition of the slave trade. In the opening chapter, Equiano states that he wrote his autobiography at the request of friends who had the 'interests of humanity in view', while also thanking 'the gentlemen called Friends or Quakers' for their 'deepest sense of benevolence and unwearied labor' (46, 240–1). Writing to the *Edinburgh Review* in June 1792, Equiano defends his African birth by relying again on the complicity of 'the friends of humanity', while Thomas Walker recommends the book to 'the Friends of justice and humanity' in Manchester, who in turn call on the 'friends of humanity in the town and neighbourhood of Sheffield' to promote the book in their circles (Equiano 255, 257, 258). Aware of such bonds of support, opponents who were eager to maximise doubts about Equiano's birth denigrated at a stroke the book and the 'friends to the Abolition' who vouched for it (Equiano 264).

Equiano's insistence on interracial friendship had notable precursors and successors. Ukawsaw Gronniosaw's 1772 short autobiography, one of the first autobiographies that painfully retraces the hardships of migrant life after emancipation, impresses on readers the life-saving bonds of friendship in the face of the adversities caused by European servanthood. Upon finding himself friendless, Gronniosaw relates to God as the archetypical friend ('I had no friend but God') with whom he pleads for human friends. More than once Gronniosaw's plea is answered when God 'rais'd me a friend indeed' (25).[17] Some fifty years later, Thomas Babington Macaulay, future cabinet minister, referred to the 'unfinished work' bequeathed to his own generation by such departed friends of humanity as his abolitionist father Zachary Macaulay.[18] Macaulay's racialised position in 'Minute on Indian Education' (1835) would make plain that much work remained unfinished even after the 1833 Slavery Abolition Act: so much that the de-racialisation of the white child continued to be a project worth tackling for Baldwin in 1964.

The Aspiring, Not Perfected, Young Cosmopolitan

The texts discussed above solicit the child firstly to endorse broadly egalitarian values that rest on the human dignity of enslaved racial others, and secondly to examine concrete socio-economic conditions that cripple and alienate the very human dignity that the Stoics deem inalienable by socio-economic externals. The solidary position traced in the *Woman of Colour* is desired for white children in *The Newtonian System of Philosophy*, *Little Truths*, *The Happy Family*, *Edward and George* and *The Slave's Friend*. Some of these texts intensify the anti-slavery strategies when they confront the guilt-ridden relationship between British consumerism and colonial economy. For instance, turning the rock that *Little Truths* leaves untouched, the older boy of *Happy Family* reprimands the racist imaginings of his little friend, telling her that behind the incommensurable suffering suggested by the image of the supplicating enslaved man lies no better reason than the sweetening of her palate. The black man toils and kneels in chains, so that 'such as you', he tells her, 'may have sugar to your tea, and you [sic] tarts made sweet and palpable' (*Happy Family* 18). Exposure to market realities makes the labouring enslaved populations protagonists in the child's understanding of colonial economy. How far removed this could be from some pro-slavery positions can be appreciated by the evening scene that opens the narrative of *Hamel*, when the sun 'relieved from his scorching rays those Europeans who toil on the northern shores of Jamaica' (Williams 55). Erased from the fields under the Caribbean sun, the back-breaking labour and lives of the multitudes of slaves are hijacked by industrious white protagonism.

Against such erasure, child readers of abolitionist literature like *The Happy Family* learn that their self-interest as consumers is bound up with the enslaved labour force. A book like *The Happy Family* stops short of championing the child's immediate activism through the boycott of colonial goods, although, by the last decade of the eighteenth century, many children were following in the steps of Fox's *Address* (Gleadle and Hanley 98). Despite this reticence to call for boycott, *The Happy Family* is alert to posterity when it assesses the present and future of British slavery in relation to the age of the legally relevant citizen. The older boy expresses an oblique dissatisfaction with adults, contemplating an alternative reality in which 'older christians [sic] than we, were to come to a resolution to break the fetters and kindly raise up these poor afflicted fellow-creatures, who are so sorely burthened' (*Happy Family* 19). The implied hope is that time will be on the side of reform, a reform substantiated when children who actually or imaginatively befriend enslaved people reach the age when they can accomplish what previous generations' endeavours did not.

A crucial reason for my choice of these children's books is their tendency to keep complacency at bay and advocate for reform out of a perceived unfulfilled duty of British civic life and politics that must involve the education of the young. Comparison with Wakefield's *Excursions*, which I previously cited for its anti-slavery views, helps make the point that the cosmopolitan consequences of abolitionist views can be enmeshed with tenacious Brito-centric values (redolent of Macaulay's in 'Minute on Indian Education'). Wakefield, wary of the financial loss resulting from the emancipation of enslaved persons, writes of the generosity rather than the obligation of slave-holders to relinquish their property and monetary claims in slaves (22, 23). In addition, she assumes a morally superior view of British youth. Appalled at the tyranny of American friends towards black children, the young Briton who accompanies the narrator of *Excursions* intervenes by 'giving lessons of humanity and moderation to his [white] companions' (66). This is also the geopolitical direction of Barbara Hofland's didacticism in *The Barbadoes Girl: A Tale for Young People* (1816), where British children educate their slave-owning cousin from Barbados in the ways of humanity and equality. Wakefield's and Hofland's tales do problematise the fact that the institution of slavery is a hindrance to the convivial socialisation of children – white and coloured, enslaved and free – in slave-holding societies. But their complacent Britishness relegates the corrective impetus from the motherland to the colonies, obfuscating the complicit ties of moral accountability stretching over the Atlantic. Their Brito-centrism vouches for a rather immaculate motherland as the only possible source of purifying enlightenment for the corrupt (former) colonies.

By contrast, the scenes discussed in some detail here do not cast the white child living in Britain as an infallible torchbearer of Enlightenment equity, but more often as an obstacle to the spread of the cause of humanity, or as a phobic subject to be re-formed into a friend of the racial other. Fear of coloured skin and a racialised, self-righteously sheltered and unenlightened childhood testify to the empire's heart of darkness. Perhaps more than the other texts, *The Woman of Colour* renders white metropolitan ignorance palpable by placing cosmopolitan hermeneutics within the powers of the mixed-race Jamaican heroine (not hero), the novel's pro-African activist and tutor to the white child. Because we do not see a Jamaica reformed under the abolitionist aegis of the woman of colour within the novel's timeframe, Olivia is an aspirational figure that circumscribes the text's imaginative impact, not least because of her return to the island's plantocratic system.[19] Cosmopolitan solidarity, however, debilitates the slave-holding complicity in which Olivia is born, when she humanises her vilified black servant Dido in the teeth of white, infantile mysophobia and when she sides with Jamaica's legally and economically dispossessed. Olivia leaves behind a reformed ex-husband, who does not just overcome his initial disgust but bestows on the wife he must relinquish the honorific 'the child of humanity, the citizen of the world' (*Woman of Colour* 103). The weight of this reformation is enhanced by the fact that Olivia's letters end with her husband's name. If Augustus Merton is allowed to close her narrative, then it is so that he can draw a line between the novel's garishly consumptive multiculturalism of characters from the metropole, the western and eastern ends of the empire and its aspiring biracial Jamaican woman cosmopolitan.

Notes

1 'Friends' prevailed over the less frequently used 'Children of Light'.
2 In agreement with Appiah, I do not capitalise 'black' or 'blacks', to acknowledge that black and white are culturally constructed racial categories 'and whatever rule applies to one should apply to the other'. Capitalising only 'Black' re-introduces the othering of people of sub-Saharan descent, while having both 'black' and 'white' capitalised confirms white supremacist practices that already write 'White' (Appiah, 'The Case for Capitalizing the B in Black').
3 I refer here to the influential neurophysiological treatises of Swiss natural philosopher Charles Bonnet, who, building on the metaphor of the statue-man popularised by the Abbé Etienne Bonnot de Condillac, offers what he calls a physiological 'genealogy of sensibility' (Bonnet xiii). See Vila 1998.
4 For a recent and rare socio-historical approach to children's anti-slavery activism in Britain see Gleadle and Hanley.
5 For a detailed discussion of the phrase see Schwarz 71.
6 Mair contradicts the prevalent belief that the majority of the fathers manumitted their mixed-race offspring. Her research on Jamaican pro-abolition society shows that out of 4,000 registered coloured children only 797 were manumitted, that is, 20 per cent (272).
7 Even Denmark, in 1792 the first country to abolish the slave trade, took longer than Britain to outlaw slavery in its colonies, with abolition only beginning in 1848 and then taking place over a twelve-year period.
8 From Frantz Fanon, *Peau noire, masques blancs* (Paris: Editions du Seuil, 1952), 90. 'Je voulous m'amuser jusqu'à m'étouffer, mais cela m'étais devenu impossible.'
9 See also *Substance of the Debates on the Bill* 103.
10 Zephaniah Kingsley wrote *A Treatise on the Patriarchal or Co-operative System of Slavery* in 1824, and revised and republished it three times until 1834. He departed from Quaker teaching, preserving only a liking for Quaker silent meetings.
11 An image of Sir Walter Raleigh exhaling a cloud of smoke appears in the volume's frontispiece 'Sir Walter Raleigh and his Man'.
12 The Dissenting pamphleteer William Fox called for boycott in the 1791 *Address to the People of Great Britain, on the Propriety of Abstaining from the Use of West India Sugar and Rum.*
13 The title page features a quotation from More, and the preface openly acknowledges the influence of More's *Strictures on the Modern System of Female Education* (1799).
14 The pet slave is all that Hartman (169) sees in Wedgwood's cameo, an intimation that I do not share and am inclined to interpret as a retrospective influence of the 1874 paternalistic Abraham Lincoln monument by Thomas Ball.
15 This remark may refer to the 1794 *Substance of the Report.*
16 Lesses insists that the Stoics offer an unconventional understanding of friendship among other classical schools of philosophy (58).

17 The expression is repeated: 'But My GOD, still faithful to his promise, raised me a friend' (Gronniosaw 36).

18 *Report of the Committee* 70–79.

19 *New Essays on The Woman of Colour* (2023) treats complicity as an open-ended question. In its essays, readers find critics that emphasise a white-washed biracial Olivia and others who situate her within black Romantic feminism. My approach via solidarity and its allegorical implications, argued in 'Lessons', valorises the oppositional, aspiring but incomplete cosmopolitanism of the protagonist (Aljoe et al. 56–58).

Chapter 4

Cosmopolitan Calling and Censure in *The Travels of Mirza Abu Taleb Khan* (1810)

A French traveller residing in early nineteenth-century London pondered with puzzlement the relationship between British institutions and their colonial subjects, especially when these subjects returned the visit: 'It is difficult to conjecture what idea an East Indian may form beforehand, of the mighty company and its august court . . . as he approaches the foot of his sovereign's throne in Leaden Hall Street' (Simond 208). The comment reflects on a West–East relationship which, after starting out as a mutual commercial endeavour, grew to be asymmetrical and culminated in the governance of two-thirds of the Indian subcontinent by the British Crown. The French traveller ushers in the main interest of this chapter: an unfamiliar gaze and a non-Western viewpoint on cosmopolitanism in the early 1800s.

During two centuries of intensive trade with India, travel accounts in Britain sought to answer the question: 'What does the British traveller and trader think of Indians and their country?' These accounts informed, entertained and instructed Anglophone, mostly European, readers in their imaginary or real travels to this far and foreign land. Less often were these readers trained to ask and learn about what Indians thought of their trade partners. Recently, scholarship on Britain, India and colonialism has been catching up with 'a mounting "counterflow" of Indians [who] entered Britain, living there and producing knowledge in ways that compelled British responses' (Fisher 1). The present chapter joins these efforts against the assumption of unidirectional knowledge production and devotes attention to the testimony of a distinguished Indian Persian scholar: Abu Talib ibn Muhammad Isfahani (1752–1805), who worked in the ranks of the East India Company, sojourned in Britain during 1800–02, and, although of no princely lineage, became famous as the 'Persian Prince'. His memoir, *The Travels of Mirza Abu Taleb Khan in Asia, Africa, Europe, during the Years 1799, 1800, 1801, 1802, and 1803*, written originally in Persian, was translated into English by the Irish scholar Charles Stewart and published in London in 1810. At the time, Stewart was professor of Arabic and Persian languages at the East India College in Haileybury and had previously taught at the Company's Fort William College in Calcutta. Almost two hundred years after the publication of Stewart's translation, Daniel O'Quinn prepared a critical edition of Abu Talib's memoir (hereafter *Travels*), contributing to the retrieval of neglected voices central to a cosmopolitan intellectual history of ideas.

Among the multitude of Abu Talib's wide-ranging commentaries, this chapter centres on a cluster of interrelated remarks that create a specific brand of world-openness, one that engages with the local in India, Britain, France, the Ottoman Empire and elsewhere with an eye on the inception and dissemination of worldwide knowledge. I understand Abu Talib's interrogating presence in many of these locations as the third position occupied by 'the cosmopolitan stranger', who is neither a friend nor an enemy of the host culture (Marotta 115). Abu Talib's version of cosmopolitanism, while largely refusing isolationism, evinces a principle of selection, and therefore exclusion, based on what he holds to be the universal primacy of knowledge over linguistic, national or religious borders. Put differently, in his travelogue otherness is assessed, valorised or critiqued in relation to what and how it contributes to the worldwide increase of knowledge. In Abu Talib's understanding of human existence, this is a universal imperative, even a vocation, because it benefits a shared human constitution.

For scholars of cosmopolitanism, the concept of colonial counterflow has particular resonance. The recognition of and conversation with the knowledge produced by (post)colonial subjects belongs to the tasks of what Walter Mignolo has termed 'decolonial' or 'local cosmopolitanism'. I agree with Mignolo that, without taking into account non-Western responses of cosmopolitanism, 'the planetary conviviality' envisioned by Western cosmopolitan projects remains a flawed principle ('Many Faces' 721–48). Crucial to his critique is that the complicity of cosmopolitanism with managerial designs appears to be a shortcoming exclusive to Western modernity (722–23).[1] In response to Mignolo's contrast between 'cosmopolitanism as a set of projects toward planetary conviviality' and 'globalization as the set of designs to manage the world', I trace porous boundaries between cosmopolitanism and management, arguing that the *Travels*' non-Western cosmopolitan conviviality is not devoid of management (Mignolo, 'Many Faces' 721). I understand conviviality, for which Mignolo offers no working definition, in the terms suggested by Paul Gilroy: 'a mature response to diversity, plurality, and differentiation. It is oriented by routine, everyday exposure to difference' (108–09).

Abu Talib's memoir contradicts Mignolo's juxtaposition: as a reading sensitive to the notion of knowledge in *Travels* suggests, cosmopolitan attitudes from the other 'side of the line', too, can co-exist with forms of management that often resist and remake cultural relativism and, thereby, reaffirm an active cosmopolitan ethos. To anchor this claim, my argument unfolds in four stages. I first argue that Abu Talib's cosmopolitanism is rooted in non-Western practices of writing and conviviality that compel us to think of cosmopolitan aspirations as being not uniquely Western. Second, imbued with non-Western (more than) literary convictions that defend the supreme value of the circulation of knowledge, Abu Talib takes on the role of the cosmopolitan critic. Third, this role is well understood by Charles Stewart: if Abu Taleb writes in Persian in order to increase human knowledge, so Stewart translates the Persian travelogue to confront Anglophone readerships with the unfamiliar viewpoints of the stranger or guest (*xenos*). This cosmopolitan opening, however, exposes certain acts of management that raise questions about the very notion of hospitality. As the fourth section lays out, Abu Taleb's censuring management is evident when he comments on specific ethnic and national stereotypes that hamper convivial exchange. This critique creates localised ramifications in his rebuke of the coffee-house culture of Constantinople, which he finds to be 'little better than an assembly of brutes' (*Travels* 280). Lastly, the lack of critical capacity lies at the core of Abu Talib's anxiety about the reception of his travelogue among his own countrymen, the majority of whom he deems to be ill-suited readers. Although both these moments, the critiques of Ottoman coffee-houses and of readers at home, may seem to perpetuate stereotypes of Oriental backwardness, this impression is contradicted by *Travels*' non-essentialist and non-deterministic treatment of national character. Abu Talib is first a reader of the foreign cultures he encounters, then a writer and cosmopolitan critic, and his refusal of ethnic essentialism is ultimately evidenced by his persistent writerly effort to shape the cosmopolitan reader at home.

Therefore, this chapter argues that Abu Talib's narrative advances a localist engagement for the sake of worldwide enlightenment, and a worldwide enlightenment for the benefit of local human lives anywhere on earth. Clairvoyantly, this synergetic commitment copes with its own utopianism and comes strikingly close to Epictetus's advice against despairing and abandoning this commitment since its completion is unattainable. Briefly referring to the reception of Epictetus in Arab cultures, I suggest that *Travels* should be regarded as a document of decolonial cosmopolitanism, whereby decolonial cosmopolitanism must be understood not as the other of the West, but as a trace, or as a thread in a web of what Sanjay Subrahmanyam calls 'connected histories', the origins of which can be found neither in the West nor in the East.[2]

Redrawing the Borders of Enlightenment

Abu Talib ibn Muhammad Isfahani was a prolific Persian scholar and writer of several works that bespeak his Persianate expertise. Exploring a wide range of genres, he authored *Lubbu-s Siyar wa Jahánnumá* (*The Essence of Biographies, and the World-Reflecting Mirror*, 1793–94), an account of the kingdoms of Europe and America; *Khulast al-Afkar* (*Purest of Thoughts*, 1791–92), a survey of ancient and contemporary poets, including the most accomplished Hindu poets of the age; *Tafzihul-Gaffilin* (*Exposure of the Negligent*, 1797), a critical history of the Lucknow ruler Asaf-ud-daulah; and *Mirj-alTauhid* (1804), a treatise on astronomy; and he edited *Diwan-i-Hafiz* (1791), a collection of the poetry of Hafiz Shirazi. To the British public, Abu Talib became known as a poet in his own right when a selection of his poems was translated and published posthumously in 1807 (*Travels* 158). Three years later, the publication of *Travels* consolidated his erudition among English readers.

His travels take Abu Talib on an extraordinary itinerary. Setting out in Lucknow on the waters of the Ganges towards Calcutta, in February 1799 he embarks on a vessel sailing across the Indian Ocean to Madagascar and the Cape of Good Hope, along the shores of West Africa next to the Canary Islands and north to Cork and Dublin, from where, after a short stay, he leaves for London. In January 1800, he arrives in London, where he spends two and a half years, hoping to establish professional connections to the East India Company as a teacher of Persian. He departs from London in July 1802 bound for Paris, Lyon, Genoa, Malta, Smyrna (today Turkish Izmir), Constantinople, Armenia, Mosul, Baghdad and Bussora, before crossing the Persian Gulf to Bombay and eventually travelling on the waterways of the Ganges back to Calcutta. The gradual changes of scenery and climate, enriched by an astounding panoply of social practices and characters, emerge out of the position of the stranger and the guest, whose well-being is precariously dependent on his hosts' welcoming and accommodating efforts. Hence, conviviality is not merely one wish among others, but the condition that makes the arduous affair of intercontinental travelling worthwhile.

In Dublin, Irish hospitality seems to counteract solitude most successfully. Abu Talib confesses to spending the most agreeable time of his life in Dublin, surrounded by people who know or want to know his country and language. These are people who endeavour through different 'acts of kindness and hospitality' to connect him to a social network that shares his love of erudite sociability (*Travels* 117). The Irish section of *Travels* spotlights the importance in Abu Talib's cosmopolitan ethos of a will to take the trouble to comprehend the stranger's meaning and, thereby, discover what William Wordsworth calls 'similitude in dissimilitude', the familiar in the stranger. This is the yardstick against which Abu Talib measures everything that follows and prompts him to condemn the exclusion of the stranger in Constantinople's coffee-house culture.

The very praise of hospitality animates the spectre of inhospitality, so that Abu Talib's reflections crystallise in the bedrock of a more or less imperfect hospitality. Nor can Abu Talib, during his travels, embrace unconditionally everything that lays claim to his hospitality in the form of otherness, of the unknown and of the uninvited. Derrida's comments on hospitality illuminate Abu Talib's experience, as they affect theories and practices of cosmopolitanism, particularly those inherited from Kant. Expanding on *Idea for a Universal History with a Cosmopolitan Purpose* (1784), in 'Toward Perpetual Peace' (1795) Kant argued for a deep and pacifying linkage between hospitality and cosmopolitanism, conceiving of hospitality as a universal right of visitation: 'a stranger [is] not to be treated in a hostile manner by another upon his arrival on the other's territory' (82). However, Derrida is troubled by Kant's hedged right of hospitality as visitation (*Besuchsrecht*), and his reaction comes with a double movement. He first raises the concept to ethos: 'Hospitality – that is a name or an example of deconstruction' ('Hostipitality' 364).[3] Then he explains that hospitality can never fully embrace the stranger, because it can never be unconditional; it can never be an open door through which the alien, the strange human, the animal, can enter and exit freely. Thus it cannot offer the absolute welcoming that it designates and strives to achieve, without setting restrictions on guest and host alike. The accommodation of the stranger implies a hierarchy – that is, decisions made by the host and expectations to be attended to by the guest. As Peter Melville explains, a practice of absolute welcome (unconditional hospitality) would imply the full acceptance and integration of the guest, so that they make themselves truly at home. But by this very definition, with the welcoming and welcomed party being at home, the difference between the host and guest dissolves and with it the very necessity of anyone being hospitable to another: 'Hospitality, if it succeeds finally in making the guest feel at home, cancels its own history. It covers up its tracks, disappearing without a trace' (*Romantic Hospitality* 14). Underneath the very presence of hospitality lingers a history of failure without which, however, the embrace of the guests, and the otherness for which they stand, would signify their very assimilation.

In this sense, for Derrida, hospitality is always to come (*à venir*). Although the tense seems to project hospitality in the future, utopian postponement (*avenir* = the future) is far from Derrida's intention. As with hospitality, democracy and cosmopolitanism, the *à venir* conjures the present as a daily training devoid of teleological certainty, in terms akin to the praxis of the aspiring sage in Stoicism. The only certainty about this training is its interminability, since it can never project a programme into the future or obtain its goal (*Of Hospitality* 15). In light of cosmopolitanism to come, I explore the moments of conviviality in *Travels* and speak of cosmopolitanism because conviviality grows out of the desire to know, and therefore de-exoticise, the other. Mostly this knowledge is used not to master the other, but to share in moments of exchange and co-existence which, nonetheless, are never without effort, if not struggles, of accommodation. Therefore, we can speak of moments of unfinished conviviality within the discourse of cosmopolitanism.

It is important to emphasise here Abu Talib's Persianate education and this education's roots in the practices of the Mughal Empire. The ethos of conviviality at the heart of *Travels* draws its essence from the cosmopolitan texture that Persianate culture developed under the pressures of successive empires and, more particularly, during the Mughal Empire. Of the five imperialist projects – the Savafid, Ottoman, Mughal, Russian and European – that traversed Persian literary humanism, the Mughal Empire was the most hospitable. According to Hamid Dabashi, Mughal India became the heartbeat of Persian literary humanism (192). Dabashi equates Persian literary humanism with the very far-reaching concept of *adab*. In Persianate culture *adab* stands for a literary production as well as codes of comportment and moral values. Dabashi argues that, upon entering Mughal courts and their religiously heterogeneous territories, *adab*, as both literature and ethos, was to face an ecumenical encounter, 'facilitating a conversation among Muslim-Hindu segments of the empire' (203). One of Dabashi's key claims is that Mughal India cultivated a syncretic cosmopolitan humanism of Persian *adab* with consequences that endured from the eighteenth century well into the twentieth (212).[4] Abu Talib does not understand his contribution to conviviality as an acquiescence to host cultures but as an ecumenical participation that redirects these cultural traditions, interrogating their realities, practices and self-assurances. In other words, *Travels*, a document of Persian literary humanism, shows that 'contrary to a major train of thought in postcolonial thinking, it is not only "Western" humanism that is capable of worlding itself' (Dabashi 199).

In *Travels*, the foundational feature of conviviality between the foreign visitor and their host culture is textual or generic. Abu Talib's account, although emerging from distant shores, shares important assumptions with European travel narratives. The recording of travels is part of the Muslim literary genre of the *rihla*. Originating from the Arabic *rahla* (to set out, to depart, to migrate), *rihla* came to designate travel accounts that combined the pursuit of religious and worldly knowledge. In Persian, these travel accounts, called *safar nama* (travel book), belong to and enact *adab*. The *safar nama* and *rihla* uphold both valences of *adab*, by being as much literary productions as templates of a cosmopolitan ethos. Stefania Pandolfo describes the *rihla* 'as physical journey and existential displacement as the style and possibility of learning . . . The imperative for traveling for seeking knowledge determined the cosmopolitan character of centers of learning, where everyone was a foreigner and everyone belonged' (315–16). Although not irreducible to classical and later European travel accounts, the *rihla* shares with them ideas about travelling that are present in both Abu Talib's and European Enlightenment travel writing. The *rihla* foregrounds, first, the importance of leaving one's home to acquire knowledge; it absorbs observations pertaining to geography, history, local mores; second, it celebrates the movement and circulation of knowledge; and, lastly, it gives precedence to knowledge gathered by eyewitnesses and supported by storytelling. The Greek 'authority of autopsy', that is, seeing with one's own eyes, corresponds to the Arabic *'iayn*, which stands for unmediated observation (Euben 16). Consistent with the *rihla* and *safar nama* as well as many European travel narratives that, since Pausianas's *Guide to Greece* in the second century CE, elaborate on the pleasures, benefits and dangers that attend a traveller's life, Abu Talib provides readers who may venture in his footsteps with advice about the safest routes and means of transport (*Travels* 78).

The emphasis on knowledge that Abu Talib's memoir inherits from the *rihla* and *safar nama* is worth scrutinising, since it has been a stubborn rather than persuasive assumption that the quest for knowledge as the main motivation for exploring beyond familiar horizons distinguishes Western civilisation and fosters its superiority. As late as at the turn of the twentieth century, Jürgen Habermas writes in a much-cited chapter that 'to gain distance from one's own traditions and broaden limited perspectives is the advantage of Western Occidentalism' ('Remarks' 162): an articulation that crops up in the works of a host of writers (some of them neo-Kantians like Habermas) and is possibly as much a part of the self-perception of the West as Kant is a towering figure of Occidental Enlightenment.[5] Yet it also is an assumption contradicted by the many English Enlightenment thinkers, writers, radical Protestants, Unitarians and Deists reconsidered in Humberto Garcia's *Islam and the English Enlightenment 1670–1840*, as they sought to revive rationality through a return to the figure of Mohammed, for them an example of enlightenment. Their efforts contradict Habermas's presumed gap between the West and the rest. Indeed, the idea of Enlightenment with a capital E in encyclopaedias and surveys of Western literature and culture – retrospectively synonymous with a particular span of time, philosophy and moment of modernity – monopolises the very metaphor of knowledge as light, so much so that a diffuse idea of Western civilisation (where does it start and end geographically, temporally, symbolically?) circulates as shorthand for a journey from darkness to light guided by an unabated yen for knowledge.

Reading Abu Talib's *Travels* as a thread in the web of connections helps us to relinquish such monopolistic fantasies. Neither light nor valorisation of knowledge springs uniquely from Western soil. In splendid imagery, involving passages between darkness and light, Abu Talib discloses that his principal reason for travelling to England is employment, namely, to prepare future teachers of Hindustani, Persian and Arabic languages who themselves would not travel but dwell in Britain and instruct Company employees who aspired to work in India:

> The plan I proposed was, that I should commence with a limited number of pupils, selected for the purpose, who were not to go abroad; but, each of these to instruct a number of others: thus as one candle may light a thousand, so I hoped to spread the cultivation of the Persian language all over the kingdom. By these means I expected to have passed my time in England in a rational and advantageous manner; beneficial both to myself, and to the nation I came to visit. (*Travels* 123–24)

The metaphor of the one candle that lights a thousand links rationalism with illumination and the spread of knowledge, in this case of unknown languages and remote cultures, through contact with someone who has the first-hand expertise of the Greek autopsy or Arabic *ʿiayn* which the '[British] self-taught masters, ignorant of every principle of the science' lack (*Travels* 124). Just to name another example of this metaphor: a prayer-poem by Emperor Shah ʿAlam conceives of justice and prosperity, in themselves results of a good government, in terms of all-encompassing light:

> illuminate the world with the light of my justice . . . let me make hill and plain prosper through my justice . . . Since you have made my name shine like the sun throughout the world, By my sun illuminate the hearts of friends and foes. (qtd. in G. Khan 7)[6]

Like the candle that kindles a thousand other candles, the light of the just government reaches indiscriminately friend and foe, familiar and unfamiliar lands. Conceived as a divine gift, this light prescribes the sovereign's calling to a cosmopolitan or, in other words, a shareable benefit of knowledge, in itself a practical orientation towards individual and social virtue. Abu Talib, too, defends his educational plan as a vocation that furthers his own rational well-being and that of a convivial world made of hosts and guests who exchange knowledge capital. For important strands of Arabic philosophy, striving after knowledge is synonymous with the pursuit of 'what constitutes true happiness: philosophy, or knowledge of the existing things that by nature are simply to be known' (Reisman 64). The reason to speak of vocation or calling rests with the idea of an 'Active Intellect' in Arabic philosophy that lies outside human intellect but whose action 'is the providence of the rational animal, to seek its attainment of the highest grade of perfection appropriate to man'. Al-Farabi, a key representative of that influential Arabic line of thought which built on and refined the Neo-Aristotelianism developed in Alexandria, likens the 'Active Intellect' to the sun and human intellect to vision, asserting that, in the absence of this sun-like 'Active Intellect', there could be neither vision or sight emerging from the human eye nor intellect from human life (Reisman 62). We also find the notion of vocation in Epictetus, who extrapolates from the providential gift of reason the 'calling' that distinguishes the 'citizen of the world' from 'wild beasts'. This calling expects citizens to refrain from prioritising their 'personal advantage', in fact '[n]ever to deliberate anything as though detached from the whole' (*Discourses* 90; II.10.4). Abu Talib's employment plan follows this principle.

Such central valorisation of knowledge bears resemblances to Kant's '*sapere aude*', or 'dare to know', that reductively has become the motto of Occidental Enlightenment. Much has been written about the entrenched individualistic and abstract rationality inaugurated by Kant's exhortation, and many critiques of Kantian revivals, like Habermasian philosophy, redress the solipsism of Western metaphysics, inherent also in a concept of cosmopolitanism obsessed with the rightful boundaries of the ego. In contrast, within everyday life exigencies, such as the necessity to make a living, Abu Talib's conception of knowledge is grounded in communitarian cosmopolitanism and mutual benefit. Knowledge is acquired to be passed on to others, to cross linguistic, ethnic and religious divides. The metaphor of candles lighting many others conveys the very act of giving that Abu Talib's memoir performs materially on the page: knowledge gathered, processed and made accessible. Although, or because, such metaphors have become part of Western cultural furniture, there is significant value in the discovery of what Subrahmanyan calls 'vocabularies that cut across local religious traditions', which by revealing 'ideas and mental constructs' in flux and circulation, make us realise that 'what we are dealing with are not separate and comparable, but connected histories' (748).[7]

Managing Cosmopolitanism and Translating Knowledge

A solipsistic economy of knowledge distribution is the main target of Abu Talib's cosmopolitan critique, when rebuking the British self-taught masters whose learning and teaching represent in the flesh the misguided self-sufficiency of a civilisation that puts more trust in its books. For example, in the inaccurate grammar and lexicons of Persian written in English, rather than in the synergetic exchange of knowledge with native scholars. Gulfishan Khan's translation of '*ustad-i ja 'li*' as 'the most ignorant pretenders' (62) drives home Abu Talib's discontent with British scholarly insularity and blind self-confidence more effectively than Stewart's rendering ('the self-taught masters', *Travels* 124). This was also the complaint of Ghulam Hussein, an intellectual and contemporary of Abu Talib, who judged British scholarship on India as suffering greatly from a poor reliance on indigenous savants (G. Khan 62). Such a propensity for elitist self-sufficiency would culminate in James Mill's myopic assertion that travelling and empirical knowledge were superfluous: 'a man who is duly qualified may obtain more knowledge of India in one year in his closet in England, than he could obtain during the course of the longest life, by the use of his eyes and ears in India' (12).

Abu Talib's collaboration with the East India Company testifies to the multifaceted value of connected histories not as inevitably unifying, but as moments of informed critique. His memoir devotes several passages to investigations of imperialism that contribute to a de-Westernisation of knowledge. Here Abu Talib's scathing critique of the Company's administration and its uncosmopolitan stance towards education deserves a mention. Moreover, the East India Company's commercial approach with no regard for public welfare, the immoral commercialism sweeping over Asia from warring European states, Abu Talib's moral autopsy of the vices and virtues of the English and his praise of Irish hospitality in the face of crippling poverty can be understood as initiating the 'delinking' of knowledge, to use Mignolo's terms, from centres of power ('Delinking').[8] Hence, it would be wrong to understand Abu Talib's concept of the acquisition of knowledge for dissemination purposes metaphorically. There is evidence that his advice to his countrymen affected the latter in their subsequent dealings with the East India Company, inspiring opposition rather than subordination to Company policy. In 1806, when the directors ordered the hiring of two Indian teachers (*munchi*) at the lowest salary paid at the Company's college at Haileybury, the Hindu and Persian scholars in question insisted that they be paid the salary proposed by Abu Talib in *Travels*. Their terms were accepted, and the teachers' work was remunerated with a salary 22 per cent higher than that of the highest-paid British professor, Charles Stewart, the translator of *Travels*, and three times higher than the salary negotiated by an Indian scholar who had applied independently some years previously (Fisher 114–15).[9] At the same time, however, Abu Talib perceptively registers that the traveller's desire to acquire and disseminate knowledge must plug occasionally into networks of power, into some kind of economy of production and distribution (Mignolo and Gastambide-Fernandez 205–06).[10] He regrets, for example, in a passage omitted in the first edition of the translation, that, due to lack of financial support and patronage, his travelogue cannot enhance the reader's comprehension with visual illustrations, maps and drawings of places, objects, and people (*Travels* 60).

Abu Talib understands the urge and need to travel and disseminate the impressions gathered on one's travels as springing from a view of the shared human passion for 'curiosities and wonders' (*Travels* 58): 'such a passion', he insists, 'has been implanted by nature in every human breast, as an honour and an ornament to the species' (60). If, as Tihanov clarifies, cosmopolitanism 'has always, explicitly or tacitly, built on the assumption of a shared (and accessible if not necessarily immediately transparent) human constitution that is being mobilized, or at least addressed', the cosmopolitan premise of *Travels* rests on the desire for shared knowledge, 'new discoveries and inventions' (Tihanov 134; *Travels* 60). Moreover, aiming 'to add to the stock of [the reader's] knowledge' and inspire 'imitation' of foreign discoveries, *Travels* participates in reconfigurations of home and the familiar through a cosmopolitan circulation and adaptation of knowledge that triggers recalibrations of political, economic and cultural powers (*Travels* 59, 60).[11] There is a point of contact between Persian and British travels and readers in this valorisation of 'wonders', 'discoveries and inventions'. What Barbara M. Benedict writes about early modern European culture, namely that '[c]uriosity became the trademark of progress itself' (1), also holds true for Abu Talib's memoir. Stating the value of curiosity at the outset of his account and sustaining it throughout with a panoply of architectural, scientific, botanical, zoological and ethnographical descriptions, Abu Talib endorses the emphasis on *aj'aib* (the strange, marvellous and unusual) that is a central convention of the *rihla* (Euben 115). It is important to stress this point against Bernard Lewis's othering of Muslim curiosity and the quest for knowledge as the unscientific and unstructured other of Western curiosity (208, 280).[12]

Attention to the scientific developments aligns Abu Talib with the networks of European and American philosophers and scientists that Schlereth calls 'the world brotherhood of knowledge', a cornerstone of Enlightenment cosmopolitanism (25–46). Abu Talib's talk of 'imitation' does not mean an uncontested replication, thus refuting the passivity of 'spectatorial cosmopolitanism' (Robbins, *Feeling* 17). He vigilantly gauges the advantages and pitfalls of European technological developments as works in progress and experiments worth examining. When discussing a manufactory of needles or a spinning engine, he carefully surveys the relation between the division of human labour and machines, surprised that the making of a basket of needles requires only two people, each of them responsible for one segment of the process, and the spinning of threads only a few women and boys. Heightened speed, Abu Talib notices, is the greatest benefit of these new technologies: speed to produce thousands of tools maximises profit (*Travels* 166–67).

Abiding as his fascination with the technological progress is, it is also checked by a critique of a future spun out of control, detrimental to both moral and physical life. Speed is singled out as one of the most dangerous aspects because it breeds impatience. According to Abu Talib, impatience, the source and product of an accelerated pace of production, is responsible for inferior products, as in the case of English muslin, which because of its 'over twisted' threads does not wear or wash as well as the manually spun equivalent in India (*Travels* 166). The over-twisted thread figures synecdochally the excess attending the Western scientific boom. Obsession with speed betrays the haste of Western progress (167), a feature of scientific development condemned later in Mary Shelley's *Frankenstein* (1818), where Victor deliberately selects big body parts for his creature to accelerate the process with no regard for the difficulties a giant would face in the outside world. As Abu Talib notices, demand for speed is an excess that predicts the degradation of the social and moral habitus in unacknowledged, uncosmopolitan ways. Prosperity and luxury, 'the bad consequences of which have not yet appeared', foster, among other defects, 'a contempt for the customs of other nations and the preference [the English] give to their own; although theirs, in fact, may be much inferior' (*Travels* 218). This contempt, he notes, can take the shape of 'obstinacy and prejudice in favour of their own customs' (217). Not referring to British condescension towards Indian customs exclusively, but towards other nations too, Abu

Talib presents his critique from a third perspective, in which the other is evaluated not merely through references to the self and the nation, but through a multitude of nations and selves. This non-binary perspective treats 'the abstract category of the world as a form of third culture' (Delanty 70). Therefore, Abu Talib's advised remedy against the moral disintegration of the English is rooted in cosmopolitan education. Abu Talib attributes redemptive potential to the reading of history, which reveals to readers the vices responsible for the downfall of powerful civilisations. For him, Occidental and Oriental histories hold equal places, 'the subversion of the Roman Empire in Europe, and the annihilation of the Moghul government in India' (*Travels* 217).

It is cosmopolitan education through exposure to foreign historiography that also motivates Stewart's translation of *Travels*. By the time of the English publication of *Travels*, Stewart had gathered considerable expertise in Eastern cultures and languages during a six-year assistant professorship at the Fort William College in Calcutta. Three years followed as a professor of Arabic, Persian and Hindustani at Haileybury College in Hertford. Stewart believed that Anglophone readers would greatly benefit from the unprecedented 'counterflow' historiography about 'the institutions of Europe' by an Asian savant ('Translator's Preface', 2009 ed., 57–58). The appearance of the second English edition of *Travels* in 1814, following on from the 1811 French translation and 1813 German translation, rewarded Stewart's faith in Abu Talib's work. However, seeing the English translation of *Travels* as an act that validates 'counterflow' historiography should not distract from its incomplete conviviality. The dedication and the note prefacing *Travels* display Stewart's uneasiness with the 'disadvantages' stemming from the tension between fidelity and adaptation that is inherent to the act of translation (Stewart, 'To the Most Noble' 56). Fidelity, Stewart admits, is imperfect because of the processes of adaptation that a new linguistic and cultural territory imposes on the guest-text. Hence, he elucidates that he had to 'curtail or omit' Abu Talib's narrative 'in very few instances' and to reshuffle 'the Chapters, in order to preserve a connexion between the subjects' (57). In a paragraph that does not appear in the second edition, he summarily writes that he has omitted 'the poetical effusions of the Author', a long list of friends Abu Talib met at particular places, a 'dissertation on anatomy' and a lengthy description of a hot-house (Stewart, 'Translator's Preface', 1810 ed., vii. These textual interventions assume that the guest-text must be filtered and reorganised to better match the taste of the hosting Anglophone readership.

To maximise the aesthetic compatibility between the Persian text and the British readers, Stewart's translation aims for a clearer distinction between travel narrative and imaginative literature. This intention leads him to discard 'the poetical effusions' of Abu Talib, tipping his hat towards the requirement for '"factual" parameters' that were coalescing in European travel writing (Leask 222). The taste for generic parameters had been trained at least since the 1660s, when the Royal Society published instructions for scientific travellers, and later through the frequent advice given by various writers to future participants of the Grand Tour. The impressive range of travel narratives published between 1550 and 1800 shows that by this period travel and travel writing had become methodologised through thousands of instructional publications and correspondence among European intellectuals and centres of learning and documentation (Stagl 47–90). As a result, Stewart's decision to restructure the translation into a familiar and increasingly standardised mould is not surprising. Despite this compliance with generic expectations, Stewart hurries to secure his translation's exclusivity over the 'books of fictitious travels, ascribed to natives of the East': for 'the first time', he writes, 'the opinions of an Asiatick, respecting the institutions of Europe, have appeared in the English language' ('Translator's Preface' 57–58).[13] The co-existence of adaptation techniques with claims to authenticity lay bare two kinds of imperial anxieties. The first concerns the journey that foreign texts took to Britain and their arrival as strange imports of unsettling potential, in need of textual supervision and management. The second points to these texts' status as potential frauds among British readers, a possibility that ultimately harbours the uncanny question: can we ever know what the foreigner thinks, in this case the Indian? Both these concerns, the danger of the strange import and its unsound reception, have a bearing on textual conviviality and hospitality.

For paradigms that tend to fetishise the source text, translation represents an act of both hospitality and betrayal: one language receives ideas that were first articulated in another language, and foreign ideas come to live and share existence with the signs of another idiom. This welcoming by and into the sign-system of another idiom has a cost for the guest-text, which must be changed and modified to fit the linguistic house of the host. In this sense, Walter Benjamin states in 'Task of the Translator' (1923) that the translator faces an impossible imperative, an impossibility present in the German title that captures the double bind of *Aufgabe* (task) and *aufgeben* (surrender, capitulate). For Benjamin, however, this capitulation has salutary consequences since a text's afterlife thrives in its translations. The eighteenth century produced its own concept of textual capitulation. Alexander Tytler's *Essay on the Principles of Translation* (1791) stressed the importance of literalness, but Tytler made it clear that literalness meant fidelity to the author and not to the text. As Matthew Reynolds explains, from Dryden to Tytler, the good translator transmits authorial intentions to the receiving readership in elegant and congenial ways. From this viewpoint, translation is an act of 'metempsychosis or transfusion' at the end of which 'the source can be buried or cast away, a dead body or a dry skin' (Reynolds 66). Transposed onto Stewart's translation, such emphasis on the author's intentions once more raises the question: 'What did the Indian author think?'

While the tradition of translation as interpretative 'metempsychosis' informs Stewart's edition, it also co-exists with the worry about fidelity that was gaining strength and would dominate nineteenth-century theories of translating, although the acculturation of the foreign text would still be the paradigm behind translation for mass production (Bassnett and France 52–53). Stewart's preface reflects this moment's dual exigencies: an obligation to the original that demands that translators acknowledge their modifications, and an obligation to modify the text in order to appeal to the taste of the host readership. The double bind then comes down to a matter of prioritising obligations to approximate a distant other – an effort that lies at the heart of cosmopolitanism. Stewart's cosmopolitan education as the translator of *Travels* is less ambiguous when he counters contemporary reviewers who reproached him for tampering with the 'Oriental' character of the work, whose 'descriptions [despoiled of the poems] are not sufficiently replete with Oriental imagery, or flights of fancy' (*Travels* 61–62, footnote). In a footnote, Stewart retorts that it is a symptom of ignorance to assume ornamental imagery or '*climaterical* warmth' in all Eastern writings. Proving wrong the exoticising and homogenising expectations of British readers, Stewart refers his detractors to the 'Descriptive Catalogue of Tippoo Sultan's Library' as evidence for a very versatile tradition: 'the Orientals can and do write in every kind of style' (61, footnote). Nonetheless, the omission of Abu Talib's poems cannot be unambiguously legitimised if we consider that poetry permeated all literate strata of Mughal society, all kinds of discourses from scientific to literary and political. Indeed, even the political vision of the just and pious government of Emperor Shah Alam reached its subjects in the shape of poetry, as illustrated above (G. Khan 7).

Stewart is outspoken about another key modification: 'the necessity of transposing the chapters in order to preserve a connexion between the subjects' ('Translator's Preface'., 2009 ed., 57). This is the only change he justifies as being an obligation towards the culture that hosts *Travels*; a culture accustomed to a certain trajectory of development, according to Stewart, 'an object little attended to by Oriental writers in general'

(57). It is in the reshuffling of the text, an intervention that seeks to compensate for an allegedly vagarious Oriental habit of travel writing, that Stewart's managerial efforts surface most clearly. It is plausible to interpret his reluctance to translate the poems of Abu Talib as an instance of the kind of resignation that Kate Teltscher encounters in some British travel memoirs of India, featuring moments where Europeans restrict themselves to communicating their 'desperate perplexity' and surrendering to the Indians' 'ultimately unknowable and independent existence' (32–33). In this interpretation, Stewart's confessed 'inability to do justice to the poetical part of the Work' ('Advertisement' 58) may exude his unwillingness to settle the Oriental poems for British readers, thus shunning a strong (Saidian) disciplinary version of Orientalism. The other omissions and the modified chapter order, however, submit the Persian text to the systemic restructuring of the translator, who takes on the responsibility of cultural mediator. Hence, Stewart's avowed caution, reservation and awe towards the text that he promotes is nonetheless not devoid of a weaker form of disciplinary Orientalism.

A helpful contrast here is the instance of a strong type of disciplinary Orientalism towards *Travels* later in the nineteenth century. In *The Biographical Dictionary of the Society for the Diffusion of Useful Knowledge* (1842), a work that aimed to provide a thorough survey of contributors of knowledge by rescuing forgotten ones from oblivion and 'put[ting] them in their proper rank', Abu Talib is listed 'as a learned and intelligent native of India' who 'received excellent education, at least what the Moslems consider such' (6: 210). This sense of British superiority and denigration of the Islamic intellectual tradition echoes T. B. Macaulay's 'Minute on Indian Education' (1835), which, nullifying the arguments of 'admirers of the oriental system of education', championed instead English as the vernacular language for Indians, a people who, in Macaulay's reasoning, 'cannot at present be educated by means of their mother-tongue' (1: 229, 231). (Abu Talib's instruction model contends that Indians can and must educate themselves in their vernacular languages.) Macaulay's eulogy of Britons as educators of Indians has the implicit support of the *Biographical Dictionary*, which explains its decision to include *Travels* with surprising reasons:

> The Persian text is admirably calculated to give the natives of India a correct idea of the Power, the magnificence, and even the manners and customs of the British Empire. The British reader will derive both instruction and amusement. (6: 211)

Where Stewart assumed an openness of reading, firmly convinced that to hear from the other is edifying (although the other's voice may require adjustments like the ones Stewart undertakes), the *Biographical Dictionary* blatantly reduces Abu Talib's analysis to an encomium of British civilisation. Invoking an imaginary ethnic homogeneity in India, such complaisance is equally oblivious of what a contemporary reviewer in 1810 had self-critically described as the 'acuteness' of Abu Talib's 'animadversions on our customs, manners, virtues and vices' (review of *The Travels of Mirza Abu Taleb Khan* 274). The *Biographical Dictionary*'s deafness hijacks *Travels* for purposes of imperial propaganda, thus containing and shoehorning Abu Talib's critique into a self-congratulatory imperial ideology. Such otherising imperial sentiments can hardly be extrapolated from Stewart's translation. Therefore, Stewart's decisions as an editor and translator of *Travels* testify to both his trust in his own judgement about the taste and practices of British scholarship and to his appreciation of the Persian original and its critique.

This brief discussion of *Travels*' debut in English lays out an ambivalence that cosmopolitanism and translation have in common. One could say that translating is the cosmopolitan act *par excellence* because it invites a text to be at home in a foreign idiom and among an unfamiliar readership. It is, moreover, a tool of cosmopolitan knowledge and education that promotes the reader's sense of world literature (*Weltliteratur*), at least since Goethe coined the phrase (Damrosch 1).[14] In the case of *Travels*, the convivial relationship between Stewart's translation and Abu Talib's Persian original is performed under mediatory managing conditions (*Travels* 57). I believe this to be an imperfect conviviality driven by a bi-directional, and therefore cosmopolitan, approach to knowledge: by Stewart's wish to promote knowledge of and from the other and by Abu Talib's intention in *Travels* to share the 'curiosities and wonders' of Europe of which many 'might with great advantage be imitated by Mohammedans' (57).

Stewart's reservations about his own translation raises a question that persists in Abu Talib's *Travels*: if cosmopolitanism is endorsed as an ethos that seeks to preserve and valorise difference, how should it face the unwelcome, the morally (even though always and only subjectively) suspect or reprehensible? Must the citizen of the world embrace difference indiscriminately in order to remain true to a vision of total inclusiveness? Perhaps the question comes down to what criticism stands for: is it a sign of hostility or can we better capture critical cosmopolitanism under Derrida's notion of *hostipitality* (blending the hospitable and the hostile), a conditioned and potentially censuring embrace of the other ('Hostipitality' 356–420)? Can 'a saving critique' (*rettende Kritik*, in the sense of rescuing), an approach associated with Walter Benjamin, inscribe both conviviality and censure in the form of a minimal managerial kernel within an ethical concern for close and distant others (Habermas, 'Bewusstmachen' 205–07)? Or to return to Gilroy's definition of conviviality as 'a mature response to diversity, plurality, and differentiation' (108–09): what qualifies as a mature response; does or could critique characterise maturity? The next section addresses this question as I consider the evaluation of coffee-house cultures in *Travels* to elaborate the complicity between cosmopolitan commitment and managerial necessity. The coffee-house, a locale of urban conviviality, provokes Abu Talib's conditional appreciation of otherness and his critique of mere multiculturalism undertaken in the name of a shared cosmopolitan economy of knowledge.

The Cosmopolitan Critic

A comparison of Charles Stewart's 1810 preface with that of the French translation in 1811 reveals a greater interest on the part of the French translator in this text's non-Europeanness. The French translator not only emphasises that the target readership of *Travels* was not European but goes on to enthuse over its representations of territories in the Ottoman Empire (A. Khan, *Les Voyages* xii). A focus that wonders not only about the Indian other, but also about that other's other, emerges in the review of *The Travels of Mirza Abu Taleb Khan* in *The British Critic* too. Less insular-minded than Stewart's preface, which centres on the memoir's connection to Britain and Britons, this review comments on Abu Talib's journey from Constantinople to Baghdad and his visits to tombs and sacred places, illustrating his interest with an excerpt about the Ottoman habit of smoking. This excerpt was reproduced frequently throughout the nineteenth century, cementing the stereotype of the indolent and tobacco-addicted 'Turks' who light their pipes even 'while riding at a brisk pace' on horseback (*Travels* 281). To my knowledge, nothing has been said about this stereotype's incorporation in the setting of the Ottoman coffee-house. Modern commentators, like Stewart, more often than not have reflected on Abu Talib's gaze on Britain or British subjects rather than on the larger cosmographic map of *Travels*. As I hope to demonstrate, the coffee-house functions as a cross-national and cross-ethnic trope that prompts readings of Abu Talib not just as a witness from the other side of the line, that is, as the other of the Western reader, but as the cosmopolitan stranger formulating a critique from a third position, as the other's other who thinks of the world as a third culture.

The coffee-house is a cultural construct of sociability that intrigues Abu Talib at several locations: in Britain, France, Constantinople and

Baghdad. By virtue of the interconnections established through this trope beyond national and ethnic boundaries, representations of the coffee-house agree with a key procedure of 'methodological cosmopolitanism' (Beck, 'Mobility' 30). The first description of the English coffee-house links this construct to print culture and dissemination. Abu Talib writes of the 'Utility of the Art of Printing', to which,

> the English are indebted for the humble but useful publication of Newspapers, without which life would be irksome to them. These are read by all ranks of people from the prince to the beggar. They are printed daily, and sent every morning to the houses of the rich; but those who cannot afford to subscribe for one, go and read them at the coffee-rooms or public-houses. (*Travels* 157)

He goes on to state that the information circulated by newspapers in the coffee-houses ranges from events, conflicts and victories at home and abroad, parliamentary debates, information on food prices, the economy and births and deaths among the powerful, to details of cultural events and entertainment (157–58). His perception corroborates the description of an eighteenth-century British observer who conveys the idea of a public sphere that gathers around different bodies of the demos. As platforms of circulation of information and knowledge, newspapers and coffee-houses energise the public sphere:

> Coffee-houses make all sorts of people sociable, the rich and the poor meet together, as also do the learned and the unlearned. It improves arts, and merchandize and all other knowledge; for here an inquisitive man, that aims at good learning, may get more in an evening than he shall by Books in a month. (Houghton 132)

When we turn to Abu Talib's assessment of French coffee-houses, all references to newspapers or the circulation of news disappear: 'In Paris, the coffee-houses are innumerable, but in general are very filthy; and as many of the French smoke segards or cheroots in them at all hours of the day, they smell shockingly of tobacco. A person is also much annoyed by beggars at these places' (*Travels* 242). Beggars in search of benefactors and consumption of tobacco, rather than daily updates on internal and foreign affairs, are the sole markers of Parisian coffee-houses. We need to compare this experience and its snobbish irritability with that of the coffee-house in Constantinople to gauge the implications of Abu Talib's tacit omission of print media.

In Constantinople, his dissatisfaction with a consumptive, sedentary, leisured coffee-house goer crystallises:

> The coffee-house and barbers' shops in this city are innumerable. The Turks, though very indolent, are not fond of retirement or solitude: they, therefore,

> immediately after breakfast, go to one of these places, where they sit smoking, drinking coffee or sherbet, and listening to idle stories, the whole day. Their conversations are carried on in a loud tone of voice, and sometimes eight or ten persons talk at the same time; it is therefore impossible for a foreigner to understand what they are saying; and, in short, the societies of these coffee-houses are little better than an assembly of brutes. The rooms are also exceedingly dirty and seldom afford any thing but thick coffee, and tobacco cheroots or pipes. (*Travels* 280)

The French and Ottoman coffee-houses resemble each other: they are unsanitary and full of tobacco-smoking customers. So are the ones in Baghdad, echoing Abu Talib's bad experience in Constantinople: 'Baghdad abounds with coffee-houses, and rooms for smoking tobacco; but are even darker and filthier than those of Constantinople' (*Travels* 315). It is noteworthy that the resemblance between French and Turkish coffee-houses, rather than that between French and English ones, undermines the idea of a monolithic West. The same effect arises through the comparison of musical traditions during Abu Talib's short stay in Genoa: 'I here acknowledge, that the Indian, Persian, and Western Europe music bears the same comparison to the Italian that a mill does to a fine-tuned organ' (263). Thus the coffee-house experience and aesthetic considerations provoke a reshuffling of expectations that undo a binary organisation of Eurasia.

Such reshuffling at the time of Abu Talib's journey is topical. In 1802, when Abu Talib set foot in Constantinople, the long-lasting alliance between France and the Ottoman Empire had only recently come to an end. Agreed upon in 1522, between Francis I and Sultan Suleiman the Magnificent, the alliance was meant to counter the powerful Habsburgs, whose territories had come into contact with the Ottoman Empire in Serbia. The alliance, which involved exchanges of embassies, trade, religious agreements and technological mentorship, ended in 1798 with Napoleon's invasion of Egypt, the campaign that should have established French presence in the Middle East. A year later, the Ottoman Empire found a new ally in Britain, but only until 1806, when the High Porte resumed its long alliance with the French. The alliance would break in 1809 upon Napoleon's failure to return promised territories to the Ottoman Empire. Filling the void left by France, Britain again became a viable but secret ally. Although 1802, when Abu Talib visited Constantinople, and 1810, when *Travels* was published in London, were years of the British–Ottoman alliance, the alignment of Paris and Constantinople through similar coffee-house practices directs our attention to the traffic of cultures, finances and interests determined by the Franco-Ottoman collaboration. The alignment of locales of sociability like coffee-houses surreptitiously attests to the fractures within the geographical and ideological construction of Europe in 'Persianate Europology' (Tavakoli-Targhi 35). Mirrored in the heart of the French capital, Constantinople's coffee-houses also confirm Ephraim and Inari Karsh's conclusion that throughout and after the Napoleonic storm, the Ottoman Empire remained 'essential to the European status quo' (17).

The coffee-house episodes make it impossible to draw a line between Eastern and Western pathologies. They reveal, however, the methods through which Abu Talib assesses local cultures and that these methods rely on a notion of hospitality that attends to individual and collective benefit. According to Abu Talib, in spite of their indolence, consumers in Constantinople share a socialising propensity that aligns them with consumers in coffee-houses in London and Paris. However, their activities of smoking, drinking and 'listening to idle stories, the whole day' convey the idea of stale conversations lacking in orientation and purpose that contrasts with the experience of the English consumer, who visits the coffee-house with the intention of socialising over information updated daily by newspapers (*Travels* 280). In comparison to the structured but vibrant circulation of news within and beyond national borders in the English coffee-house, the Ottoman's 'idle stories', exchanged boisterously and among several speakers simultaneously, exclude the foreigner. This milieu corroborates Abu Talib's early observation in the context of Dublin's sociability that profitable, inclusive conversation suffers in the presence of noise and interruption (118). Hence, the coffee-house in Constantinople goes against the ethos Abu Talib experiences and endorses in Ireland, where hosts take upon themselves 'the trouble to comprehend your meaning, to make themselves useful to you [the foreigner]' (111). Constantinople's coffee-house fails to promote a commerce of ideas between people of different languages, striking the experienced narrator of *Travels* as an inhospitable place, 'an assembly of brutes', enclosed in a loop of storytelling to which the foreigner is unable to contribute (280).

Had this been written by a European traveller, it would readily confirm the Saidian paradigm that sees representations of Oriental backwardness as produced by the prejudices of Western observers. But this is not the case for Abu Talib's memoir. His account draws on a different paradigm that opens a way out of an East–West polarisation of perspectives. If we read *Travels* as *adab*, that is, a literary form and codes of conduct, then the trope of the coffee-house functions as a *hikayat*, an exemplum, a central strategy through which the literary form *adab* transmitted *adab* as social conduct and advice. The exemplum in *adab* consists of the pairing of contrasting representations of the same trope that, standing as a synecdoche, mediate the need for moral intervention (Kia 288, 291). In the trope of the coffee-house, the contrast drawn between inclusive and objectionable sociability illustrates a moral standpoint and as *hikayat* aims to lead to a moral transformation. Read within the social conduct conveyed by *adab*, Abu Talib's critique builds on cosmopolitan values because it foregrounds the flow of knowledge between strangers and remote parts of the world. It is in this respect that Abu Talib finds the coffee-houses in France, and more explicitly those in Constantinople and Baghdad, flawed. There is a sense that the foreigner in the setting of the Turkish coffee-house is reduced to visibility and ornament: foreigners are seen but cannot participate. Their muted presence and their denied ability to co-steer the traffic of knowledge questions the utility of the coffee-house as a promoter of conviviality which involves dialogue among cultures, a practice Bryan Turner terms a 'cosmopolitan virtue' that counteracts the isolation of multiculturalism (45–63). The juxtaposition of good and bad social phenomena, in this case coffee-houses, signals a type of antagonism which can plausibly be associated with what Kant calls curative or productive resistance (*heilsamer Widerstand*) in the sense that such resistance 'strives for equal standing among others' (Muthu 245).

The idea that the foreigner is useless in some coffee-house culture and that the sociability of the coffee-house is of no use to the foreigner can be appreciated if we recall the high rank that utility holds in Abu Talib's appreciation of novelty, including new aesthetic pleasures. A few lines after the observations on the coffee-house, the 'Turkish costume' is judged in these very terms. It is depicted and admired as an epitome of cosmopolitan collaboration: 'composed of the choicest manufacturers of various nations', of 'European broad-cloths and satins', Indian muslin, Persian embroidered silk and shawls (*Travels* 281). Yet this collaboration results in heavy clothing, layers heaped upon layers that make movement difficult and foster indolent habits. Only a few years later, Lord Byron would flaunt his Albanian costume at dinner parties, embodying the pleasures of exhibitionist, exotic cosmopolitanism, albeit not only of that. Abu Talib's version of the Turkish costume registers the aesthetic value of the cosmopolitan product but subordinates it to the same category of utility and comfort that also guides his appreciation of architecture, coffee-house cultures, discoveries and, broadly speaking, achievements of human labour. Both his knowledge of the provenance of the disparate parts of the costume (European, Indian, Persian) and its inscription in the activities of ordinary life dispel the aura of exoticism that surrounds Oriental clothing in the West, of which Byron's Albanian costume is perhaps the most famous example. Furthermore, the costume as a patchwork of national differences materialises within the frame of Ottoman imperialism, hinting at the violent side of cosmopolitanism's conviviality with indolent consumption and colonisation (discussed in more detail in Chapter 5).

Abu Talib's stereotype of the 'indolent Turk' deserves attention, as it indubitably challenges the understanding of this passage as a cosmopolitan assessment. For this reason, it must be noted that indolence is a vice that Abu Talib does not restrict to the Ottomans. *Travels* opens with a dejected reflection on 'the want of energy and the indolent dispositions' of Abu Talib's countrymen – that is, the very readership of his travelogue (59). Later he identifies indolent disposition with India itself, elaborating also on his own fatigue and frequent desire to repose while living there (114–15). The dichotomy that might suggest itself here between Eastern indolence and Western agility starts to dissolve first when 'desire of ease, and a dislike of exertion' (209), the dissipative use of time thrown away 'in sleeping, eating, and dressing', and the urge to 'pamper their appetites' appear in Abu Talib's chapter on British flaws; and second, when moral character is linked to climate (*Travels* 115).[15] First, desire of ease and idleness seem the symptoms of subjects living in the greatest contemporary empires: the British and the Ottoman. Second, an environmentalist explanation of character brings Abu Talib in close proximity to Montesquieu's *Spirit of Laws* (1750), which argued that climate and modes of living affect morals, manners and consequently modes of government.[16] The last decades of the eighteenth century registered the culmination of climate-theory in Britain, during which 'Britons discussed human differences' by way of 'frequently linking the condition of the body to the development of the mind' (Wheeler 242).

Abu Talib's own experience, however, discards notions of ethnic essentialism. Arguing that the human body can adapt to diverse geographical conditions, he pictures identity as moveable and modifiable. For example, he illustrates adaptability and climatic contingency through his own process of adaptation: although raised in India, subdued easily by a one-mile walk, even when dressed in light fabric, and accustomed to sleeping several times a day without feeling refreshed, in the cold Irish weather Abu Talib covered in heavy clothes would walk seven to eight miles daily and sleep less than in India without feeling fatigued: 'on the contrary, I had a keen appetite, and found myself every day get stronger and more active' (*Travels* 114). Such a view of human 'cosmopolitan fitness' guided thinkers like Montesquieu, but also philosophers of the American Enlightenment, against another model of climate and humoral theory that defended the essential incompatibility between certain kinds of constitutions and climates (Schlereth 34; Wheeler 263).[17] More importantly, the discourse of adaptability grounds Abu Talib's national stereotypes in a larger frame of universal human constitution that could serve as the very basis for a cosmopolitan critique.

This is relevant to his non-essentialist yet scathing depiction of Constantinople's coffee-house: apart from being a discouragement to foreign travels, whose understanding and voice are drowned in the din of local conversation, could this depiction also stand for a 'saving' cosmopolitan critique? And if so, on what idea of sharedness is this critique based? One possible avenue in this area of reflection is opened by Abu Talib's repeated engagement with indolence as the nemesis of the motivation that compels him on his long journey in search of employment: cultural, scientific and spiritual knowledge (as it is often the case in the *rihla*, the last part of his tour is a pilgrimage). Strikingly, this juxtaposition between indolence and knowledge, although sharpened by his experience of the Ottoman coffee-house, germinates in his critique of the English 'desire of ease and dislike of exertion' as a defect that 'prevents them from perfecting themselves in science, and exerting themselves in the service of their friends' (*Travels* 209–10). Indolence curtails that curiosity for knowledge that Abu Talib deems 'an honour and an ornament' of the human species alone, a passion planted in everyone and awaiting cultivation through exertion (60). This is the shared propensity at the foundation of Abu Talib's cosmopolitanism, and is very similar, one might add, to the propensity endorsed by the European Enlightenment, which 'reconceived curiosity as the very identity of mankind, the mark of our difference from both beasts and angels' (Benedict 22).

It must be emphasised, however, that I am suggesting points of convergence, rather than that Abu Talib's cosmopolitan ontology were modelled upon a Western version or his treatment of curiosity as a replication of Western yen for knowledge. His anthropocentric valorisation of curiosity as 'an honour and an ornament' is redolent, for instance, of Wollstonecraft's ascribing to curiosity the power to 'fructify the faint glimmerings of mind which entitles [humans] to rank as lords of the creation' (*Short Residence* 65). This convergence testifies to views simultaneously shared by people of different ethnic and religious backgrounds as well as to a common eagerness to think about what makes humans human and those shared properties among them that give rise to countless particularities. In other words, such convergences bear testimony to a desire to think of a bonding origin and constitution, if not calling.

For Abu Talib, his travels confirm and cultivate a prior belief in a commonality preceding and surpassing ethnic or national properties. His account proposes itself as a narrative of inter-civilisational dialogue in which comparative criticism is a marker of reflective engagement with otherness and a remedy for cultural isolationism and relativism. In such a light, a critique of imperialistic gluttony (British and Ottoman), at work in both sedentary and over-productive economies that undermine the quest for knowledge either by abandoning it or by perverting its utility to commercial profit, can be a saving critique as long as this critique seeks to preserve the shared propensity. As Gerard Delanty propounds: 'Cosmopolitanism cannot be entirely separated from the normative vision of an alternative society and . . . this imaginary is also present as a cultural model within the cultural traditions of societies as a form of immanent transcendence' (64). Moreover, cosmopolitanism cannot be unconditioned hospitality, but cannot but contain a censuring *hostipitality*. In Abu Talib's travelogue, the juxtaposition of de-essentialised indolence with knowledge-seeking curiosity and the dissemination of achievements, rendered in the metaphor of one candle that lights a thousand, follows a defining trait of the cosmopolitan imaginary. It is a symptom of this sensibility – as well as of the power of metaphorical thinking – that the coffee-house in Baghdad is the worst because it is the darkest.

The recurrence of the coffee-house in different geographical and ethnic settings exemplifies procedures of methodological cosmopolitanism. Ulrich Beck coins the term 'methodological cosmopolitanism' to describe 'an experience "at ground level"' and 'bodily materialized' grappling 'with the complex realities of the "excluded others"' ('Mobility' 31). The cosmopolite must be in a state of fluctuating moments of association and dissociation, in which a question such as 'who are we as a nation or ethnic, religious group?' is increasingly replaced by 'who am I as a person because and despite my roots in a certain national, ethnic or religious group?' (31). It is telling that such fluctuations occur during Abu Talib's stay in Turkey, his place of origin by descent, and during his frequent encounters with Muslims and Indians. Interestingly, this is the segment in *Travels* with the strongest identity shifts and moments of elitist dissociation that disrupt ideas of a homogenous Eastern or Oriental identity. He declines, for example, an introduction to a group of Indian Fakeers residing in a monastery in Constantinople, on the assumption that they must have been an 'assemblage of low, ignorant people, smokers of opium' (*Travels* 287). A little later, his Muslim companions take offence at Abu Talib's preference for the comfortable house of a Christian (the English Consul at Constantinople) over the arrangement suggested by a Mohammedan of Pasha's rank, a decision that Abu Talib explains as a choice between 'the uncomfortable mode of living of the Turks' and 'the hospitable reception' of the English (335). Complex reconfigurations of ethnic varieties in the regions of the Ottoman Empire, foreshadowed already in France and Italy, seem to call forth Abu Talib's hankering for England, its cleanness, structures, comforts and hospitality. In an amicable but important altercation due to his impatience (in his book, ironically enough, an English flaw) to return home, he reproaches the representative of the East India Company in Bussora for having 'forgotten all his English principles', to which the man replies that, 'spoiled by the luxuries and attention of the people in London', Abu Talib has become 'impossible to please' (*Travels* 342). It is almost as if a process of Anglicisation takes root as the Indian traveller approaches home. Such confused boundaries of ethnic character between the Indian who cannot have enough Englishness and the Englishman who thinks the Indian has had too much of it are not only ironic but also symptomatic of the complexities to which a burgeoning literature on cosmopolitanism seeks to do justice.

Despite these instances of dissociation from local cultures, ascribing aloofness to Abu Talib – a marker of Diogenes's cosmopolitan renouncement of the polis – would under-appreciate all the encounters that enrich him with a sense of a shared humanity where least expected, especially in the form of hospitality and conversation, like his stay with a learned and religious Sunni Muslim (Abu Talib is a Shiite), the head of a multi-ethnic household (*Travels* 334). At a certain point, even an anthropocentric ethos relaxes when animals are mentioned as agents of help and are included in the company of co-travellers that have made Abu Talib's journey easier. Highlighting the importance of gratitude (like Epictetus, see Introduction) and lending spiritual flavour to the idea of utility, Abu Talib writes in praise of the perseverance of Arabian horses that 'we ought to be grateful to every person or thing that has been useful to us' (309). Indeed, this thickness of identification tends to invalidate the neo-Stoic view of the cosmopolitan self as neatly inhabiting several concentric circles of identification, with the closest circle being that of the immediate family and the furthest representing an allegiance with the world community. The messiness of (dis)associations, especially in the latter part of *Travels*, bears out 'cross-cutting allegiances' – whether ethnic, racial, religious or inter-species – that require a more sophisticated approach to cosmopolitan subjectivity than the neo-Stoic revival of Hierocles's metaphor discussed in the Introduction (W. Connolly 184). This not to say that the metaphor of concentric circles has no validity for Abu Talib, but that *Travels*' aspiring cosmopolitanism cautions against oversimplification. Admittedly, this model may be a point of departure but not the whole story of the cosmopolitan experience. Because Hierocles considers it to be 'the task of a well-tempered man . . . to draw the circles together somehow towards the centre', movement and cross-cutting circles enter the picture, while the idea of this task as an ongoing process replaces that of a static diagram (Long and Sedley 1: 349).

The Cosmopolitan Local Reader

The critique of specific practices exemplified by the case of the coffee-house in Constantinople couches Abu Talib's earnest investment in the local. His five-year nomadic cosmopolitanism and the 'sense of intensive interconnectedness' that goes with it respond to a vocation in local investment when his sits down to write his memoir for the benefit of local readers (Braidotti 5–6). The very act of writing materialises cosmopolitan interconnectedness on the native shores where he returns, and whose sight moves him to tears (*Travels* 352). An unbounded synecdoche for home, the native shore is where he commits to paper the impressions stored in memory about the foreign cultures and customs, flora and fauna encountered during his journey on three continents.

Strikingly, his book also starts with an address to his local readership: an address imbued with both a desire for conviviality and the necessity of criticism. Writing for his compatriots substantiates Abu Talib's stubborn belief in the endurance of conviviality, despite its being fraught with a nagging apprehension of failure. He fears that very few of his countrymen will seize on, disseminate and adapt the knowledge provided by his narrative. There is a risk that it may not even exceed the circles of like-minded friends, so that his work may end up being little more than preaching to the already converted. The reason for such misgiving harks back to the aspect of national character, in particular 'the want of energy and the indolent disposition of my countrymen, and the many erroneous customs which exist in all Mohammedan countries and among all ranks of Mussulmans' (*Travels* 59). Although indolence in *Travels* is temporarily linked to climate theory, Abu Talib parts ways with a deterministic view of national character in the style of Montesquieu.

Abu Talib's analysis retains nothing of this climate-induced determinism but opts instead for a socio-economic autopsy of Indian society. Like that in Goldsmith, Wollstonecraft, *The Woman of Colour* and some abolitionists texts, Abu Talib's analysis engages with environmental and societal factors to show how they shape human behaviour, capacities and even reading practices. Wary of both resignation and a generalised assessment of things as they are, he specifies the factors operating in different social strata. The wealthy and leisured members, he maintains, although financially endowed with means to promote knowledge, are 'intoxicated with pride and luxury' and imprisoned in the provincial circuit of 'scanty achievements'; at the other extreme, the resources of the poor are exhausted by the sheer struggle to make a living, so that little time remains to nurture curiosity; while the large mass of readers, who derive from reading no other benefit than entertainment, 'under pretence of zeal for their religion', will dismiss a book that mediates foreignness (*Travels* 60). Abu Talib's discontent with the rich, his justification of the poor and his critique of readers who read for little more than entertainment find numerous echoes in contemporaneous British critics of print culture, in particular opponents of the novel genre, who complained of an undiscerning and sensation-seeking bourgeois readership. Significantly enough, Abu Talib targets a taste diluted by 'Tales and Romances' (60). Once more, his critique is double-edged and cuts across the East–West divide. An opinionated and self-complacent elite, poverty, religious fanaticism and a reading culture oriented towards consumption can obstruct the circulation of a book that, because of its immersion in experiences of alterity, Abu Talib admits, requires 'more than a first glance' and 'a little time for consideration' (60). By indicating deficiencies in the socio-economic conditions of his readership, he signals where change must happen, while also pegging down the key trait of the cosmopolitan reader: patient perseverance that surmounts the estrangement of the first contact, and without which curiosity either wanes or succumbs to exoticism.

As the writer of *Travels*, a *safar nama* about an impressive journey, Abu Talib reminds his readers that curiosity without perseverance, engagement or 'consideration' produces no knowledge. And where there is no knowledge, appreciation of otherness drifts in the shallow waters of exoticism. Tzvetan Todorov brilliantly observes: 'knowledge is incompatible with exoticism, but lack of knowledge is in turn irreconcilable with praise of others: yet praise without knowledge is precisely what exoticism aspires to be' (264–65). Although the fear of slow change looms over Abu Talib's expectations, he relates his travels in written form, because the horizon of his expectations for his country's future is not framed by immutable indolence, submission to despotism (as Montesquieu speculates) or an equanimity that considers socio-economic conditions as mere externals which should leave the wise man unperturbed. The latter signals Abu Talib's difference from Stoic thought.

Interestingly, the possibility of change through Abu Talib's testimony rings as real as its completion is impossible when Abu Talib takes comfort in an Arabian proverb that combines Stoic poise and perseverance. His proverb could inform a decolonial vision of cosmopolitanism, whether understood as a personal ethos or a political, legal and economic option: 'We are not to abandon the whole, because we cannot obtain the whole', the proverb goes (*Travels* 60). Comfort is needed to clairvoyantly cultivate the good passions (*eupatheia*) for the sake of the world as a good place (*euthopia*), an investment that is constantly in tension with censure and utopian impracticability. The proverb echoes Epictetus's equanimous resolution not to 'cease to make any effort . . . merely because I despair of achieving perfection' (*Discourses* 9; I.3.37). The agreement I suggest between Abu Talib and Epictetus has a mirror image in the broader investigation of points of contact and convergences between Arab and Muslim philosophy and the Greco-Roman Stoa. Epictetus and Marcus Aurelius appear to be the earliest influences on Byzantine Greek-speaking scholars east of the Mediterranean, while Epictetus, despite missing textual links of transmission, may have influenced al-Kindī, one of the founding figures of Arab philosophy (Sellars 4; Adamson, *Great Medieval Thinkers* 17; Adamson, 'Al-Kindī' 37, 50). As mentioned in the Introduction, a worry regarding utopian and unattainable goals already surfaces in the Greek Stoa, prompting Panaetius of Rhodes to shift focus from perfected sagehood to the daily training of the '*aspiring* sage' (Reinhardt xvi). Likewise, the proverb selected by Abu Talib welcomes a relaxation that neither makes daily imperfect cosmopolitan practices conditional on the completed task of cosmopolitanism nor yields to indifferent resignation.

The whole, the world conceived as a *eutopian* good place or dwelling of sociable, unperturbed and unconditioned conviviality, free of censure and management, may be unattainable, but this impossibility does not translate into a premise of surrender, aloofness or indolence, to refer for one last time to the vice that Abu Talib considers to be both a source of and an excuse for negligence. Ultimately, unsaturable success implements an incentive to hone the local eye to view home as a structuring pattern of the unfinished but interconnected whole.

Notes

1 Mignolo offers the following distinction and alternative: 'Narratives of cosmopolitan orientation could be either managerial (what I call global designs – as in Christianity, nineteenth-century imperialism, or late twentieth century neo-liberal globalisation) or emancipatory (what I call cosmopolitanism – as in Vittoria, Kant or Karl Marx, leaving aside the differences in all of these projects), even if they are oblivious to the saying of the people that are supposed to be emancipated. The need for a critical cosmopolitanism arises from the shortcomings of both' ('Many

Faces' 722–23). It is debatable how critical cosmopolitanism can keep clear of managerial moves.

2 I refer here to Mignolo's insistence to propose decolonial cosmopolitanism as fundamentally anti-Western, and very often cosmopolitanism itself as a uniquely Western preoccupation. Raschke, for example, argues that Mignolo tends to disregard the divergences, trajectories, and re-appropriations of Western and non-Western knowledge by local (decolonial) cosmopolitanism. A similar counterargument is mounted by Delanty, who suggests that even at what we take as its inception among the ancient Greeks, cosmopolitanism was not a Western construct but the coalescing of Western and Eastern influences (18–19). Derrida's concept of the 'trace' helps exit the maelstrom of the inception of cosmopolitanism by defying the concept of origin itself, because the trace 'is not only the disappearance of origin . . . it means that the origin did not even disappear, that it was never constituted except reciprocally by a non-origin, the trace, which thus becomes the origin of the origin' (*Of Grammatology* 66).

3 On the impossibility of hospitality that deserves its name, see Derrida, 'Hostipitality' 386. In several interviews, Derrida calls unconditional hospitality 'pure' hospitality.

4 A noteworthy moment in *Travels*, the encounter between Abu Talib and the Bishop of London is an instance of the ecumenical conviviality characteristic of the Mughal Persian literary humanism (*adab*).

5 Pratap Banu Mehta critically addresses the currency of this conceit (638).

6 Shah 'Alam's *Diwan-I Aftab*, Bodleian Library, Persian MS. Ouseley 94, cited by G. Khan 7.

7 Subrahmanyam considers the co-existence of millenarianism in Europe, Asia and Africa to be, first, a trigger of modernity and, second, the basis for the ambition of a universal kingdom underlying imperialist conquests, European and other. Thus millenarianism qualifies as a cosmopolitan impetus, albeit a not uniquely Western one; neither are its implications in imperial practices uniquely Western. For a more detailed analysis of cosmopolitanism and imperialism see Chapter 5.

8 For Abu Talib's critique, see also Khan's commentaries drawn from the original manuscript (G. Khan 251).

9 Eventually, the directors of the East India Company asked specifically for Abu Talib to fill one position, but after detailed enquiry, it became known that Abu Talib had passed away a couple of months earlier.

10 Mignolo explains this restricted and temporary participation in dominant structures to be compatible with delinking attitudes, insisting that this is no surrender. He answers, in other words, the question about complicity with colonial power addressed at the close of Chapter 3.

11 Tihanov calls cosmopolitanism a 'marker' of 'recalibrations' of the polis, where the polis includes not only the demos of the nation-state, but also sub-nationally and transnationally formed communities (Tihanov 134).

12 The centrality Abu Talib accords to curiosity sharply contrasts with Lewis's insistence on a lack of curiosity among Muslims. When Abu Talib voices dissatisfaction with many of his countrymen's uncultivated curiosity, he makes this contingent on socio-economic factors.

13 Earlier opinions of Indian intellectuals were translated and published especially by the Asiatick Society, but such statements were not widely circulated and would have been experienced as literary rarities by the readers. See also G. Khan 70.

14 In 1827, Goethe advised his assistant and disciple Johann Peter Eckermann to turn his attention to works from foreign cultures and nations and embrace and promote the new 'epoch of world literature' (Damrosch 1).

15 The British are judged somewhat less indolent than the apathetic 'smokers of opium of Hindoostan and Constantinople', but the comparison implies an underhanded virtue (*Travels* 210).

16 A prominent expounder of climate-theory was the German anthropologist Johann Blumenbach, who in his *On the Natural Variety of Mankind* (1775) maintained that different developments of the human skeleton are due to climate and conditions of living, but that these distinctions are not profound enough to suggest polygenesis.

17 Schlereth mentions Thomas Jefferson who, on the grounds of this 'cosmopolitan fitness' (Schlereth 34) justified the mission of humankind to explore and found new societies all over the earth: a line of thought that reveals the proximity and entanglements of cosmopolitanism with imperial ambition and mission, as discussed in Chapter 5.

Chapter 5

Air of the World and the 'Murky Night of the Empire' in *The Last Man*

'I read the histories of Greece and Rome, and of England's former periods, and I watched the movements of the lady of my heart' (M. Shelley, *The Last Man* (hereafter *LM*) 61). These words capture the double focus of Lionel Verney, the character in Mary Shelley's *The Last Man* (1826) who narrates the microcosmic fortunes of his circle of friends and the macrocosmic demise of a humanity made almost extinct by a deadly disease. A common association of Britain with Greco-Roman civilisations rings in Verney's words, an association that Shelley's novel explores in profound ways. Ending with a scene in which the works of Shakespeare and Homer are loaded onto the boat of the titular last man, who leaves Rome for Africa, the novel revisits but also undermines Greco-Roman legacy. Curiously, Verney refrains from taking works by Roman poets, philosophers or politicians on his journey. The most conspicuous absence in his boat is Virgil's *Aeneid*, the foundational tale of Roman civilisation that informs the very narrative frame of *The Last Man*. It is this omission that spurs my investigation.

To do justice to the sophistication of Shelley's approach, this chapter maps out four intersections. First, it addresses the anti-imperial Sibylline affiliations of the 'Author's Introduction' to stress the narrative's gender inflections. A historicisation of the Cumean Sibyl and the *translatio* of her cult from Greece to Italy supports the dissident voice of the Aeneidan Sibyl, who warns about the destructive force unleashed by the transfer of power from Troy to Rome. Second, I trace the relevance of *The Aeneid* for the historiographic casting of the British Empire as a new Troy and inheritor of the Roman imperial legacy to argue the novel's severing of this continuity. The third intersection elaborates the narrative's decolonial choices by scrutinising anti-cosmopolitan, imperialist mentalities as they are parsed through Shelley's exploration of the passions. Attention to destructive passions aligns *The Last Man* with an eighteenth-century line of thought that discerns a symbiosis between human psychology and the mimetic attraction of power driving civilisational narratives of conquest. Luminaries like Abbé de Fénelon, Adam Smith, Comte de Volney and Germaine de Stäel are representatives of this approach. Shelley dramatises the 'serious' correlation between 'the nature of individual and political felicity' that de Staël had defended twenty years earlier in her 1796 *Influence of the Passions on the Happiness of Individuals and of Nations* (2). The last intersection draws together epidemiology and imperial agents. Carried literally and metaphorically by the plague, the air of imperialism suggests that poisonous air literalises the fatal ideologies and practices of imperialism – framed as an ambition for dominion – and reveals the novel's opprobrium for projects that assent to the concomitance of cosmopolitanism with imperialistic warring.

Readers of the eighteenth century encountered such an assent in Plutarch's *Morals*, translated into English in 1684–94 and revised in 1718. *Morals* eulogised the ethnic diversity resulting from the conquests of Alexander the Great, this man of war, whom Plutarch credits with the realisation of the Stoic ideal of a human fellowship formed by people of diverse provenances, unified 'as in a festival goblet' (*Morals* 448).[1] An 'arbiter of all nations', Plutarch's Alexander implemented a top-down type of cosmopolitanism, 'mixing lives, manners, customs, wedlock, all together' and 'ordain[ing] that every one should take the whole habitable world for his country' (*Morals* 449). This passage has compelled scholars of cosmopolitanism to argue for more interdisciplinary histories of cosmopolitanism that integrate ancient historiography in 'histories of cosmopolitan thought "proper"' (Inglis and Robertson, 'Cosmos' 300). A thorough interdisciplinary approach, however, should also include the questioning of celebratory conflations of imperial warring with cosmopolitanism like Plutarch's enlisting of citizens of the world as beneficial products of empire. This would imply questioning a 'transposition of Stoic cosmopolitanism onto empire' that was well known in the Roman world (Atkins 245). Shelley, too, knew Plutarch's *Moralia* well, and her novel prompts readings which undo this transposition by decoupling cosmopolitan ethos from empire. The novel suspects the deceitful, propagandistic language that serves imperial aspirations: the 'gently sounding . . . terms that compose the style' of royal or imperial 'might' in a manner akin to Plutarch's exulting metaphor of a convivial 'festival goblet' (*LM* 44). Suggestively, *The Last Man* is also suspicious of Caesar, another imperial magnate whom Plutarch's historiography dignifies and who, like Alexander, is a precursor of antiquity emulated by Raymond in the novel and by Napoleon in real life. If Shelley 'mourns for a certain type of universal vision', as Barbara Johnson believes (263), my analysis suggests that the object being mourned is a cosmopolitan ideal instrumentalised and hollowed out by imperial mentality and practice.

Verney's study of Greece, Rome and England's former periods alongside the study of his beloved Idris entwines two historiographical traditions: a classically oriented historiography and Scottish philosophical history. While the first, relying on the template of *translatio studii et imperii* inherited from medieval historiography, investigated Europe's and Britain's roots in Greco-Roman antiquities, Scottish philosophy pursued a methodology with more universal applications that sought to understand how human societies developed from a state of savagery to societies regulated by manners and mentalities encapsulated by the concept of civil society (Curtius 28–29; Allan 319). The emphases of these two approaches to historical sense-making differ. If Scottish philosophical history, also called stadial or conjectural history, deliberated world history in terms of the evolution of human communities and psycho-social habitus alongside evolving means of subsistence, the theory of *translatio imperii et studii* linked the transfer of knowledge from one people or group of peoples to another with the transfer of political rule. *Translatio* was a westward-moving process from the old Eastern civilisations towards Europe and, as some foresaw with resignation, towards the colonies planted in the so-called New World.

When Shelley's narrator connects his intellectual initiation into civil society with the historiography of ancient Greece, Rome and England, he taps into the tradition of *translatio imperii et studii.* After he has transitioned from his native wilderness to 'the order and beauty' of this historiography, Verney's focus also incorporates his beloved Idris, thus intoning the gender relations that interest Scottish stadial theory, eloquently delineated in John Millar's *The Origin of the Distinction of Ranks* (1771) (*LM* 120). The subtitle of Nicholas Miller's recent study, *John Millar and the Scottish Enlightenment: Family Life and World History* (2017), reads as a paraphrasis of the quote at the start of this chapter, if not as a fitting subtitle to Shelley's *Last Man.* A professor of civil law at Glasgow between 1761 and 1800 and recipient of Hutcheson's notion of human sociability, Millar linked the rank and emancipation of women with the degree of development achieved by a given society (Sebastiani, 'Beyond' 826). The correlation of civilisation and gendered life particularly undergirds those substantial parts of Shelley's narrative that delineate the minutiae of evolving heterosexual relations within the social unit of the family. Unlike Scottish philosophical history, traditional historiography, guided by an interest in transfers of political and military power, focused on the state as a political entity and was espoused by influential theoreticians like Hobbes and Locke

(*LM* 137). This tradition limns 'the conventional politico-diplomatic historical narrative' that Shelley acknowledges by making her narrator a 'diplomatist' amid the 'giddy whirl' of European diplomacy (Hargraves 262; *LM* 29). In her novel, diplomacy falls short of achieving what Machiavelli's *Prince* thought to be the mission of diplomatic relations: the prevention of physical violence and its substitution. The 'conventional politico-diplomatic historical narrative' may be just the type of history that Austen's Catherine Morland in *Northanger Abbey* finds tiresome: 'The quarrels of popes and kings, with wars or pestilences, in every page; the men all so good for nothing, and hardly any women at all' (79).

Shelley's novel engages with both these traditions, by interweaving a critical story of international wars, diplomacy and pandemic with intimate examinations of the lives of women and men whose passions are the ultimate movers of human history (*LM* 5). Her method resembles that of Scottish narrative historians, who produced historiography on the assumption that warring and governing 'could be illuminated and amplified by reference to deeper lying structural features of human existence in particular conditions', in other words, by 'relating particular detail to a broader process of "systemic change"' (Allan 321; Hargraves 263). The mereological structure of *The Last Man* ties the obliteration of familial sociability with the annihilation of state power, which both signify the destruction of human 'universal happiness' that Hutcheson learned from Marcus Aurelius to value as the 'noblest Desire' and objective (Hutcheson 40). The novel explores systemic change by referencing the *translatio imperii*, a template appropriated by the eighteenth-century subgenre of the 'progress poem' (Gidal 143–44). Virgil's *Aeneid* (29–19 BC) mediates this template in Shelley's narrative, which opens in the cave of the Sibyl and ends with an evocation of Homer, whose *Iliad* looms over Virgil's epic about the war-ridden Trojan resettlement in Italy. In between these narrative poles, awareness of the ravaging effects of the plague, repressed for a while by a false sense of isolationist security, erupts as a visitation from Roman history: 'The Rubicon, I felt, was passed' (*LM* 204). So Verney confesses, when the progress of plague is felt to be as unstoppable as Caesar's crossing of the river Rubicon, the event that unleashed Rome's Civil Wars (49–30 BC) and which has metaphorically conveyed the point of no return ever since. The aborted voyage of the last three survivors, Verney, Adrian and Clara, after contemplating a new start in Greece, the cultural womb of European civilisation, signifies that no return is possible.

Although, with its focus on the little society of the family unit, Scottish philosophical history may seem at odds with the rather impersonal account of *translatio imperii*, Shelley works out consequential relationships between domestic personhood and civilisational narratives. The novel internalises de Staël's lesson that 'Without the interference of the passions, governments would be a machine fully as simple as so many levers' (*Influence* 5). And both de Staël and Shelley knew Comte de Volney's *Les Ruines, méditations sur les revolutions des empires* (1791), published like de Staël's *Influence* in response to the French Revolution. Reverberating in the nearly sixty appearances of the word 'ruin' in Shelley's novel, Volney's essay provided her with a diagnosis of the backbone of *translatio imperii*, the rise-and-fall pattern which Volney made contingent upon human psychology. For Shelley, human psychology is both home-bred and propagated by cultural memory. On Volney's 'tragic scene of the passions', she crafts a story about what she calls 'the stormy and ruin-fraught passions of man' (Volney xii; *LM* 5). These disastrous passions kindle the imagination of the author/translator/editor, engendering a critique of empire, of eminent European narratives and concepts like liberty and civility.

The novel's melancholia advocates a decolonial exit from the violent, acquisitive rise-and-fall loop of *translatio imperii*, which also involves an intellectual disidentification that is implied by the exclusion of Virgil's *Aeneid* in the novel's ending. *The Last Man* delinks from Britons' appraisal of their past and future via the paradigm of *translatio studii et imperii*. To delink from empire and the tales, myths and ideologies that sustain, disguise and disseminate its legacies means to decolonise, and for this reason Shelley's critique is decolonial. *Translatio*, when paired with knowledge and empire, siphons a public and political type of passage, that is, 'the transferral of one civilization's culture and knowledge (*studii*) and empire or political authority (*imperii*) to another' (Bell 13). By making the main narrative dependent on Sibylline prophecies, the novel's structure offers ample incentive to ponder the transferral trope. Yet it requires more argumentation to claim that Shelley's conflation of the vatic tradition with her own tale of disaster decouples *translatio studii* from the *translatio imperii*, adapting the first to her goals while jettisoning the latter. It is this chapter's core argument that the novel concurs with decolonial cosmopolitanism, in that it does not stop at making space for otherness within the Eurocentric field of thought and practice, but queries 'the legitimacy and validity of the previously accepted parameters – both historical and ethical' on which Eurocentrism has traditionally operated (Bhambra 326). I conclude with Shelley's recognition that effective disaffiliation demands the confrontation of Western historiography and ethics with the figure of the 'wretch', a figure of dispossession foreshadowed in *Frankenstein* and embodied by the dying black man, who is the only Africanist presence in *The Last Man* (*LM* 265).

Sibylline Affiliations

In *Enquiry Concerning Political Justice* (1793), Godwin professed that 'The true instruments for changing the opinions of men are argument and persuasion', and therefore to 'improve the social institutions of mankind, we must write, we must argue, we must converse' (*Political and Philosophical Writings* 202). The conversation inscribed by *The Last Man* makes readers ponder past, present and future connections and, in the face of (imaginative) disaster, makes them ask what went wrong. Fusing vatic and poetic traditions, the implied author merges her own authority with that of the Sibyl, the prophetess of the Apolonic cult in Cumea near Naples. Critics have insisted on the vatic tradition and on the prophecies that frame *The Last Man*, and on how 'the traveler to the Sibyl's cave resets Verney's thoughts and words within the scope of her own vision of life' (Ruppert 145). Not emphasising, however, Shelley's 'visionary poetics' over her investigation of 'the pre-Victorian imperialist mind', as Timothy Ruppert does (153), I approach them dialogically. The visionary poetics mediated by the Sibyl of Cumea are entangled with the process of *translatio imperii* adumbrated in *The Aeneid* through the voyage of the Trojan survivors, their ordeals on the way to Italy and wars over Italian territory.

A contriving stratagem, the 'Author's Introduction' refers only obliquely to Shelley, whose identification is further delayed on the novel's title page. There, Shelley appears not by name but by reference to *Frankenstein*, her first novel, which also deployed narrative framing as a guiding hermeneutical device. *The Last Man* cajoles readers to suspend their disbelief regarding the author's arcane discovery in Cumea and to comply with her plot of presenting Verney's life story as a product of co-authorship with the ancient prophetess. The scattered state, the multilingualism and the cross-temporality of the Sibylline leaves that launch Verney's story enhance suggestiveness.[2] Once deciphered, translated and interpreted by the 'author', some of the leaves yield Lionel Verney's story in the memoir genre to which Daniel Defoe had given the name 'journal' in *A Journal of the Plague Year* (1722). *The Last Man*'s frame tale signals the intensification of a culture of persuasion and dialogue. With authorship being shared between the Sibyl, the author/translator/editor and the character of Verney, this novel's main narrator is more of a composite of selves than the homodiegetic narrators of *Frankenstein* and *Mathilda*. The 'Author's Introduction' inscribes polyphony onto Verney's character. According to Mikhail Bakhtin, the polyphonic character is created by the author but 'created in such a way that it can develop to the full its inner logic and independence *as someone else's discourse*, the word of the *character himself*' (65). The author props up the 'illusion of the character having an autonomous word' so as 'to call forth readers' unmediated response' (Vice 115). Because it is impossible to extricate the voice of the implied author from that of the Sibyl and the voice of the Sibyl from Verney's, this orchestrated polyphony spawns multiple references to the transferral trope of *translatio studii et imperii* that are first invocated by the Sibylline prophecies. The very disorganised state of the leaves as well as the fragmentary translations by the 'Author' undermine the unbroken linearity of *translatio studii et imperii.*

The opaque conflation of the Sibyl's creative powers with those of the author/translator/editor works to raise the stakes of this seemingly peripheral vatic figure. Verney's narrative is not what the visiting couple find in the cave: the 'sacred remains' excavated by the two are only a 'selection of such of the leaves, whose writing one at least of us could understand' (*LM* 3–4). Left behind are all the leaves composed in ancient and modern languages that the companions cannot translate. The Sibylline leaves represent a cosmopolitan document, if 'cosmopolitan' can be taken to mean that which welcomes the inclusion of more than one specific region, culture, language and time of human community and history. Additionally, the ethnic versatility of the prophetic leaves is part and parcel of the pan-planetary narrative that the author constructs from the fragments she and her companion choose, even though their linguistic limitations are avowed from the start. Hence, the novel, while emerging from a cosmopolitan pool of knowledge, also spotlights incompleteness, indicating the unperfected state of any attempted cosmopolitan project, including the narrative of *The Last Man*.

For Godwin, human perfectibility represented the cornerstone that held together the idea and arduous work of reform. Perfectibility has been a point of discussion among critics of *The Last Man*.[3] My position is that, although the implied author concedes imperfection, the desire for betterment inspires her attempt to make intelligible the Sibyl's 'pristine' but 'unintelligible' leaves (*LM* 4). This means that Shelley separates the drive towards perfectibility from the teleological attainment of a perfect physical, moral and social state. Therefore, she instructs readers on the capacity for betterment but also on the incompleteness of cosmopolitan psychology and its actualised social arrangements. On this point, my argument shares common ground with Lauren Cameron's assertion that Shelley subtly joins in the controversy between Malthus and Godwin, sparked by Malthus's *Essay on the Principle of Population* (1798), and sides with Malthus against her father's creed that 'human nature can be perfected' (Cameron 178). Yet as long as the distinction between a state of perfection and the capability to improve remains intact, disbelief in a perfected state need not and does not preclude the novel's standpoint that betterment must be strived for. The pristine message of the oak leaves, albeit deserving of an immaculate *translatio studii*, remains untransferable into English and, therefore, unattainable for readers of English, including the implied author herself. And yet attempts at creative, subjective reconstruction breathe life into a narrative that the narrator explicitly associates with personal improvement: while being transferred onto paper, the story had the therapeutic effect of assuaging the writer's 'real sorrows and endless regrets' (*LM* 5). As for the novel's ameliorating impact among socially and temporally diverse readerships, that extratextual potential becomes incommensurable not least through the prophetic affiliations ushered into the main narrative by the frame tale. Hence, the implied author's assurance that the 'main substance [which] rests on the truths' of the Sibylline prophecies is carried into Verney's story could signify that it is possible to do better even while the absolute best remains unfeasible (*LM* 4). The admonishment to do better may be the very Sibylline substance that survives the transfer.

The Sibylline tradition is complementarily anticipated in the novel's epigraph, taken from Milton's *Paradise Lost*: 'Let no man seek / Henceforth to be foretold what shall befall / him or his children' (XI. 770–72). This is when Milton's epic transforms 'the familiar biblical story into a shocking personal tragedy' (Stafford 15). In this moment, communitarian and intimate lives meld in Adam, who suffers a father's woes as he views the killing of his descendants by the relentless flood. This moment resonates with *The Aeneid*, that predecessor of *Paradise Lost* in which tribal and individual suffering merge poignantly, and a book which Shelley read and reread at several points in her life, including a few years before *The Last Man*'s composition (Morrison and Stone 5).[4] Importantly, Anchises' words to Aeneas – 'don't press to know your people's awesome grief' (*Aeneid* VI.1002) – are keenly echoed in the passage Shelley chose from *Paradise Lost*. Anchises speaks these words in the Sibyl's presence in the underworld, which *The Last Man* reconfigures through the Sibylline cave.

Suffering was at the genesis of the Sibylline tradition that developed in Cumea near Naples. Cumea, the first known Greek settlement in Italy c. 750 BC, was founded by Euboean colonists (mentioned in *The*

Aeneid). These came to know the Sibylline cult through contact with refugees who fled Polycrates, Samos's tyrannical ruler, and settled in neighbouring Dikaearchia (modern Pozzuoli) in 531 BC (Johnston 14). Among the many refugees who left Samos for southern Italy, enduring harrowing episodes of forced displacement, was also Pythagoras. The cult survived thanks to refugees and colonists, people who historically embody what Peter Sacks, in his seminal study on elegy, calls 'figure[s] of fertility' that revitalise what is mourned as a loss (28). The forced migration of the Sibyl's cult, together with *The Aeneid*'s refugees turned colonists, laid the foundation for the series of displacement and dispossession of communities and peoples in Shelley's novel. *The Last Man* closes with the impending migration of a figure of fertility, Verney, as he ponders what is lost and what may be worth revitalising.[5]

Virgil makes the Sibyl the mediator between Aeneas and his dead father Anchises, the chief spokesperson for the Trojans' forceful occupation of Italian territories. In the Sibyl's cave, Aeneas, an archetypal agent of fertility, seeks and receives confirmation about the future of the Trojan survivors who follow him. By having the Sibyl mediate the temporal gulf separating the Trojan refugees' arrival in Italy from their colonisation of foreign lands, Virgil lends weight to the Sibyl's prophetic interpretation of Aeneas's future empire-building, especially because her oracle is antonymic to Anchises' confirmation. Prophecy, a crucial trope of colonisation narratives that communicates directions to the colonialists, is of even more consequence in *The Aeneid*, where 'directional prophecies are not just geographic but also historical' (Fletcher 23). One specific historical aspect of the Sibylline cult resonates closely with Virgil's and Shelley's narratives. Despite the presence of several regional Sibyls in the ancient Mediterranean world, scholars of antiquity underscore the fact that all these Sibyls retain their personality. Their subordination to the deities whose oracles they communicate does not supplant the Sibyls' own interpretations of these communications. This trait distinguishes the Sibyl(s) from all other Mediterranean prophetesses or priestess, who shed their personality to become 'mouthpieces of their deities' (Johnston 13). *The Aeneid*, too, preserves the Sibyl's autonomy, and this decision introduces a seed of dissidence against empire in *The Last Man*. Dissenting from Anchises' high-flown speech, the Sibyl spells out the belligerent future of mass killings and regret ingrained in the very colonisation that *The Aeneid* seeks to legitimise. Her prophecy brims with pessimism, refusing to be consoled by the prospect of the Trojans' ethnic survival or by discourses of triumph and fame. With piercing frankness, the Sibyl discloses to Aeneas the carnage upon which Trojan resettlement is predicated:

you Trojans will reach
Lavinium's realm – lift that care from your hearts –
but you will rue your arrival. Wars, horrendous wars,
and the Tiber foaming with tides of blood, I see it all! (VI.101–04)

After this terse and severe speech, Anchises attempts to obscure the awfulness that the Sibyl's prophecy has revealed to Aeneas. Eventually, Anchises' verbose patriotic and militaristic projection into the future weakens the heart-wrenching effect that the Sibyl's depiction of wars and streams of blood has upon Aeneas.

Anchises' glorifying rhetoric of the *translatio imperii* that secures Trojan survival wins Aeneas over and permeates European history in far more visible ways than the Sibyl's dissidence. In the sixteenth century, Aeneas provided the chief model upon which to 'characterize [Christopher] Columbus by framing' the latter's travels 'within a pre-existing discourse of colonization and imperial power' (Bartosik-Vélez 560). Peter Martyr's *Decades de orbe novo* (1515–30), a seminal historiography of the euphemistically named Spanish 'discoveries' in America, cast Columbus as a new Aeneas and protagonist of a superb new chapter of *translatio imperii.* Martyr's historiography even capitalised on Columbus's foreign origin to legitimise his achievement by tracing his pedigree back to Virgil's Aeneas. Consequently, the early modern European expansion bequeaths to later generations a 'Columbus [who] is not only a Ligurian, a descendant of the hearty stock praised by Virgil as the strength of the Roman Empire, but also the agent responsible for the westward transfer of empire' to what Europe called the New World (Bartosik-Vélez 568). Virgil's dissident Sibyl, it seems, made little impression on European champions of Columbus, including Shelley's contemporaries.[6]

As much a domestic as a civilisational and political narrative, Shelley's novel revives the public weight that Sibylline prophecies carried in ancient Rome (Fletcher 4). The Sibyl's role as a neglected legislator surfaces in Goldsmith's *Citizen of the World*, read by Shelley in January 1817: 'Their laws i.e. [of the British people] may be compared to the books of the Sybils, they are held in great veneration, but seldom read, or seldomer understood' (*CW* 2: 45). Historically, three surviving books of Sibylline writings were preserved in the temple of Capitoline Jupiter and, after the burning of the Capitol in 83 BC, were kept in reconstructed form in the Temple of Palatine Apollo. In times of crisis, fifteen trained men, the *Quindecemviri*, minutely analysed the books for guidance (Johnston 14). Among Shelley's contemporaries, de Staël most famously referenced this political Sibyl. In *Corinne* (1807), which Shelley read in 1815, de Staël's eponymous *improvisatrice* steps onto the political and religious arena of Rome as an incarnation of the ancient oracle, a 'triumphant Sibyl' honoured by a cheering public in the Capitol in front of the highest representatives of state power (24). In its last pages, *The Last Man* contemplates Corinne's Sibyl-like ascension to the Capitol, drawing the Sibyl of the 'Author's Introduction' closer to de Staël's passage (*LM* 361). The Sibylline references at the start and end of the novel liken the narrative to an instructive document in critical times, without excluding a speculation about future planetary disaster. I agree with Lisa Vargo that Shelley's interest in de Stäel's Sibylline *improvisatrice* nods to Godwin's faith in conversation as a tool of reform ('Shelley' 171). In Godwinian spirit, the novel's readers, like modern-day *Quindecemviri*, are drawn to invest in a culture of conversation, debate and persuasion through their own hermeneutical interventions.

The Sibyl's cave in the 'Author's Introduction' harks back to earlier models of *katabasis*, the descent of a character into the underworld, with Homer's Ulysses and Virgil's Aeneas as two enduring classical predecessors. Another author, highly valued by Shelley and Godwin, who reworked the motif of *katabasis* was Abbé de Fénelon. Fénelon's *Adventures of Telemachus* (1699) presented Shelley with a modified *katabasis*. Written in the tradition of the 'mirror of princes' (*speculum principis*), Fénelon's picaresque novel seeks to instil personal virtue and just political principles in his pupil, the Duke of Burgundy (1682–1712), future heir to the French throne. In *Lives of the Most Eminent Literary and Scientific Men of France* (1838–39), Shelley underscores a didactic mission that Fénelon's novel conveyed less openly than, say, Seneca's advisory epistles to Nero. The invented story of Ithaca's prince thinly disguises the tutor's critique of the policies of Louis XIV, a fact well noted by the Sun King. Telemachus's encounter with his dead grandfather – tellingly not mediated by the Sibyl – is a dialogue between men who ponder the human potential for good or virtue, and evil or vice, especially when combined with the political power wielded by kings. Shelley adopts the moral censure of Fénelon's *katabasis,* which is voiced only by the Sibyl in *The Aeneid* and almost drowned out by Anchises' long speech and the poem's implicit celebration of Augustus as the emperor who ended civil strife (Kantzios 198).[7] *The Aeneid* says little about Augustus as an authoritarian ruler, so that Aeneas's success aims to provide readers with 'a view of what Italy can become' and 'a glimpse of the imagined community that Italy will be under Augustus's (Kantzios 198; Fletsher 11). Fénélon, by contrast, interrogates state power, and it is in his footsteps that Shelley follows. One substantial difference between her and Fénélon, however, devolves upon gender. While there is no Sibyl in Fénelon's *katabasis*, Shelley spotlights the presence of the prophetess outside and within Verney's narrative. Omission would have curtailed the importance of female prophecy and authorship: without the Sibylline leaves, it would be harder to demonstrate that the novel leans on a female-gendered assessment of empire and cosmopolitan justice.

The capacity of the Sibyl as a figure that has traditionally emphasised transferrals between the past and the present has relevance for *The Last Man*. In *The Aeneid*, the past is represented by older deities like Juno and the younger deity Apollo who replaces Juno, the goddess to whom the Sibyl was previously subordinated and whose wrath must be satisfied before Aeneas's people can settle in Italy. The Sibyl and her hermeneutic autonomy prevail during the transfer of power from Juno to Apollo. She also offers a counter-imperial commentary to processes of transferral. She refuses to justify the violence that propels the *translatio studii et imperii* endorsed by *The Aeneid* as a good confirmed by the great cities built upon the ruins of older ones. The city of Pallanteum serves as an example to boost Aeneas's progress inland. Just as in the years of Roman ascendancy Pallanteum was built upon the ruins of the Etruscan cities Saturnia and Janiculum, so Aeneas is supposed to replant what remains of ruined Troy's life and culture on Italian ground (VIII.355–58). The idea of replanting and replacement explains why only 'in Italy do the Trojans begin to use a new type of name, the personal names of people on the voyage', to rename the places they colonise (Fletcher 19).[8] Because 'renaming a place is, in turn, a sort of refoundation', the practice remakes the land in the newcomers' images and language, declaring their ownership of these territories (19). The violence concomitant with transfers of land ownership is what Virgil's Sibyl anticipates with dismay.

Shelley's Virgilian echoes blend fictional materials with contemporary concerns, and her own Sibylline critique produces a counternarrative. Looking ahead to a journey into the unknown, unlike the Trojans who journey to a divinely ordained home, *The Last Man* cancels refoundation or, to use a different name, the *renovatio imperii* (renewal of empire). The modest gesture of the transfer of knowledge represented by the volumes of Homer and Shakespeare on Verney's boat as it is bound for Africa and India carries no promise of the renewal that stabilises narratives of colonisation/refoundation. *The Last Man* stages the very opposite, that is, a narrative of decolonialisation at the end of world empires. The ideological countermovement of the narrative is initiated by the countermovement of the classical *katabasis* in the 'Author's Introduction'. Shelley's cave may prefigure the underworld, but the way to the Sibylline leaves points upwards (*hyper*) rather than downwards (*kata*). Together with the labyrinthine galleries starting from the mouth of the cave, the 'ascent' into a 'wide cavern with an arched dome-like roof' recalls the womb (*LM* 2). The critique advanced by Verney's narrative bears the image of an inception, a new beginning, so that what presents itself as a last-man story actually can be a firstling of a line of narratives that deny the renewal or the resurrection of the parameters serving the *renovatio imperii*. The Sibyl's cave then is the locus where something new is born, a decolonial narrative that launches the protagonist towards the world.

Nevertheless, before transforming the cave into her text's birthing place, Shelley confronts death and decline. Redolent of Botting's point about Wollstonecraft's shifting symbolism that imagines the family as both a cave and a prison, Shelley's cave too is a trap and a tomb where lies the 'perfect snow-white skeleton of a goat' which 'had fallen headlong' (Botting 131; *LM* 3).[9] This glaring snow-whiteness, a persistent proof of the goat's missteps, connotes error and self-inflicted tragedy, which as this chapter argues, *The Last Man* elevates to civilisational errors. Perhaps 'The Rime of the Ancient Mariner' (1798) with its two 'hosts of contagion', the decaying white bird and the leprous woman who 'destroy the myth of white purity' of the 'British bride', linger behind Shelley's lethal whiteness (D. Lee 687). In fact, Verney's narrative frequently associates whiteness with lethality. White can be the colour of disease, death and fall: it is the colour on Perdita's lips announcing her suicide and the hue of 'threatened dissolution' over the 'ashy paleness' of human faces (*LM* 41; 58); of the black spectre's 'ashy pale' face and of the sun that grows 'paler and paler' (321; 320). Death awaits in 'the white crests of the murderous' breakers that kill Adrian and Clara, fatefully reducing Verney to desolate solitude (345); death haunts the Italian cottage's sheets 'of snowy whiteness' which fail to lull Verney into the illusion of revived domesticity (353). A *mise en abyme* of the 'white flimsy substance' enveloping leaves and objects in the Sibyl's cave, these are the white linen on the coffin of the European home, a funereal whiteness, visible from afar in the message Verney leaves in white paint and with little hope before departing for Rome: 'Verney, the last of the race of Englishmen, had taken up his abode in Rome' (3, 355). His white words in three languages grasp at the illusion of a resurrected European community. It is just a few pages later that readers learn that neither Rome nor Europe at large is a viable home for Verney.

Paleness and whiteness evoke Britain, Europe and Christianity – the multitudes 'clad in white' seeking solace from plague in churches (*LM* 176). Already in the early days of their friendship, Verney regards Adrian as the keeper of 'the paled demesne of civilization', architecturally embodied by the royal forest of the ancestral estate with its 'white gate' swinging behind its inhabitants one last time (21, 260). Adrian's name bears echoes of civilisational defeat bringing to mind the battle of Adrianople in 378 AD, where the Eastern Roman army succumbed to the Gothic uprising. In search for a humanist compass after Adrian's death, Verney resorts to fancy and imagines the Pope 'in his white stole' blessing throngs of believers (360). Temporarily, the 'white stole' at the centre of this vision holds together the mirage of a functioning Roman, European and Catholic – in the sense of universal – communion of human beings. So powerful is the charm conjured by this tableau that coming out of its bubble strikes Verney not merely as an abrupt end but as a brutal plunge: his 'soul . . . stooping from its wheeling circuits round and round this spot, suddenly it fell ten thousand fathom deep, into the abyss of the present' (361). Verney's abyss refers readers back to the novel's first casualty in the Sibyl's cave: the goat which had dropped into the cave and met its demise. Illusion precedes both the animal's and Verney's falls. Illusion also animates the dazzling spectral presence of the plague-stricken artist, a 'figure all in white, apparently more than human stature', who deliriously imagines himself being on stage as if performing one last dance for the little band of British survivors, who look aghast upon the scene (320). It is the grotesque last dance of a 'pale' civilisation that measured the progress of other civilisations against the sophistication of its own artistic aptitude.

Rome, Greece and Britain's *translatio imperii*

The cave-womb with its Sibylline intra- and intertextualities fosters an understanding of Mary Shelley as an author who was raised and bred inside the discourse of *translatio imperii*, but who also conjectures an exit and outside to this discourse. Shelley's 'outside in' position requires a double movement that both acknowledges complicity with master narratives and imagines ways to delink from them.[10] Shelley deploys this double bind to mount an internal critique of empire-building narratives and their participation in primarily, albeit not uniquely, white imaginaries of political, military and epistemological power transfers. To make this point about complicity and delinking, I now turn to seminal circulations of the transferral trope that may have prompted Shelley's critique.

If nowhere else, in Spenser's *The Faerie Queene* (1590–96), which Shelley read in 1815 and quoted throughout her career, she encountered the trope of *translatio imperii* as it was applied to draw a continuous line between Britons and *The Aeneid*'s Trojans. Spenser's epic provides a view of Britain's history that is seamlessly appended to the fate of the first Troy conquered by the Greeks and of the second Troy raised by Aeneas on Latin ground. Book 3, canto 9 of *The Faerie Queene* establishes that 'noble Britons sprong from Trojans bold, / And Troynovant was built of old Troy's Ashes cold' (lines 341–42). The canto's whole argument is about showing Britons' Trojan 'auncestry' and the transfer of power, arts and sciences from old Troy via Rome to London. As the following sequence in this lineage, the third Troy is expected to grow by the banks of the river Thames: 'It Troynovant is hight, that with the Waves / Of wealthy Thamis washed is along' (lines 397–98). Keeping the Trojan-Roman-British line of transfer continuous, Brutus, great grandson of Aeneas, is celebrated as the founder of the city by the Thames:

> The Trojan Brute did first that citie fownd,
> and Hygate made the meare thereof by the west,
> and Overt gate by north. (lines 406–08)

This genealogical discourse consolidated the Tudor reign only to become historically questionable towards the end of Elizabeth I's rule. What matters in terms of the history of ideas is that '[w]hen the Tudors ascended to the throne of England, so runs the myth, the ancient Trojan-British race of monarchs once more resumed the imperial power and brought in a golden age of peace and plenty' (Yates 50). Aligned with this myth, the metamorphosis of Shelley's narrator from a wild youth 'as uncouth a savage as the wolf-bred founder of old Rome' into a subject of history begins in the bust-studded library of Adrian, a connoisseur of the classical civic order who acquaints Verney with the wisdom of 'the old Greek sages, and of the power which they had acquired over the minds of men' (*LM* 11, 20). Thus inducted, Verney learns to approach history linearly as a chain of transfers of power and knowledge from the Mediterranean to the British Isles: 'I read the histories of Greece and Rome, and of England's former periods' (61). Even for warfare strategies against the Turkish usurpers of modern Greece, the male characters peruse classical models: 'We read of centre and wing in Greek and Roman history' (140). So does the novel's war of liberation hark back to the concept of 'just war' that preoccupied Cicero in *De republica* until he could integrate the contentious idea of empire within the Roman republic (Atkins 232).

Suspicions about the novel's 'just war' and the republican acceptance of empire accumulate in the portrayal of Raymond, head of the British Protectorate and of the British troops against the Turks. When he diminishes the victories of the Greek armies by calling them 'all his own', thus casting Greece as too weak to emancipate itself, Raymond replicates Cicero's 'paternalistic argument for empire' in *De republica* (*LM* 31; Atkins 235). Cicero's paternalism invokes the right of stronger states to protect and rule over weaker ones so that universal justice is assured. The cosmopolitan bedrock of this argument, which Jed Atkins demonstrates to be Stoically inspired, shows in Cicero's justification of the 'Roman Empire inasmuch as it made possible the defence of Rome's provinces and allies as the protectorate of the world' (Atkins 235; Cicero, *On Duties* 72; II.27). Paternalism rings in the word 'protectorate', which translates Cicero's '*patrocinium*' and can describe the 'relationship of patron to client or ex-slave' and, in republican discourse, the 'relation of ruling state to subject' (*On Duties* 72; II.27). Shelley may be working from within a sceptical view of this relationship already voiced by Wollstonecraft, when she chastises Rousseau's eulogy of Roman incorruptibility for forgetting that 'in conquering the world, the Romans never dreamed of establishing their liberty on a firm basis, or of extending the reign of virtue' (*Vindication of the Rights of Woman* 31). So does Shelley's scenario warn that the lofty wish for a protectorate of the world can be utilised to mask self-aggrandisement and so annul the dignity, or worthy standing (*dignitas*), of this allegedly cosmopolitan undertaking? I use the word 'allegedly' because the first act projected in Raymond's reveries as the future 'King of England' is the union of the British and Greek armies against the Turks in a joint conquest of Constantinople, envisioned as the gateway to British rule over all Asian peoples (*LM* 44–45). Historically, this projected conquest would mend the line of Roman and Christian dominion in the region, which was broken when Sultan Mehmed II, named 'the Conqueror', captured Constantinople in 1453. On a personal level, the restoration of Constantinople to Christianity answers Raymond's ambition for exceptional politico-military 'aggrandizement' as the British 'Conqueror' (*LM* 31). Fixated on Constantinople, Raymond seeks to avenge that loss which Gibbon's *Decline and Fall of the Roman Empire* (1776–88) considered to be the landmark military campaign that sealed the demise of the Roman Empire. This British-ruled Constantinople, which Raymond flaunts to his soldiers as the recuperated 'seats of your ancestors, your own inheritance' (*LM* 15)', revives the pervasive idiom of heredity from Burke's reactionary *Reflections on the Revolution in France* (1790). The novel's central war, then, is a revanchist offensive to reconstitute empire under a new Christian leader who thinks of the liberation of Greece as the breakthrough to imperial acquisition. Shelley insists on the European scale of this enterprise by highlighting the commercial ties that uphold the British alliance with the states of Continental Europe in their joint defence of Greece against the Turks: no humanitarian obligations but primarily 'extensive commercial relations', Verney explains, 'gave every European nation an interest in their success' (*LM* 123). But the regaining of Constantinople is an act of transfer and *renovatio imperii* that the novel refutes.

Spenser's view of Britain's classical parentage is no isolated instance. '[T]he idea of the passing on of civility from the Romans to the British' in writings of the sixteenth and seventeenth century is well attested (Hingley 158).[11] The eighteenth century brought new nuances to this narrative. On the one hand, contemporary archaeological work among the remains of military posts along Hadrian's Wall and the Antonine Wall imprinted a dominantly military interpretation of Roman sites and influence in Britain. As a consequence, the revelation of bellicose relations between the Romans and the colonised islanders, laying bare Roman violence against indigenous resistance during the supposed *translatio imperii* from Rome to Britain, rendered less attractive the claim about Roman classical civility as the foundation of Augustan Britain (Hingley 160). But the second half of the eighteenth century mitigated this violent view when archaeological excavation shifted from military sites to sites of Roman habitation, making it possible for Roman influence to be interpreted not solely in military terms. Another narrative emerged when a formidable Roman colonisation could be remapped onto Britain's own imperial expansion. Roman military character was utilised to appraise British military acquisitions abroad and to uphold imperial interests to the extent that '[a]ccounts claiming that Britain had improved on the territorial achievements of classical Rome had become commonplace during the eighteenth century' (Hingley 226). In this vein, Edward Barnard's *The New, Comprehensive, Impartial and Complete History of England* (1790) tapped into Spenser's metaphor and likened Britain to 'a young phoenix' rising from the ashes of 'its mother', the Roman Empire, upon whose demolished body 'a magnificence structure of British glory might be raised' (233). The trend of writers legitimising the growing British empire through 'the turn to ancient Rome' and comparisons of Greater Rome to Greater Britain would continue well into Victoria's reign (Vasunia 39). Commonly, the attitudes of British writers towards Roman imperial historiography hinged on their views of the rising British Empire. In many aspects, as Phiroze Vasunia concludes, the *translatio imperii* was the 'driving engine' of these narratives (58).

The Last Man explores this correlation in ways that delegitimise and delink from European imperialism. Only briefly does the novel entertain the possibility of planting a British colony in Rome, when Adrian, Clara and Verney discard the idea of following in Childe Harold's steps in Albania. Instead of the 'savage uncultivation' of Albanian lands, they choose Rome (*LM* 343). Paradoxically, though, a grieving and solitary Verney reverts to the 'uncouth' state of his youth in Rome. Re-becoming as 'savage as the wolf-bred founder of old Rome', he undoes the fine civilising work effectuated by the influences of Adrian and Idris, the paragons of British civilisation. If, as some strands of eighteenth-century historiography argued, over time the rule of the Roman Empire bred Romanised Britons, Verney's devolvement signifies de-Romanisation in the very heart of Rome. Eventually, Verney abandons Rome without packing any of Virgil's works, choosing to neglect the Augustan court poet over whose celebration of imperial Rome Romantic and Victorian British writers enthused (Vance 141). In this detail, the novel shares a key insight with Edward Said by positing empire-building as being assisted by desires and intentions. As Said shrewdly argues, what precedes, inspires and aspires to the enterprise of empire is the very 'idea of having an empire' together with 'all kinds of preparations [that] are made for it within a culture' (11). Verney's exit from Rome and his omission of *The Aeneid* repudiates some of the elements that had accumulated for centuries, enabling the survival and promotion of the idea of empire. Therefore, arising in the context of past and contemporary imperial aspirations, *The Last Man*'s pandemic emergency disrupts what Thomas Harrison calls 'the perpetuation of ideological conditions necessary for empire' (34).

Disruption symptomises Shelley's alignment with critics of Britain's past and future. For this group, Britain's loss of the thirteen American colonies that fought for political and economic self-determination and the ongoing insurrections in the West Indian plantocratic colonies were red flags of imperial catastrophe. If Britain had exceeded the territorial expansion of its parent (Roman) empire, could its failure be proportionately more harrowing? Moreover, did the Roman model, bolstered by claims of common ancestry, provide the best model upon which to build the present and the future? What about the Greek paradigm of empire? There were historiographers like James Abercromby, who maintained in *Magna Charta for America* (1774) that the Greek colonisation was politically different from the Roman one upon which Britain had ill-advisedly modelled its colonising projects (Abercromby 185; Vlassopoulos 46). Two years later Smith's *The Wealth of the Nations* devoted a chapter to this issue that distinguished between Greek and Roman precursors, preferring the former of the two. Smith saw a laudable model in Athens as a parent that treated its Mediterranean colonies as 'emancipated' children who did not depend 'on the approbation or consent of the mother city' (585). Abercromby and Smith had the backing of other Enlightenment thinkers who maintained that, by borrowing from the Athenian model, Britain 'could avoid the destiny of the Roman Empire' (Vlassopoulos 42). However, despite scholarly efforts to arrive at a cohesive view of what the Greek and Roman experiences encompassed in the long eighteenth century, no unified picture of these classical models emerges. As Krishan Kumar sums up: 'The Greeks were at one time, and in one aspect, exemplars of liberty and intellect; at another time, and from another aspect, they spelled the failure to find an adequate and lasting solution to their political problem' (82). As for the Romans, they could be appreciated as both 'carriers of the civilizing mission to the world and the prime expression of imperial brutality and oppression' (82).

A text whose influence can hardly be overstated when it comes to connecting the dots between eighteenth-century views of the Roman Empire and *The Last Man* is Machiavelli's *Discourses on the First Ten Books of Livius Titus* (1531). There, Machiavelli attributed the collapse of the Roman Republic, for him a prelude to the fall, to luxury and selfishness. Machiavelli judged that these social vices emanated from a military type of masculinity characterised by an avidity for glory and personal wealth, thus eroding the civic spirit that sustained the republic. What ensued was a catastrophic desire for warfare: 'armed forces and grandiose ideas wiped out all republics with all their civic institutions' (Machiavelli 279). In *The Last Man*, Adrian's intellectual and suave approach to political leadership, in addition to his final failure to offer a political solution to the plague crisis, suggests a Greek approach. Raymond's military training and thirst for public acclaim are reminders of Machiavelli's ambition-drunk leaders whose version of historiography as a parade of great personalities is not unlike the gallery of portraits and statues that Shelley's Raymond erects to mark his rule. If one wonders why the pursuit of glory could have such an all-enveloping effect, one can turn to de Staël, who explains that the sublimity of the passion for glory consists in its capacity to 'absorb all the other affections of the soul, and its pleasures, as well as its pains' (*Influence* 66). It is an absorption to which the novel subjects Raymond, its most illustrious military man.

Machiavelli's assessment of the Roman Empire may be the foundation that Shelley's critique of Raymond-like agents of the *translatio imperii* shares with Volney's universalist rebuke of imperial psychology in *Ruins* (1791). In Volney's analysis, Shelley finds a correlation of micro- and macro-psychology that delineates the interplay between the individual human psyche and an imperial mentality. The cluster of ideas that *The Last Man* develops from such influential thinkers can be made sense of through 'critical cosmopolitanism', which, as Rebecca Walkowitz explains, is a position that investigates dynamics of 'cosmopolitanism, prompted by skepticism towards Western superiority as a worldwide agent of the civilizing process' (4). *The Last Man* can be described as critically cosmopolitan because it values collective social ethics and projects but also purges them from the vainglorious and dispossessing violence ingrained in the *translatio imperii* that, as Plutarch blithely stated about Alexander the Great, promoted such social projects. By refusing to acquiesce to cosmopolitan aspirations that camouflage imperial endeavours, Shelley's novel validates the wish and necessity for a cosmopolitan order without imperialism.

Plague and the Passion of Imperialism

In drawing attention to Volney's Enlightenment historiography, I join critical efforts to recover a philosophy 'underrated by interpretative traditions', despite *Ruins* being perhaps the most influential text of the 1790s (Abbattista 406; Kim 222). While many have treated Volney as a progressive stadial historian (and some connections to Scottish stadial theory emerge from my reading of *The Last Man*), Minchul Kim insists that Volney be understood as 'a worried republican steeped in the Enlightenment's historiographical tradition and engaged in the heroic attempt to find a way out of the menacing deadlocks of his age' (224). Crucially for the hermeneutics of *The Last Man*, much of Volney's worry stems from the history of European civilisation and its relationship with the Ancients (Kim 223). Like Shelley, Volney rejects the unexamined reverence for Greco-Roman antiquity in his 'detailed and elegant critique of civilizations' (Kim 227). Marcus Aurelius's self-censuring admonishment 'Take care that you are not turned into a Caesar' (51; VI.30) is aligned with Volney's scrutiny of Roman legacy. Volney saw a nefarious precedent in ancient Rome's transition from a republican to an imperial form of governance that he wanted the unstable new French Republic to avoid. His ultimately justified dread of a new French Caesar rose from such a dangerous return to the Ancients that would compromise the republican ethos of the revolution. Additionally, at the psycho-social level, *Ruins* ventured to explain the decline of once powerful states: 'The fate of the state depended on both the society and the individuals, since a state could prosper only upon its citizens' virtuous manners, but these were men whose natures were also guided by passions' (Kim 241). Religious passions and the cupidity of political leaders emerge as two key destabilising factors. However, cupidity, the vice singled out by Machiavelli, represented the greatest threat for Volney too. Shelley's interrelated emphasis on passions and the acquisitive appetite of rulers who spur people to war is of a piece with my understanding of imperialism as an infection of the human mind that spreads onto the nations. The fact that only human life is vulnerable to plague, while both flora and fauna continue to exist intact, accentuates the human problem. Dismissed by implication, human life is not indispensable to the survival of other life forms on the planet.

More often than not, Volney appears in interpretations of *Frankenstein*, with critics referring to this passage from *Ruins* (rarely quoted in full):

> Was it the charity of your gospel that led you to exterminate whole nations in America, and to destroy the empires of Mexico and Peru; that makes you still desolate Africa, the inhabitants of which you sell like cattle, notwithstanding the abolition of slavery that you pretend your religion has effected, that makes you ravage India whose domains you usurp; in short, is charity that has prompted you for three centuries past to disturb the peaceable inhabitants of three continents, the most prudent of whom, those of Japan and China, have been constrained to banish you from their country, that they might escape your chains and recover their domestic tranquillity. (307–08)

The Last Man's dystopia suffers under this indictment of European and British imperialism more directly than *Frankenstein*. The guilt of Britons for disturbing 'peaceable inhabitants' surges in the streams of migrants from North America and Ireland that force a confrontation between the British metropolis and its past colonial schemes. The first hint that *The Last Man* wrestles with a disease of empire lies with the plague's first appearance in the Nile region, where the British, French and Ottomans vied for control in 1789 at Aboukir, a campaign the British won under Horatio Nelson. Moreover, the novel's plague spreads in the East, that geopolitical space which Volney sees as a body 'ravage[d]' and 'usurp[ed]' by European imperial rivalry (309–10).

Shelley met with echoes of Volney's analysis in Coleridge's and Byron's work, to name two key influences. Coleridge's 'Fears in Solitude' (1798) condemns the wars in North Africa. They unleash a string of sickening episodes in the Anglo-French contest for the 'cup of wealth' that exudes 'pollutions' and is mired in 'vain, speech-mouthing' theatricals (lines 59–63). Byron's *The Curse of Minerva* (1811) followed Volney's searing critique of European influence in the East, starting with Lord Elgin's removal of the Parthenon artworks before turning to the Indian subcontinent, 'where Ganges' swarthy race / Shall shake your tyrant empire to its base' (lines 220–21). Here Byron also offered another interpretation of the Hellenistic legacy: British imperialism, in a *translatio* gone awry, had misappropriated Greek philosophy, and hence the Juvenalian speaker thunders the curse of Athena (Minerva), the goddess of law and justice: 'So may ye [Britons] perish! Pallas, when she gave / Your free-born rights, forbade ye to enslave' (lines 226–27). Byron's amalgamation of Greek heritage with the philosophy of inalienable human rights – the embattled ideal of the American, French and Haitian Revolutions – lends additional significance to Verney's choice of Homer's epics as a journey companion steeped in a tradition that enshrined notions like democracy and justice (Anagnostopoulos and Santas 1–13).

The ethnic and religious implications of Volney's critique, not often discussed by Shelley scholars, are relevant to *The Last Man.* The passage above appears in the speech of the Muslim representatives in *Ruins*, a narrative mostly conceived as an agora where delegates of diverse religious and ethnic belonging assemble to debate the current and future states of a humanity rent by doctrinal and military conflict. The passage targets Christian and European delegates, who spread ruin under the noxious pretext of their charitable 'gospel' (Volney 309). What Volney conjures is a rhetorical face-off between Christian and Muslim self-representations and actual practices which *The Last Man* transposes onto the battlefield, particularly in the blood-soaked streets of Constantinople where Turks, Greeks and Britons fight to capture the city. Volney's rhetorical confrontation and Shelley's military conflicts denounce two of the largest empires of their time, the British and Ottoman. Like Volney, Shelley assumes these empires' acquisitive avidity and, consequently, has plague befall all parties indiscriminately. In response to the Muslims' charges, *Ruins*' Christian delegates mount a critique of Ottoman expansion on a similar accusatory premise. A mirror-image of the ravaging practices of Christian empires, the Muslims' merciful religion has been 'converted into a torch of discord and an incentive to war' that 'has never ceased for twelve hundred years to whelm the earth in blood and spread ravage and desolation from one extremity of the ancient hemisphere to the other' (157). In the end, *Ruins* insists that such misappropriations flagrantly hollow out the cosmopolitan foundation of both religions: 'a beneficent and merciful God, the common parent of the whole human race' (157). As a basis on which to build a cosmopolitan order of justice and peace, the conviction of this common parentage that makes humanity into one worldwide household (*oikos*) motivates Volney's analysis of the imperial rise-and-fall cycle.

Common parentage is a sturdy enough foundation on which to strive for conviviality in Shelley's novel. Adrian, the spokesperson of this aspiration, recognises both the justice of the Greek cause for freedom from Turkish rule and the crude fact that humanity dies every time a human life is extinguished on either side of the conflict: 'But let us not deceive ourselves. The Turks are men; each fibre, each limb is as feeling as our own, and every spasm, be it mental or bodily, is as truly felt in a Turk's heart or brain, as in a Greek's' (*LM* 123). One hears in Adrian's words the cosmopolitan ethos of Fénelon's Mentor in *Telemachus*, although Adrian more openly than Mentor builds on the shared 'neurophysiological property of sentient beings' defended within natural philosophy by the monogenetic theory and the neuroscience of sensibility (Steiner, 'Cultures' 136–38). Abstaining from an adversarial vocabulary that casts the Turks as foes, Adrian admonishes his companions not to 'prate of war' while right there, in a Constantinople turned slaughterhouse, '[e]very breathing creature within the walls was massacred. Think you, amidst the shrieks of violated innocence and helpless infancy, I did not feel in every nerve the cry of a fellow being?' (*LM* 123). Human fellowship undergirds the morality of cosmopolitan responsiveness that articulates an idiom of commonality instead of warmongering, ethnic and religious partisanship.

In *The Last Man*, cosmopolitan moral responsiveness represents a counter-ideology to the 'prate of war' predominantly associated with Raymond and, by extension, to 'the brutal force' which, according to Wollstonecraft, 'has hitherto governed the world' (*A Vindication of the Rights of Woman* 56). Adrian's advice, 'let us not deceive ourselves', contravenes the camouflaged military agenda fed and led by 'an adventurer in . . . wars', as Verney guardedly calls Raymond (*LM* 31). Raymond, a charismatic 'adventurer', rallies the Christian troops with talk of enemies, forceful entry, incentives of spoils and hereditary possession: 'The enemy is already vanquished; the pleasant places, the noble dwellings and spoil of the city are already yours; force the gate; enter and possess the seats of your ancestors, your own inheritance!' (*LM* 151). 'Spoil' has contemporary resonances, as Angela Esterhammer delineates in the works of Felicia Hemans and Byron. Reacting to the Italian artworks shipped to Paris by Napoleon, Hemans calls the latter a 'spoiler' who must restore the artefacts to their rightful owner (Esterhammer 31–32).[12] Byron's chief 'spoiler' is Lord Elgin, while Elgin's ancient precursors, according to Byron, are the spoilers of the Roman Empire, whose eventual disintegration proves that loot and empire do not last. Compared with the Romans', Elgin's spoils are even more objectionable 'because they are not acquired through any initial act of heroism' (Esterhammer 33). Shelley radicalises this critique by writing of heroism as an offshoot of 'patriotic fury' and disguised adventurism (*LM* 151). It is the leadership's adventurism, Verney intimates, that fans the dangerous flames of populist patriotism. Therefore, Verney repeatedly queries the conscious and unconscious motivations driving Raymond's military and political careers as these intertwine, while steering towards imperial conquest. With the word ‘adventurer’, Verney offers readers an interpretative tool through a notion that Samuel Johnson’s *Dictionary* (1751) had linked to hazardous and monetarily motivated actions. The *Dictionary*’s explanatory quotes contextualise the adventurer as a military fortune-seeking figure rising at the inception of British imperialism and mercantile piracy.[13] Johnson’s historical source for this meaning was the Adventurer’s Act, passed in 1642 by the English Parliament to attract investors in a future English invasion of Ireland that promised to repay investors and adventurers with Irish lands. These are the earlier historiographic and lexical contexts that fold into Shelley’s critique of British imperial adventurism.

Further signs of critique transpire in the novel’s depictions of conquests neither celebrative nor commendably heroic. The North American migrants who force their way into Ireland are portrayed as plunderers ‘with mad desire for change’ and the ‘blind’, ‘insane fury’ and a ‘senseless spirit of conquest and thirst of spoil’ that ‘deluged the country in ruin’ (*LM* 231, 234). The adventurer’s heroism miscarries when Raymond attempts to rally his troops with grandiose speeches about inheriting Constantinople and its fabulous spoils only to find his soldiers un-moved and reluctant to ‘die in heaps, like dogs poisoned in summer-time by the pestilential air of that city’ (151). Yet, uncannily, the destructive legacy of spoils and imperial adventurism lives on in Raymond’s corpse, ‘[s]uch as he had now become, such as was his terrene vesture, defaced and spoiled’ (162). Raymond’s body, ‘the burthen in our arms’, exits the narrative as friends and family carry the thwarted adventurer away from Constantinople (163). In an ironic reversal, the spoiler turned spoiled negates heroic explanations of adventurism and imperial warring.

We need to complement this view of adventurism with Shelley’s sketching of passions as definers of personal and world history, a view advanced by classical Stoics and later by Scottish philosophical history and Volney. All these influences agree with the novel’s psycho-genetic approach to history, that is, the ‘ruin-fraught passions of men’ mentioned in the ‘Author’s Introduction’, a phrase echoing ‘the tragic scene of the passions’ contemplated by Volney’s inquisitive wanderer (*Ruins* xii). Passions also occupy a central place in ‘Principal Causes of Misery’, a note possibly written by Shelley in 1818 and revisited in the aftermath of Percy’s drowning. Eileen M. Hunt, writing during the health crisis of COVID-19, has recently drawn attention to the words ‘Hate-Strife-Revenge’ in Shelley’s note (6, 11). My attention is rather engrossed by the lines in the middle of this text, which read: ‘~~A love~~ The want of being admired – Ambition – Envy – Jealousy –.’ The visual ordering at the centre of the short, list-like note evokes this quartet of passions as triggers of human miseries which express themselves in 'Hate-Strife-Revenge'. De Staël's *Influence of the Passions on the Happiness of Individuals and of Nations*, yet another mournful rumination on the heels of the Reign of Terror, may be one of the sources tersely reflected in Shelley's note, because the passions of 'love of glory', 'ambition' and 'vanity' open de Staël's essay (45, 73, 97). At the heart of Shelley's list stands out a cocktail of passions that worries de Staël too and constitutes a persisting theme from *Frankenstein* to at least *Lives of the Most Eminent Literary and Scientific Men of France* (1838).

In *Frankenstein*, passions are responsible for the individuation of the self, calling forth actions that set the self apart from the undifferentiated mass of other selves. So Victor explains how he came to think of his daring experiment:

> when I would account to myself for the birth of that passion, which afterwards ruled my destiny, I find it arise, like a mountain river, from ignoble and almost forgotten sources; but, swelling as it proceeded, it became the torrent which, in its course, has swept away all my hopes and joys. (67)

Unlike her scientist, Shelley learned from 'the virtuous, calm and wise' Fénelon to search the depths of an 'erring passion-tost [*sic*] humanity' (*Lives* 372). It is a depth that *The Last Man* plumbs with Frankensteinian self-involvement when Raymond describes his life as one lived at the passions' behest: 'I cannot rule myself. My passions are my masters; my smallest impulse my tyrant', which intimates a bond between passions and tyranny, a kind of pre-Freudian inevitability: 'where *id* is, there ego goes' (*LM* 117). Raymond's assumption contradicts Wollstonecraft's, which maintains that human beings are endowed with passions so that 'by struggling with them they might attain a degree of knowledge denied to the brutes' (*Vindication of the Rights of Woman* 28). Staying close to Wollstonecraft, the novel does not corroborate Raymond's determinism. Shelley's insistent evocation of cultural models of idolised acquisitive masculinity endorses Volney's and the Stoics' position that passions are learnable and thereby subject to change and reform. This conviction incites Volney's genius to teach truths about fallen empires and to conjure up a debate in a multi-ethnic interreligious assembly. The genius of *Ruins* offers a Stoically inspired instruction on how we humans may 'take a more comprehensive view of our relations, and be exalted above the atmosphere of our passions' (Volney 135). (The phrase 'atmosphere of our passions' holds a profound meaning that I explore in the next section.) In the context of learnable passions, Volney's most straightforward Stoic antecedent is Seneca, whose 'On Anger' takes great pains to teach young Nero how to shore up the pull of ambition, anger and retaliation and, in their stead, make place for communitarian or, at least, conciliatory passions. This teaching is shared by Epictetus, who advises his audience to counteract 'this inclination to take offence and vent hatred' with passions like pity, mercy and tolerance (*Discourses* 42; I.18.9–10) – the kind of *eupatheia* also embraced by Fénelon in Shelley's *Lives* and Adrian in *The Last Man*.

The point I want to make here is that, while Shelley may not exclude an ontological explanation for humanity's failure to build sustainably peaceful communities, her novel investigates a culturally constructivist view of human history for which Raymond's adventurist characterology is a case in point.[14] Raymond's hubristic ambition is less ontological than engendered and nurtured by imperial psychology, as discussed in historiographies both fascinated with and appalled by military supremacy. From the lives of larger-than-life V/victors like Alexander the Great and Caesar, Raymond learns to aspire to greatness like theirs (*LM* 44). Theirs is the type of ambition that writes history in *The Aeneid*; they are the conquerors Raymond looks up to, the ones who carry on the voice and logic of Anchises. Like Aeneas, Raymond's character is chiselled by the keenly felt loss of a formerly illustrious pedigree that longs for vindication, no matter what the cost. In *The Last Man*, historiography and biography converge to shape a constructivist personal ambition eager to yield to what René Girard calls 'the mimetic attraction of violence' exuded by models of imperial masculinity like Caesar and, in Shelley's time, by Napoleon (837). Accordingly, Verney notes that Raymond's 'first wish was aggrandizement; and the means that led towards this end were secondary considerations' (*LM* 30). His character bears the mark of what Coleridge's 'Fears in Solitude' denounced as the defining trait of imperial Britishness, of a nation so 'passionate for war' that it has 'swell[ed] the war-whoop' (90). Raymond wishes to join the ranks of 'darling[s] of fame' like Caesar, men enabled by and reigning over a 'wonder-loving world' hungry for extraordinary sensations (*LM* 30). Parallel to this public Raymond, Shelley develops Raymond's characterology in domestic scenes, first as the offspring of impoverished aristocrats, then as Perdita's and Evadne's lover, Clara's father and the friend of Adrian, Verney and Idris. This carefully constructed synergy explains why a weakened domestic life precedes Raymond's defeat in the political realm and why a merely ontological conceptualisation of passions, vices and virtues is implausible.

In this, the narrative shows affinities with Scottish historiography, which adapted Stoic moral psychology to reconceive history as a narrative akin to the (then new) genre of the novel. Scottish historiography participated in the culture of sensibility popularised by the novel via a 'pronounced stress upon the psychological and cultural origins of individuals' behaviour' and upon the historiographer's effort 'to seek to cultivate empathy and increase identification between modern readers and those who had lived in the past' (Allan 332–33). Hugh Blair, for instance, in his defence of James Macpherson's forged *Works of Ossian* (1765) declares that the chief interest of history resides in the investigations of feelings and thoughts that precede or accompany individual behaviour, summed up as the 'curious spectacle' of 'human manners' (1). History fulfils its mission to instruct when it familiarises readers with 'human imagination and passion' because these ultimately determine the history of communities and societies at large (Blair 1). His argument rehearses Seneca's conclusion in 'On Anger' that the tyrant's negative passions misshape the entire nation. As for the continuity between ancient Greco-Roman civilisations and contemporary European history, it appears in some strands of Scottish socio-psychology: Hume's socio-genesis, for instance, maintains that whoever wants to learn about the temper and passions of the Romans and the Greeks should study the behaviours of their French and English successors. Hume also lists ambition, a passion that preoccupied classical Stoicism, as the first in a series of passions not organised in vices and virtues (*Enquiry* 60).[15]

More explicitly attuned to classical Stoicism, Adam Smith treated ambition as a passion typical of rulers and monarchs (*Theory* 86), as did William Robertson in his description of Charles V and Columbus. Ambition, Smith argues, obtains the monarch's exalted state and demonstration of power through conquest and acquisition. Prefiguring Shelley's 'wonder-loving world' (*LM* 30), Smith thinks of crowd psychology when he illustrates the singular attraction emanated by the monarch with the powerful impression that the monarch's misfortunes make on the multitudes: 'All the innocent blood that was shed in the civil wars, provoked less indignation than the death of Charles I' (*Theory* 86). Smith roots this spectatorial phenomenon in human 'disposition', but he also develops it in culturally evolutionary terms to make a point about the birth of social inequality: 'Upon this disposition of mankind, to go along with all the passions of the rich and the powerful, is founded the distinction of ranks, and the order of society' (88). In Shelley's novel, this pull first emerges in Verney's attraction to the royal Adrian, but once Adrian's character readily disassociates himself from a lust for power, the careerist Raymond enters the novel and propels the friends' microcosm towards political prominence and warring projects. From then on, the comforting predictability of what Adrian calls 'our pastoral life' starts petering out (*LM* 74).

Perhaps the strongest evidence for Shelley's awareness of this Smithian insight is the novel's sabotaging of latent sympathies for militaristic rulers, when the spectre of a pestilential Raymond emerges in Verney's 'disturbed' dreams (*LM* 158). Lastness enters the narrator's consciousness with Raymond posturing as a magnanimous Timon of Athens hosting the last meal for his friends. To Verney's horror, it is a meal of fetid vapours recalling the fatal air of plague-infested Constantinople; a meal presided over by the distorted and ever-swelling shape of Raymond's phantom, 'bearing on its brow the sign of pestilence' (158). 'Sign', *signum*, that is, 'an identifying mark', in addition to having the apocalyptic ring of the Biblical 'mark of the beast', turns Raymond's body into the banner of the plague, a banner with planetary emanations. Distortion already surfaces in the imperial traces that taint Raymond's cosmopolitan warring on behalf of the Greeks while he is alive. Cosmopolitan warring, in the Stoic sense and practice of the word, may signify that the citizen of one country chooses to fight in the emancipatory cause of another country (Kleingeld and Brown). Among other things, participation in a foreign war has prompted comparisons of Raymond with Byron. Yet the differences between the two may be even more telling. Raymond follows a duplicitous career in his pursuit of becoming both 'the conqueror of Stamboul, the liberator of Greece' (*LM* 156). Order matters – first conqueror of the heart of the Ottoman Empire, second liberator of Greece – in that it indicates Raymond's priorities: imperialist intentions precede and even cannibalise cosmopolitan pretexts of emancipation. Verney's dream and Raymond's spoiled body convey the novel's reckoning with the instrumentalisation of such cosmopolitan aspirations as universal happiness and peaceful conviviality. What Paul A. Cantor writes about Byron's uneasy toying with the epic genre in *Childe Harold* and *Don Juan* can illuminate Shelley's exploration of leadership (Raymond, Ryland, Adrian) during *The Last Man*'s planetary crisis. Shelley's epic of medical sublime, like Byron's poems, 'search[es] for greatness in the modern world that will not be so destructive' as the greatness of Alexander, Caesar and, most alarmingly to Shelley's contemporaries, Napoleon (Cantor 393).

The moment Raymond's phantom fills and bursts beyond the 'vault that bent over, sustaining and enclosing the world', his ambition becomes synonymous with plague and anti-cosmopolitanism (*LM* 158). Verney's dream is also a verdict. No less a nightmare for Verney than for humanity, Raymond's rupture through his friend's subconscious resembles what de Staël, in the wake of the terror of the French Revolution, calls 'a universal moment' that hurriedly compels survivors to stir up the 'very *dead*' so that they may be 'judged anew' (*Influence* 1). Because human annihilation follows the trail of the plague's poisonous air, thus destroying human citizenship on earth, plague is an anti-cosmopolitan agent. It is another bitter irony that only in death, when his phantom enfolds the world, does Raymond garner the aggrandisement he pursued in war and politics, as if ambition had outlived its host. But this is the novel's point: the ambition of a Caesar or an Alexander lives on after their death, not least, through storytelling and historiography. Verney's traumatic dream of Raymond bursting at the threshold of a Constantinople depopulated by plague bequeaths to the figure of the imperial adventurer the unbounded recklessness that Smith identifies in the relation that a person of such ambition entertains with the world:

> With what impatience does the man of spirit and ambition, who is depressed by his situation, look round for some great opportunity to distinguish himself? No circumstances, which can afford this, appear to him undesirable. He even looks forward with satisfaction to the prospect of foreign war, or civil dissension; and, with secret transport and delight, sees through all the confusion and bloodshed which attend them, the probability of those wished-for occasions presenting themselves, in which he may draw upon himself the attention and admiration of mankind. (*Theory* 94)

Shelley had only to turn to Wollstonecraft to complement Smith's diagnosis with the figure of the adventurer: 'Alas!' writes Wollstonecraft, 'what unheard of misery have thousands suffered to purchase a cardinal's hat for an intriguing obscure adventurer, who longed to be ranked with princes, or lord it over them by seizing the triple crown' (*Vindication of the Rights of Woman* 29). The nightmarish subconscious of Shelley's novel implies that the recklessness of adventurers dies hard. Raymond's last appearance as a miasmatic apparition conflates fetid air with the spirit of imperialism. The enterprise of empire, about which the novel's Sibylline references warn, is active in a British leader's desire to force Asia into submission through a war that becomes the bedrock of pestilential formations.

Cosmopolitanism without Empire

Plague in the novel is conceived as residing in and travelling through airways. Air can be not only inimical to human life but also imagined to turn noxious under human influence. For instance, bitterness leads Verney to write that 'the air seemed poisoned' by Adrian's presence, a prejudice swiftly abandoned (*LM* 18). Similarly, in the air Raymond sees the nemesis to human passions such as 'love, hate or ambition' (56). But in his antagonistic psychology, these passions can master atmospheric hostilities 'stemming the opposing air in triumph', a belief roundly disproved when miasmic air annihilates his imperial dream (*LM* 56). In the Biblical tradition, reinvigorated by the philosophy of Giambattista Vico (1688–1744), aerial phenomena like wind and thunder are the most common elements of theophany. By implication, miasmic air can represent an actor of divine reckoning. However, what I want to argue here by drawing attention to the conflation of miasmic air and the spirit or ethos of imperialism is the (anti-)cosmopolitan and decolonial thrust of plague.

There are early indications in the novel for understanding air as the conveyor of human intentions, spirit and presence: for example, Verney recalls that '[t]he spirit of Idris hovered in the air I breathed' (*LM* 48). Percy Shelley's equation of air with a new and revitalising spirit, ethos and mindset in 'Ode to the West Wind' (1820) is the most obvious model, but Wollstonecraft's calling the passions 'the winds of life' and her evocation of 'a pestilential vapour' that 'hover[s] over society' as the result of human crimes, vices and 'vile intrigues' has more in common with *The Last Man*'s aerial conflation of moral and physical pathologies (*Vindication of the Rights of Woman* 32, 137). Volney's phrase 'atmosphere of our passions' is another explicit influence that grounds such pathologies in the mismanagement of drives, desires, impulses (135). Greek philosophy and science underlie these models. Hippocrates wrote of air 'and its articulation in breath' as the element that holds all beings in sympathy (*sympatheia ton holon*), so that 'there is one common flow, one common breathing' (qtd. in D. Macauley 31). The central role of breathing and its ubiquitous, generally taken-for-granted occurrence in and around the earth prompted Aximenes to single out air as 'the element that can explain all that exists' (D. Macauley 32). In the correspondence between a macrocosm and a microcosm, attested very early in Western thought, air is both 'a thin "material" and a metaphysical glue', while 'the life-soul (or breath-soul)' is likened to cosmic air that is also 'alive and animate' (33). By being both a metaphysical connector and a breath-soul, air takes on primordial cosmopolitan qualities, making its opposite, global pestilential air, the most disintegrating and anti-cosmopolitan element. In Shelley's novel, imperial ideology that survives the death of fictional colonisers (Aeneas, Raymond) or real ones (Caesar, Columbus as Neo-Aeneas, Napoleon as Neo-Caesar) causes this 'metaphysical glue' to mutate into a divider and conqueror of human communities.

Epidemiologically, the non-contagiousness of the novel's plague has cosmopolitan ramifications. Unlike the plague of 1665, when a contagionist diagnostics justified restrictions on mobility and the controversial shutting up of houses of the sick, *The Last Man*'s plague is not transmitted from human to human. This contrast, frequently pointed out by Verney, gestures to the most intense debate of contemporary epidemiology about the transmission of the 'big three' epidemic diseases: plague, cholera and yellow fever. Shelley wrote her novel during the first cholera outbreak of 1818–24, which fuelled sparring between the contagionist and non-contagionist camps. Each camp's position stood not only for distinct medical policies to prevent and manage epidemics but also for a set of differing worldviews.

Contagionism, for several centuries the medical rationale behind preventive measures like quarantine and governmental policing, was suspect to the non-contagionists who, in addition to being scientists, also were reformers wary of the fetters of state control, and therefore propagated the right of people to international trade and mobility. This cosmopolitan politico-economic aspect of anti-contagionism 'contributed probably no less than its scientific aspects to its gaining over the majority of those parts of the medical profession that were independent of the state' (Ackerknecht 9). Thus non-contagionists defended a position that did not justify fear of the human other on the grounds of the migration of plague, and *The Last Man* largely endorses this position. When the novel's mass migrations from North America and Ireland stir up fears of annihilation, the crisis is resolved under Adrian's non-antagonistic leadership. To double down on his integrating policies, the narrator shows the futility of xenophobic measures when fear of contagion leads to isolation and death, as happens to Ryland. One inconsistency, as critics note, unsettles the novel's non-contagionist stance, when Verney catches the plague (or so he thinks) from a black man, whose significance I discuss at the close of this chapter.

This inconsistency draws attention to the social and aetiological hermeneutics of plague, which points to the novel's absorption of insights gained from diseases provoked by wars. Because Verney is unable to explain his recovery from plague, it has been argued that 'there is no logically adequate way of construing' the disease in Shelley's novel (Snyder 436–37).[16] Aerially transmitted infection that does not involve human exhalation seems impossible to square with the germ theory that Robert Koch proposed in the 1880s, refuting anti-contagionist interpretations ever since. Shelley's anti-contagionist aetiology, however, does not seem to have been an impossibility in the 1820s. It is worth remembering that disease, whether contagious or not,

> has in itself no meaning: it is only a micro-organism. It requires meaning and significance from its human context, from the ways in which it infiltrates the lives of the people, from the reactions it provokes, and from the manner in which it gives expression to cultural and political values. (Arnold 151)

War was the human context for what is perhaps the first pandemic recorded in human history: the disease outbreak that followed Rome's gruelling but ultimately successful wars in Persia in 165 AD. Called the Antonine plague after Emperor Marcus Aurelius Antoninus Augustus, this virulent disease 'was a crucial factor in the demise of the Pax Romana' (Elliott xxiii). War was also the context of disease in Shelley's generation. Imperial wars triggered numerous outbreaks, creating fertile ground for teaching in medical schools and intensive medical investigation (Pickstone 141). If we take into account the fact that the first cholera outbreak occurred in British India in 1817 during the expansion of the East India Company in the Indian subcontinent, it seems that war-provoked diseases grotesquely literalised the spirit of British imperialism. Cholera spread and travelled as British troops marched from Bengal to the north (Punjab) to fight and eventually win the third war against the Maratha Empire.[17] For more than a decade before reaching Europe in 1831, what Europeans dubbed *cholera asiatica* or *cholera indica* was known in the British mainland through the devastation the disease wreaked in British military stations and campaigns in Asia (McGrew 61). Brits at home, for instance, learned that within just one week in November 1817 no fewer than 764 soldiers in Lord Hastings's troops succumbed to cholera. And for the next fifty years, cholera would wage 'an intermittent guerilla warfare against the common British soldier' (Arnold 127). Arnold rightly calls it a 'guerilla warfare', for India's indigenous populations, discerning the hand of divine reprisal, attributed the disease's virulence to the just indignation of the idol 'Yagatha Ummah' at British rule over Hindustan (Jonnès 114).

War was a recurring context for aetiologic sense-making. Sir John Pringle, president of the Royal Society (1772–78), prioritised military environments in *Observations on the Diseases of the Army* (1753), explaining miasmatic air as being caused by the 'putrefication' of dead matter and bodies (169–70).[18] So too did Joseph Priestley and Charles Maclean. The latter's anti-contagionism was concomitant with his critique of military medicine, which was based on both his experiences as a surgeon in the East India Company's hospital in Calcutta in 1792–98 and his subsequent service in the Levant Company. A researcher and plague survivor who contracted the disease in Istanbul (*The Last Man*'s war- and plague-ridden city), Maclean published the two-volume study *Results of an Investigation, Respecting Epidemic and Pestilential Diseases* (1817–18), where he concluded that non-contagious plague was entirely dependent on atmospheric influences. Extending Maclean's correlation of war and disease four years after Shelley's novel, Thomas Southwood Smith's *Treatise on Fever* (1830) relied on war reports to maintain a localist and anti-contagionist view of yellow fever and plague. Smith suggested that the interplay between air and decomposed matter (vegetal, animal, human) engendered the poisonous air called miasma (362). In accounts like Smith's, whose anti-contagionist ideas she encountered in the *Quarterly Review* in 1825, Shelley read about war bringing together large masses of people and animals in crowded encampments causing great amounts of vegetal, animal and human waste, in addition to human and animal casualties (McWhir 25). The anti-contagionist position maintained that this decaying matter reacted chemically with the air, resulting in poisonous effluvia. This may be the kind of disease that Shelley hypothesises in her novel and that the nineteenth century called a zymotic disease, that is, a disease caused by processes of fermentation. As late as 1886, despite Koch's discovery of the *Vibrio cholera*, Koch's opponent, the chemist Max Pettenkofer (1818–1901), continued to maintain an anti-contagionist aetiology of cholera akin to the zymotic aetiology of Shelley's pandemic. For Pettenkofer, the *Vibrio cholera* was not poisonous *per se*. Once, however, the *vibrio* penetrated the soil and groundwater and met with enabling conditions there, it could develop and release poisonous substances into the air as if it were a plant (Snowden 257). In short, contemporary explanations and disagreements among contagionists and anti-contagionists show that there existed no stable and consistent aetiology for virulent diseases like plague, yellow fever and cholera for most of the nineteenth century. Hence, the varied measures of prevention advocated in the world of Shelley's novel recreate conflicting aetiologies in the medical field.

I veer into medical interpretations of the novel to highlight connections between epidemiology and war so as to point out that Verney's contact with the diseased 'negro half clad' accentuates a polyphonic and already opaque understanding of plague (*LM* 265). Verney's unexplained contagion (if contagion it really is) and subsequent recovery contradict but also co-exist without resolution with his non-contagionist stance. This lack of explanation represents the polyphonic *pièce de resistance* in the medical sublime to which Shelley subjects her narrator. It is an epistemological absence typical of the polyphonic character, which treats with silence the contradictory responses to the sublime that terrifies but does not kill Verney. Polyphony intensifies the self-consciousness rather than the objective truths of *The Last Man*'s homodiegetic narration, or, more unsettlingly, makes truth a matter of self-consciousness. It is worth recalling that, because polyphony ensures the autonomy of the character from the author, Verney's voice must not be collapsed with Shelley's (Vice 121). Shelley allows Verney to continue his narration without elucidating an inconsistency that she, however, makes plainly visible for readers to see. The passage stands out by centring on raw physicality and on the wordless duel for survival between a suffering black man brought low by plague and a healthy but distraught white man. The enigmatic encounter alerts readers to the fact that the whole narrative is produced by this white male's perspective, his gaze, senses, contemplations and prejudices. As readers, we do not witness the plague's presence in the breath of the black man, but rather the effects of Verney's reckoning that plague rages in his breath. Even before this episode, Verney's sense-making explicitly registers effects rather than scientific truth. He relates a 'tale' about the strange meteorological occurrence of the black sun in Asia and Africa, adding that '[w]hether this story were true or not, the effects were certain' (*LM* 176). The effects, be they illusionary or not, make the stuff of Verney's story. The effects of plague are sheer 'panic', and panic permeates Verney's wrestling with the sick black man (176). Fear of celestial blackness or of contagion from the black body are psychologically active and not epistemologically proven. What we are assured of are the effects on the perceiving subject(s) and not the cause of the said effects.

This passage gives postcolonial readers pause; it would be troubling if it did not. I find illuminating Dan Bivona's evaluation of Western modernity's relationship to the concept of civility which is central to eighteenth-century sensibility or sympathy, since there is a blatant failure of sympathy in this passage ending with Verney's physical rejection of the black man: 'I . . . threw the wretch from me' (*LM* 265). Bivona writes that 'discussions of "modernity" need to consider modernity's complex and tortured relationship to the "civility" that it both celebrates itself for treasuring and that it belies in its periodic exercises of highly efficient brutality' (130). The epithet 'tortured' befits this incident. The dying stranger, whose half-dressed state connotes uncouthness and dispossession, has been civilly admitted into Verney's home, and a deeply agitated Verney has enough empathy to retrospectively fathom the agony of the 'wretched' black man. But between the act of hospitality and Verney's recognition of the man's suffering, Verney's terror aborts civility by egregiously refusing practical compassion and brutally treating the black body as an abject thing to cast aside while it still throbs with life. Yet have not readers been already warned about Verney's 'tortured' relation to Western civility? After all, he is the narrator who confesses: 'I continued my war against civilization, and yet entertained a wish to belong to it' (*LM* 14) – a war that has its solitary showdown among the ancient monuments of Rome, where Verney will desperately arouse himself one last time with visions of great Roman personalities, bright like 'meteors' in what he sees as 'the murky night of the empire' (360). It is needless to repeat that one such meteor, Virgil, is at the genesis of Shelley's interest in the Sibyl.

The failure of sympathy towards the half-clad, dying Africanist presence conveys Shelley's recognition that the litmus test for contemporary white, Western, self-adulating 'civility' is the black body, this Fanonian 'wretched' of the world whose agonising weight of unrelieved plight brings into sharp relief white moral blindness, a state the novel regards as a symptom of the 'spirit of conquest' and the 'thirst of spoil' (*LM* 234). It is plausible to read the passage's snapshot of human failure as a compensatory gesture for Shelley's own omission of Volney's condemnation of the transatlantic slavery in *Frankenstein*'s anti-imperialist critique. The New World, Peru and Mexico do appear in *Frankenstein*. What is missing, though, is her reference to the accusation mounted by Volney's Muslims against European enslavement of Africans: 'you still desolate Africa, the inhabitants of which you sell like cattle, notwithstanding the abolition of slavery that you pretend your religion has effected' (Volney 157). A compensatory reading may explain Shelley's choice of the word 'wretch', which Coleridge probably borrowed from Wilberforce's twelve propositions against the slave trade, 'that wretched brutishness', presented to Parliament in 1787 (Howse 35). Coleridge's 'Fears in Solitude' describes those wrecked by British 'slavery and pangs' as 'wretches', the 'Brethren' whose 'groan of accusation pierces Heaven' (lines 45–51). Thus, like *Frankenstein*'s crisis with its fiascos of scientific irresponsibility, *The Last Man*'s global pandemic drives home its critique by absence: we wish Victor had fathered the creature and thought of Elizabeth's vulnerability in the face of the latter's revenge; we wish Verney had alleviated the misery of the dying African and recognised the epidermal othering behind his panic. Guided by this paradigm of critique-bearing absences, I understand Verney's presumed contagion to be a product of his 'diseased fancy', that imaginary infection underpinning European notions of superiority that hindered cosmopolitan solidarity and justified the subjugation of Africans in Britain's slave-labouring colonies (*LM* 158).

Reading racism as an infection of the mind complements the Sibylline dissidence I discern in Shelley's attitude towards narratives of colonisation and 'foundational quasi-mythical pasts, which previously served as generation-transcending fixed points' (Levy and Sznaider 197). To reiterate the 'outside in' double bind using José E. Muñoz's words, *The Last Man* 'works on and against' narratives that instil an imperial mindset, stepping towards a disaffiliation from mythical pasts which have held sway over many generations and centuries (Muñoz 12). This does not infer the ultimate eradication of an imperial mentality, but that a critique typical of disidentification has occurred: 'a strategy that tries to transform the cultural logic from within' (12). Shelley is too shrewd to give into utopianism by suggesting that Verney roams the world free of his European legacies. Such disidentification would court disembodiment and amnesia. His tormented loitering in Rome, spiked with moments that fetishise Roman cultural artefacts in the aftermath of catastrophe, conveys his deep attachment. Eventually, though, he treats Rome's unpopulated aesthetics as 'externals', to use the Stoic term for those elements of existence that do not make or break human happiness. By abandoning Rome's long-lived artefacts, Verney heeds Epictetus's advice not to attach ourselves to these elements by 'overvaluing' them (*Discourses* 63; I.29.3). Epictetus's word for externals is 'materials', a word better suited to the human-made objects that surround Verney in Rome. Just as Epictetus argued that our virtue is specified by our choice to value without attachment certain materials more than others, Verney's preference for Africa and India over Rome is indicative of his cosmopolitan disidentification from the revered materials and things of a civilisation annihilated by its own errors. Verney severs himself from those objects which, according to Cicero, bind the citizens of the same city into 'intimate' fellowship by them sharing that city's 'forum, temples, porticoes', 'ancestral memorials' and 'tombs' (*On Duties* 23; I.53–55). That this disidentification does not mean that Verney can and will operate outside his past conditioning and cultural memory is conveyed by such formative authorities as Homer and Shakespeare whose works Verney loads onto his boat. Yet a critical stance is implicated even by this choice if we recall that the Caesar venerated by Raymond becomes 'prey to laughable grandiosity' in Shakespeare's *Julius Caesar*, retaining little of the dignified aura Plutarch had bestowed on him (Gray 161). As for Homer, one of his epics warningly opens with the eruption of plague in a war zone ridden by conflict, military ambition and arrogant cupidity.

Verney's move away from imperial legacies is and cannot be complete. Yet his narrative firmly rejects the *renovatio imperii*. If there is any hope for regeneration, that is not expected to come from Europe but from the libraries of the world with which Verney will 'renew' his stock of books once he has left behind Rome, 'the Niobe of nations', and the Mediterranean with its tales of colonisation, eulogies of colonists and ruined schemes of empire (*Childe Harold* IV.79.703, Byron, *Major Works* 171). For Verney as a new, counter-Ulysses, his Ithaca is the world. His polyglot prospect, the only ray of hope at the end of a grief-stricken narrative, honours the multilingual Sibylline prophecies. Journeying in Africa and India, Verney plans to learn about their lands, empires and populations in their own libraries, temples, caves and tombs, suggesting new intimate fellowships and critical deliberations. There at the source, the (perhaps) last citizen of a world blasted by the spirit of empire will learn to 'renew' himself in a series of ongoing re-identifications (*LM* 360). His is a direction towards epistemic decolonisation, a turn indispensable for what Ngugi wa Thiong'o calls the 'decolonising the mind', which inscribes onto future readers of *The Last Man* a decolonising of cosmopolitanism.

Notes

1 The influence of *Morals* on Shelley and particularly on *The Last Man* has been demonstrated (Morrison and Stone 343).
2 Coleridge titled his 1817 collection of poems *Sibylline Leaves*, alluding to the fragmentary and scattered state of the volume.
3 Mellor suggests that Shelley shows readers how to come to an improved state through an embracing of the other ('Blake' 144); Bennett offers a reading that aligns Shelley with her father's belief that governments should serve the well-being of all citizens (150); Cameron argues that Shelley rejects Godwin's vision of perfectibility (184).
4 In January 1818 and March 1820.
5 Although the absence of a female companion thwarts biological reproduction, the novel's ending on the open sea does not exclude it.
6 Curtius elaborates on the earliest applicability of the *translatio* narrative (28–29). In Barbauld's 'Eighteen Hundred Eleven' (1812), colonisation appears as innocuous a process as horticultural planting: 'Nations beyond the Apalachian hills / Thy hand has planted and thy spirit fills' (83–84). In Hemans's *Modern Greece* (1817), Columbus is a welcome visitor: 'But thou, fair world! whose fresh unsullied charms / Welcomed Columbus from the western wave' (122). Instead of people, it is an impersonalised *terra nullius* that appears to be the welcoming host. In both poems, the colonising of this 'fair' New World unfolds without indigenous uprooting, conflict or disease.
7 Similarities between Augustus and Napoleon may have been a further source of inspiration for Shelley.
8 Up to this point, they have used real place names such as Troia or Pergama to commemorate their past.
9 Bailes detects in the goat passage the geological knowledge that Shelley encountered in William Buckland's *Reliquiae diluvianae* (1823), whose theories contributed to contemporary cave mania (Bailes 681).
10 I am indebted to Spivak's concept of the productivity of the 'outside in' double bind (*Outside* xi).
11 Hingley singles out studies by Sweet (Hingley 161) and Ayres (87–88).
12 Hemans took the opposite position in the Parthenon controversy, deeming Britain to be the best guardian of the Greek marbles.
13 Johnson quotes Sir John Davies: 'The kings of England did not make the

conquest of Ireland their own work; it was begun by particular adventurers, and other voluntaries, who came to seek their fortunes in Ireland.' The other explicitly pejorative use of 'adventurer' comes from *Aestrae redux* (1660), Dryden's panegyric for the restoration of Charles II: 'Their wealthy trade from pirate's rapine free, / our merchants shall no more advent'rers be.' 'Adventurer, n.s.', S. Johnson, *Dictionary*.

14 I see some validity in a Malthusian Shelley who believes that 'there is a brutish part of human nature that cannot be eliminated and that overpowers benevolence, particularly in a crisis situation' (Cameron 184).

15 '[A]mbition, avarice, self-love, vanity, friendship, generosity, public spirit' (Hume, *Enquiry* 60).

16 Peter Melville's reading of the passage offers valuable insights ('Problem').

17 Another surge happened during the Mutiny years 1857–58 (Arnold 126).

18 Pringle writes: 'moisture arises from stagnating water in which plants, fish and insects die and rot, then the damps being of a putrid nature not only occasion more frequent but more dangerous fevers' (169–70).

Afterword: Expansive yet Particularised Moments

Between 1750 and 1753, the Italian painter Giovanni Battista Tiepolo worked on the magnificent ceiling fresco in the Prince-Bishop's new residence in Würzburg, one of the independent states that would eventually become part of Germany. Tiepolo's masterpiece has been praised by critics like Roberto Calasso for being no less than the 'anthropological experiment' that best visualises the concept of cosmopolitanism: 'If ever the word cosmopolitanism had a meaning, it is on that ceiling' (ch. 3). To those who, like me, are convinced that the eighteenth century is a crucial moment in the tradition of Western cosmopolitanism, Calasso's assessment represents a confirmation that is further strengthened by book covers, conference leaflets and talks on cosmopolitanism where photographs of Tiepolo's frescos are used to convey what the concept could look like in a concrete, embodied form. The fresco's prominent human figures gesture to the exterior orientation defended by Wollstonecraft and Spivak (discussed in Chapter 2), an orientation that Calasso detects even in the fresco's animals:

> Where it is clear that all the characters, including the animals, would be able to understand one another, talking a lingua franca made up of facial features, fabrics, and colors. But without any of this implying a conciliatory attitude. All would cling to their own nature, which can also make them enemies, traitors, or indifferent. (ch. 3)

Exemplifying his own conceptual framework with an eighteenth-century artefact, Calasso leads readers into thinking that eighteenth-century cosmopolitanism was about little more than traffics of knowledge and trade which left all parties as they had been since the dawn of human society. It seems far from clear why, while every breathing creature remains intrinsically unchanged by physical and linguistic communication, partial to 'their own nature', animosities and indifferences, the ability to speak a common language deserves to be called the best actualisation of cosmopolitanism, and not, say, of multiculturalism or transnationalism. Upon reading Bruce Robbins's *Perpetual War* (2012) only a year after Calasso's commentary on the fresco, I could better grasp Robbins's alarm at what he considered a postmodern tendency to evacuate cosmopolitan thought and practice 'of all ethical substance, leaving nothing more than a marker of transnational movement' (14). As I have argued in the Introduction and Chapter 1, this critical tendency was neither unknown in the long eighteenth century nor unchallenged by ethically committed and even activist performances of cosmopolitanism.

There are at least two 'meanings' of Tiepolo's fresco (not addressed by Calasso) that are features of and lessons from eighteenth-century cosmopolitanism in the ways I have traced in this book. First, Tiepolo's concentration of an imposing number of life forms (animals, plants, and humans of different races, genders, ranks and religions) throwing their lot together in the limited space of the planet, transposed on the spatial limits of the ceiling, co-exists with an expansive yet particularised view of humanity enabled by the sheer size of the fresco and the proximity of the animal and human figures. The planet-like ceiling represents the shared physical ground which is the earth's surface, that geographical fact that Kant takes as the starting point for his world history with a cosmopolitan purpose and whose despoilment by human progress Wollstonecraft anticipated with dread. This expanded geographical awareness is fostered in early modern and Enlightenment natural philosophy which found its way to an ever-increasing array of genres and readerships, including children's literature. The second feature is an absence for which Tiepolo cannot be faulted: there is no Australia in his fresco of the continents. The first European landfall on *Terra Australis* was made by the Dutchman Willem Janszoon in 1606 and, to greater acclaim, by James Cook in 1770, but during Tiepolo's time the Australian continent was called New Holland and viewed as an extension of India. It was only in 1803 that the first circumnavigation of the continent by the British explorer Matthew Flinders led to the increasing popularity of the name 'Australia'.

This absence, together with the codified racial distinctions circulating within the European Republic of Letters, is a marker of the situationality and limits of the fresco's cosmopolitanism, reminding us that the specific place and time Tiepolo occupied on earth restricted his (un)conscious abilities to imagine worldwide conviviality. Like Tiepolo, we cannot escape the gaps and absences created by situationality. Escape would mean submitting to 'agentless abstraction', and a cosmopolitanism without an agent betrays the *kosmopolitēs*' belonging to an actual world (F. Cooper 17). This is a lesson beautifully captured in Goldsmith's

Citizen of the World: resembling the course of 'rivers whose streams are not only encreased but refined, as they travel from their source', the knowledge and abilities of cosmopolitan personhood are predicated on ever changing physical and spatio-temporal factors and boundaries (*CW* 2: 41). Therefore, the question 'what does cosmopolitanism want?' also queries what cosmopolitanism lacks. Especially when conscious, this lack can provoke a salutary self-critique that holds on to the idea of betterment, unabated by the realistic limits of human situationality. As Abu Talib's proverb prescribes, 'We are not to abandon the whole, because we cannot obtain the whole' (*Travels* 60).

The key contribution of this book is to identify and examine the potential of salutary critique in eighteenth-century century moments of cosmopolitanism that both respond to inherited material and contest to improve on this material. I have brought the performances discussed here into dialogue with Stoic practice, advice and rhetoric to test my hypothesis that certain continuities and contestations showcase the adaptability of a cosmopolitan sense-making of texts and their contexts. The eighteenth century, in step with classical Stoicism, presents us with cosmopolitanism as a concept open to innovation and of cosmopolitan performances as indications of a life-long training, a self-scrutinising apprenticeship that aims for more ecumenical and egalitarian distributions of justice. In the eighteenth century, more than in classical Stoicism, this scrutiny extends to the political and social conditions that constitute the self and cannot be treated as indifferent externals. While these case studies by no means offer an exhaustive picture of eighteenth-century cosmopolitanism(s), they demonstrate that ideas about 'tolerance, inclusiveness, hospitality, personal autonomy, emancipation' were salient well before the emergence of new cosmopolitanism within twentieth-century cosmopolitan and postcolonial studies (Werbner 156). These ideas already operate meaningfully in Goldsmith's *Citizen of the World*, Wollstonecraft's work, Abu Talib's travelogue, abolitionist literature and Shelley's novel. Appraising them as instructive, explicit or implicit engagements with cosmopolitan ethics can be relevant for studies of eighteenth-century and postcolonial cultures.

Wishing to delineate some of the specificities and innovations of eighteenth-century cosmopolitanism in relation to the classical predecessors that inform it, however, without making this a study about the reception of Stoic cosmopolitanism, I can think of no better illustration for my hermeneutical method than Margaret Atwood's words in *Cat's Eye* (1988): 'You don't look back along time but down through it, like water. Sometimes this comes to the surface, sometimes that, sometimes nothing. Nothing goes away' (3). Such a relationship to the past as neither lost nor accessible in unadulterated form has guided my decision to speak of cosmopolitan performances rather than expressions, a distinction made by performance, gender and postcolonial studies. To speak of expressions would imply that the texts I discuss in this book, their rhetorical situations and their spokespersons enact an original (Cynic, Stoic or other) script, or to put it absurdly, a manual of how to be cosmopolitan. By contrast, the notion of performance befits the context-based, voluntary but also unintended processes of selection and actualisation of ideas about cosmopolitan living. In some of the texts I have chosen, the phrase 'citizen of the world' stands for an honorific which, even when bestowed for no clearly defined criteria, is sustained by some ethical grounding that demands human responsibility in specific historical contexts and encounters with alterity. Anchored in 'highly mediated conditions of relations that exceed a straightforward, self-other model of cross-cultural encounter', the notion of performance particularises the opaqueness of the criteria perpetuated by the figure of the 'citizen of the word' in eighteenth-century literature, a century routinely criticised for its obsession with universalising narratives (Yang 15).

To regard cosmopolitan citizenship under the aegis of performance means to appreciate the potential for interpretation in new contexts rather than the replication of a prior and immutable 'core or substance' of the citizen of the world (Butler 136). Like Thomas Wentworth Higginson, whose 1865 translation of Epictetus was based on Elizabeth Carter's, this book has argued that the teachings of Seneca, Epictetus and Marcus Aurelius are not displaced, but that 'new versions of them constantly appear', proving that despite, or perhaps because of, their 'fragmentary and unsystematic' transmission they lend themselves to adaptation rather than mimicry (qtd. in Risinger 215). For example, although we are told that the teachings of the emancipated slave Epictetus were highly esteemed in the 'camp of coloured soldiers' led by Toussaint l'Ouverture, the Haitian Revolution fought against a type of discrimination and for ways of liberation from a dehumanising, inheritable slavery that differed greatly from the one Epictetus had endured. So too did the strategies and the political and social outcomes of this liberation differ from those of emancipated enslaved persons in antiquity (Epictetus, *Works*, trans. Higginson, 336). Hence, every time this study discusses eighteenth-century cosmopolitanism in relation to Stoic thought, it assumes, to use the words of Roland Barthes, 'the return of the different' (16). And this difference, so goes my argument, consists of a wide-ranging critique and, in some cases, innovative emancipatory contestations that modify and enrich received cosmopolitan wisdom.

These modifications occurred in parallel with and in response to misappropriations of Stoic indifference (equanimity), contemporary scepticism towards the utopianism of the Stoic or Cynic ways and a lingering tendency to reduce cosmopolitanism to a type of geographical mobility that warranted aloofness from concrete human experience. The eighteenth-century print culture compelled readers to ponder ethical ways of co-existence between humans and animals which, without universalising, radicalised Seneca's concept of *commune ius animantium*; to turn to historiography and socio-economic analyses produced by colonised subjects and to validate the intellectual and physical lives of female citizens of the world; to make human suffering integral to cosmopolitan ethics and to enquire into specific contemporary social, racial and economic conditions; to decolonise European cosmopolitanism by unmasking deeply entrenched narratives of empire building; and to rid the instruction of the young from racial phobia and anti-cosmopolitan mechanisms of othering. None of these innovations of Stoic inheritance achieved completion during the eighteenth century, nor have their trajectories been linear and uninterrupted movements towards actualisation ever since. However, in the measured yet firm words of Marcus Aurelius, 'You should not hope for Plato's ideal state, but be satisfied to make even the smallest advance, and regard such an outcome as nothing contemptible' (88; IX. 29), eighteenth-century readers, writers and activists met with encouragement to both practise tolerance and persevere in their efforts, thereby becoming a source of instructive encouragement for us and generations to come.

Bibliography

Abbattista, Guido. 'The Historical Thought of the French Philosophes'. *The Oxford History of Historical Writing: 1400–1800*, edited by José Rabasa et al., vol. 3, Oxford UP, 2012, pp. 406–27.

Abercromby, James. *Magna Charta for America*. 1774. Edited by J. P. Greene, C. F. Mullet and E. C. Papenfuse. Philadelphia: American Philosophical Society, 1986.

Ackerknecht, Erwin H. 'Anticontagionism between 1821 and 1867'. *International Journal of Epidemiology*, vol. 38, 2009, pp. 7–21.

Adamson, Peter. 'Al-Kindī'. *The Cambridge Companion to Arabic Philosophy*, edited by Peter Adamson and Richard Taylor, Cambridge UP, 2005. pp. 32–51.

———. *Great Medieval Thinkers: Al-Kindī*. Oxford UP, 2007.

Agnew, Lois Peter. *Outward, Visible Propriety: Stoic Philosophy and Eighteenth-Century British Rhetorics*. U of South Carolina P, 2008.

Aljoe, Nicole, Kerry Sinanan and Mirjam Wassif, eds. *New Essays on The Woman of Colour*. Special issue of *Eighteenth-Century Fiction*, vol. 35, no. 1, 2023.

Allan, David. 'Identity and Innovation: Historiography in the Scottish Enlightenment'. *A Companion to Enlightenment Historiography*, edited by Sophie Bourgault and Robert Sparling, Brill, 2013, pp. 307–41.

Anagnostopoulos, Georgios, and Gerasimos Santas, eds. *Democracy, Justice, and Equality in Ancient Greece: Historical and Philosophical Perspectives*. Springer Verlag, 2018.

Anderson, Margaret. 'The Stoic Construction of Virtue in *The Vicar of Wakefield*'. *Journal of the History of Ideas*, vol. 69, no. 3, 2008, pp. 419–39.

Appiah, Kwame Anthony. 'The Case for Capitalizing the B in Black'. *The Atlantic*, 18 June 2020.

Aravamudan, Srinivas. *Tropicopolitans: Colonialism and Agency, 1688–1804*. Duke UP, 1999.

Arnold, David. 'Cholera and Colonialism in British India'. *Past & Present*, vol. 113, no. 1,1986, pp. 118–51.

Atkins, Jed. 'Empire, Just War, and Cosmopolitanism'. *The Cambridge Companion to Cicero's Philosophy*, edited by Jed W. Atkins and Thomas Bénatouïl, Cambridge UP, 2021, pp. 231–51.

Atwood, Margaret. *Cat's Eye*. Bantam Books, 1995.

Aurelius, Marcus. *Meditations*. Edited by Christopher Gill, translated by Robin Hard, Oxford UP, 2011.

———. *The Meditations of the Emperor Marcus Aurelius*. Edited by J. Moore and M. Silverthorne, translated by F. Hutcheson and J. Moor, Liberty Fund, 2008.

Austen, Jane. *Northanger Abbey*. Edited by James Kinsley, John Davie and Claudia Johnson, Oxford UP, 2003.

'Avertissement des éditeurs'. *Encyclopédie ou Dictionnaire raisonné des sciences, des arts, et des métiers*, edited by Denis Diderot and Jean le Rond d'Alembert, vol. 3, Paris: Briasson, David, Le Breton, Durand, 1752–72.

Ayres, Philip. *Classical Culture and the Idea of Rome in Eighteenth-Century England*. Cambridge UP, 1997.

Bailes, Melissa. 'The Psychologization of Geological Catastrophe in Mary Shelley's *Last Man*'. *ELH*, vol. 82, no. 2, 2015, pp. 671–99.

Baker, Chris. *The SAGE Dictionary of Cultural Studies*. SAGE Publications, 2004.

Bakhtin, Mikhail. *Problems of Dostoevsky's Poetics*. Edited and translated by Caryl Emerson, U of Minnesota P, 1984.

Baldwin, James. *Blues for Mister Charlie*. 1964. Vintage Books, 1995. EPUB file.

Balibar, F., P. Büttgen and B. Cassin. 'Moment'. *Dictionary of Untranslatables: A Philosophical Lexicon*, edited by B. Cassin et al., Princeton UP, 2014, pp. 683–89.

Barbauld, Anna Laetitia. *Eighteen Hundred and Eleven: A Poem*. London: J. Johnson, 1812.

Barnard, Edward. *The New, Comprehensive, Impartial and Complete History of England*. London: Alex Hogg, 1790.

Barthes, Roland, *S/Z*. 1973. Translated by Richard Miller, Blackwell, 1990.

Bartosik-Vélez, Elise. '*Translatio imperii*: Virgil and Peter Martyr's Columbus'. *Comparative Literature Studies*, vol. 46, no. 4, 2009, pp. 559–88.

Bassnett, Susan and Peter France. 'Translation, Politics, and the Law'. *The Oxford History of Literary Translation in English, 1790–1900*, edited by Peter France and Kenneth Haynes, vol 4, Oxford UP, 2006, pp. 48–58.

Beck, Ulrich. *The Cosmopolitan Vision*. Cambridge, MA: Polity P, 2006.

———. 'Mobility and the Cosmopolitan Perspective'. *Tracing Mobilities: Toward a Cosmopolitan Perspective*, edited by Wert Canzleer et al. Ashgate, 2008, pp. 25–35.

Beddoes, Thomas. 'Kant: Zum ewigen Frieden'. *The Monthly Review*, vol. 20, 1796, pp. 486–90.

Bell, Kimberly K. '*Translatio* and the Constructs of a Roman Nation in Virgil's *Aeneid*'. *Rocky Mountain Review*, vol. 62, no. 1, 2008, pp. 11–24.

Bellanca, Mary Ellen. 'Science, Animal Sympathy, and Anna Barbauld's "The Mouse's Petition"'. *Eighteenth-Century Studies*, vol. 37, no. 1 2003, pp. 47–67.

Benedict, Barbara M. *Curiosity: A Cultural History of Early Modern History*. U of Chicago P, 2001.

Benjamin, Walter. 'The Task of the Translator: Introduction to the Translation of Baudelaire's *Tableaux parisiens*'. *The Translation Studies Reader*, edited by Lawrence Venuti, translated by Harry Zohn, Routledge, 2014, pp. 75–85.

Bennett, Betty T. 'Radical Imaginings: Mary Shelley's *The Last Man*'. *Wordsworth Circle*, vol. 26, 1995, pp. 147–52.

Berry, D. H. 'The Criminals in Virgil's Tartarus: Contemporary Allusions in *Aeneid* 6.621–4'. *Classical Quarterly*, vol. 42, no. 2, 1992, pp. 416–20.

Bhambra, Gurminder K. 'Cosmopolitanism and Postcolonial Critique'. *The Ashgate Research Companion to Cosmopolitanism*, edited by Maria Rovisco and Magdalena Nowicka, Routledge, 2018, pp. 313–28.

The Bible. King James Version. International Bible Society, 1987.

The Bible. New International Version, 3rd ed. Biblica, 2011.

Bickham, Troy. 'Preparing for an Imperial Inheritance: Children, Play, and Empire in Eighteenth-Century Britain'. *Journal of British Studies*, vol. 60, 2021, pp. 658–88.

The Biographical Dictionary of the Society for the Diffusion of Useful Knowledge, vol. 6, London: Longman, 1842.

Bivona, Dan. Review of *Epic and Empire in Nineteenth-Century Britain*, by Simon Dentith. *Nineteenth-Century Literature*, vol. 62, no. 1, 2007, pp. 27–130.

Blair, Hugh. *A Critical Dissertation on the Poems of Ossian*. London: T. Becket and P. A. De Hondt, 1763.

Blake, William. *Blake's Poetry and Designs*. Edited by J. E. Grant and M. L. Johnson, Norton, 2008.

Bonnet, Charles. *Essai analytique sur les facultés de l'âme*. Copenhagen: Frères Philibert, 1760.

Borot, Luc. 'Subject and Citizen: The Ambiguities of the Political Self in Early Modern England'. *French Journal of British Studies*, vol. 21, no. 1, 2016.

Botting, Eileen Hunt. *Family Feuds: Wollstonecraft, Burke, and Rousseau on the Transformation of the Family*. State U of New York P, 2006.

Bourdieu, Pierre. *The Logic of Practice*. Translated by Richard Nice. Polity P, 1990.

Boyle, Robert. *Experiments and Considerations Touching Colours*. London: Henry Harringman, 1664.

Braidotti, Rosi. *Nomadic Subjects: Embodiment and Sexual Difference in Contemporary Feminist Theory*. Columbia UP, 1994.

Brooks, Christopher. 'Goldsmith's *Citizen of the World*: Knowledge and the Imposture of "Orientalism"'. *Texas Studies in Literature and Language*, vol. 35, no. 1, 1993, pp. 124–44.

Brown, Christopher Leslie. *Moral Capital: Foundations of British Abolitionism*. U of North Carolina P, 2006.

Brown, Vincent. '*Social Death* and Political Life in the Study of Slavery'. *The American Historical Review*, vol. 114, no. 5, 2009, pp. 1231–49.

Brubaker, William Rogers. 'The French Revolution and the Invention of Citizenship'. *French Politics and Society*, vol. 7, no. 3, 1989, pp. 30–49.

Burke, Edmund. *Philosophical Inquiry into the Origin of Our Ideas of the Sublime and Beautiful*. Edited by Adam Phillips, Oxford UP, 1990.

Bushnell, Rebecca W. *A Culture of Teaching: Early Modern Humanism in Theory and Practice*. Cornell UP, 1996.

Butler, Judith. *Gender Trouble: Feminism and the Subversion of Identity*. Routledge, 1990.

Byron, George G. *The Curse of Minerva*, 5th ed. 1812. Paris: Galignani, 1821.

———. *The Major Works*. Edited by Jerome McGann, Oxford UP, 1986.
Cahill, Samara Anne. *Intelligent Souls? Feminist Orientalism in Eighteenth-Century English Literature*. Bucknell UP, 2019.
Calasso, Roberto. *Tiepolo Pink*. Random House, 2011. EPUB file.
Camarda, Julie. 'Keats's Chameleon Poetics, or, the Natural History of "Ode to a Nightingale"'. *Keats–Shelley Journal*, vol. 68, 2019, pp. 40–71.
Cameron, Lauren. 'Mary Shelley's Malthusian Objections in *The Last Man*'. *Nineteenth Century Literature*, vol. 67, no. 2, 2012, pp. 177–203.
Cantor, Paul A. 'The Politics of the Epic: Wordsworth, Byron, and the Romantic Redefinition of Heroism'. *The Review of Politics*, vol. 69, no. 3, 2007, pp. 375–401.
Carlyle, Thomas. 'Burns'. *Edinburgh Review*, vol. 48, Dec. 1828, pp. 267–312.
Carter, Elizabeth. 'Introduction'. *Works of Epictetus*. 1758. Translated by Elizabeth Carter, London: F. Rivington, 1768, vol. 1, pp. i–xl.
Catto, Michela. 'Atheism: A Word Travelling to and fro between Europe and China'. *The Rites Controversies in the Early Modern World*, edited by Ines G. Županov and Pierre Antoine Fabre, Brill, 2018, pp. 68–89.
Celkyte, Aiste. 'The Soul and Personal Identity in Early Stoicism: Two Theories?' *Apeiron*, vol. 53, no. 4, 2020, pp. 463–86.
'Chantre'. *Encyclopédie ou Dictionnaire raisonné des sciences, des arts, et des métiers*, edited by Denis Diderot and Jean le Rond d'Alembert, vol. 3, Paris: Briasson, David, Le Breton, Durand, 1752–72.
Chater, Kathleen. *Untold Histories: Black People in England and Wales during the Period of the British Slave Trade, c.1660–1807*. Manchester UP, 2009.
Chen, Xunwu. 'Confucianism and Cosmopolitanism'. *Asian Philosophy*, vol. 30, no. 1, 2022, pp. 40–56.
Cicero, Marcus Tullius. *De finibus bonorum et malorum, recognovit*. Edited by Th. Schiche, B. Teubner, 1915.
———. *On Duties*. Edited by M. T. Griffin and E. M. Atkins, Cambridge UP, 1991.
Clarke, Norma. *Dr. Johnson's Women*. Hambledon and London, 2000.
Cochran, Elizabeth Agnew. *Protestant Virtue and Stoic Ethics*. Bloomsbury: T&T Clark, 2017.
Cockburn, J. S. 'Punishment and Brutalization in the English Enlightenment'. *Law and History Review*, vol. 12, no. 1, 1994, pp. 155–79.
Coleridge, Samuel Taylor. *The Collected Works of Samuel Taylor Coleridge*. Edited by K. Coburn and B. Winer. Routledge and Kegan Paul, 1970. 23 vols.
———. 'Fears in Solitude'. *Major Works*, edited by H. J. Jackson, Oxford UP, 1985, pp. 92–98.
Colish, Marcia L. 'Seneca on Acting against Conscience'. *Seneca philosophus*, edited by Jula Wildberger and Marcia L. Colish, De Gruyter, 2014, pp. 94–110.
———. *Stoic Tradition from Antiquity to Early Middle Ages*. Brill, 1990.
Connolly, Paula T. *Slavery in American Children's Literature, 1790–2010*. U of Iowa P, 2013.
Connolly, William. *Neuropolitics: Thinking, Culture, Speed*. Minnesota UP, 2002.
Cooper, Frederick. *Colonialism in Question: Theory, Knowledge, History*. U of California P, 2005.

Cooper, Thomas. *Some Information Respecting America.* London: J. Johnson, 1794.

Cormier-Hamilton, Patrice. 'Black Naturalism and Toni Morrison: The Journey Away from Self-Love in *The Bluest Eye*'. *MELUS*, vol. 19, no. 4, 1994, pp. 109–127.

'Cosmopolitain ou cosmopolite'. *Encyclopédie ou Dictionnaire raisonné des sciences, des arts, et des métiers*, edited by Denis Diderot and Jean le Rond d'Alembert, vol. 4, Paris: Briasson, David, Le Breton, Durand, 1752–72.

Cossy, Valérie. 'Isabelle de Charrière, Jane Austen, and Post-Enlightenment Fiction: Writing the Shared Humanity of Men and Women'. *Humanities*, vol. 11, no. 150, 2022.

Craciun, Adriana. *British Women Writers and the French Revolution: Citizens of the World.* Palgrave Macmillan, 2005.

Cresswell, Tim. 'Vagrant/Vagabond: The Curious Career of a Mobile Subject'. *Geographies of Mobilities: Practices, Spaces, Subjects*, edited by Tim Cresswell and Peter Merriman, Ashgate, 2011, pp. 239–54.

Cumberland. Richard. *A Treatise on the Laws of Nature.* 1727. Translated by John Maxwell. Liberty Fund, 2005.

Curtius, Ernst Robert. *European Literature and the Latin Middle Ages.* Translated by Willard R. Trask, Princeton UP, 1990.

Dabashi, Hamid. *The World of Persian Literary Humanism.* Harvard UP, 2012.

Damrosch, David. *What is World Literature?* Princeton UP, 2003.

D'Argens, Marquis. *Lettres chinoises, ou correspondence philosophique, historique et critique.* The Hague: Pierre Gosse, 1751. 5 vols.

Darton, William. *Little Truths Better than Great Fables.* London: W. Darton, 1787.

'The Deaf, and Dumb, and Blind'. *The Slave's Friend*, vol. 3, no. 2, 1837, p. 4.

Dean, Dennis. *James Hutton and the History of Geology.* Cornell UP, 1992.

Delanty, Gerard. *The Cosmopolitan Imagination: The Renewal of Critical Social Theory.* Cambridge UP, 2009.

Delgado, James P. *The Beaver: First Steamship on the West Coast.* Horsdal and Schubart, 1993.

De Loos, Onésime. *Diadème des sages, ou Démonstration de la nature inférieure.* Paris: Mérigot, Lesclapart, 1781.

Derpmann, Simon. 'Solidarity and Cosmopolitanism'. *Ethical Theory and Moral Practice*, vol. 12, no. 3, 2009, pp. 303–15.

Derrida, Jacques. *Dissemination.* Translated by Barbara Johnson, Chicago UP, 1981.

———. 'Hostipitality'. *Jacques Derrida: Acts of Religion*, edited by Gil Anidjar, Routledge, 2002, pp. 356–420.

———. *Of Grammatology*. Translated by Gayatri Chakravorty Spivak, 4th ed., Johns Hopkins UP, 2016.

———. *Of Hospitality*. Translated by Rachel Bowlby, Stanford UP, 2000.

Diagne, Souleymane Bachir. 'Négritude'. *The Stanford Encyclopedia of Philosophy,* edited by Edward N. Zalta.

Diderot, Denis. *Le Neveu de Rameau.* Plon, 1981.

Dombrowski, D. A. *The Philosophy of Vegetarianism.* U of Massachusetts P, 1984.

Du Bois, W. E. B. *Writings.* The Library of America, 1986.

Duchesne-Guillemin, J. *The Western Response to Zoroaster*. Clarendon P, 1958.

Duncan, Ian J. H. 'Animal Welfare: A Brief History'. *Animal Welfare: From Science to Law*, Fondation Droit Animal Éthique et Sciences, 2019, pp. 13–19.

Eccles, W. J. 'The Fur Trade and Eighteenth-Century Imperialism'. *The William and Mary Quarterly*, vol. 40, no. 3, 1983 pp. 341–62.

Edward and George, or Lessons from Real Life: For Children of Early Years. London: Darton and Harvey, 1818.

Eliot, George. *Middlemarch*. 1871–72. Edited by G. Maertz, Broadview, 2004.

Elliott, Colin. *Pox Romana: The Plague That Shook the Roman World*. Princeton UP, 2024.

Enns, Peter, and Tremper Longman, editors. *Dictionary of the Old Testament: Wisdom, Poetry & Writings*. InterVarsity P, 2008.

Epictetus. *Discourses, Fragments, Handbook*. Edited by Christopher Gill, translated by Robin Hard, Oxford UP, 2014.

———. *The Works of Epictetus*. Translated by Elizabeth Carter. 1758. London: F. Rivington, 1768. 2 vols.

———. *The Works of Epictetus*. Translated by Thomas Wentworth Higginson. Boston: Little, Brown, 1865.

Equiano, Olaudah. *The Interesting Narrative of the Life of Olaudah Equiano, the African*. Edited by Angelo Constanzo, Broadview, 2004.

Esterhammer, Angela. 'Translating the Elgin Marbles: Byron, Hemans, Keats'. *The Wordsworth Circle*, vol. 40, no. 1, 2009, pp. 29–36.

Euben, Roxanne L. *Journeys to the Other Shore: Muslim and Western Travelers in Search for Knowledge*. Princeton UP, 2006.

Evans, J. Claude. *With Respect for Nature*. SUNY Press, 2005.

Fan, Ruiping. 'How Should We Treat Animals? A Confucian Reflection'. *Dao*, vol. 9, 2010, pp. 79–96.

Fanon, Frantz. *Black Skin, White Masks*. 1952. Translated by R. Philcox, Grove P, 2008.

Favret, Mary. *Romantic Correspondence: Women, Politics, and the Fiction of Letters*. Cambridge UP, 1993.

Fénelon, Abbé de. *Les Aventures de Télémaque*. Paris: J. B. Tilliard, 1699.

Ferguson, Arthur. *The Articulate Citizen and the English Renaissance*. Duke UP, 1965.

Figaro, no. 344, 10 Dec. 1833.

Fine, R. 'Taking the "Ism" Out of Cosmopolitanism: An Essay in Reconstruction'. *European Journal of Social Theory*, vol. 6, no. 4, 2003, pp. 451–70.

Fisher, Michael H. *Counterflows to Colonialism: Indian Travellers and Settlers in Britain 1600–1857*. Longman, 2004.

Fletcher, K. F. B. *Finding Italy: Travel, Colonization, and Nation in Vergil's Aeneid*. U of Michigan P, 2014.

Foltz, Richard. 'Zoroastrian Attitudes toward Animals'. *Society and Animals*, vol. 18, 2010, pp. 367–78.

Forman-Barzilai, Fonna. *Adam Smith and the Circles of Sympathy: Cosmopolitanism and Moral Theory*. Cambridge UP, 2010.

Forster, Thomas. *An Apology for the Doctrine of Pythagoras as Compatible with that of Jesus Christ*. Boulogne sur Mer: C. Aigre, 1858.

Foss, T. H., and D. F. Lach. 'Images of Asia and Asians in European Fiction,

1500–1800'. *China and Europe: Images and Influences in Sixteenth to Eighteenth Centuries*, edited by Thomas H. C. Lee, Chinese UP, 1991, pp. 165–88.

Gandhi, Leela. *Affective Communities: Anticolonial Thought, Fin-de-Siecle Radicalism, and the Politics of Friendship*. Duke UP, 2006.

Geist, Christopher D. '*The Slave's Friend*: An Abolitionist Magazine for Children'. *American Periodicals*, vol. 9, 1999, pp. 27–35.

Gellius, Aulius. *The Attic Nights of Aulus Gallius*. Translated by W. Beloe, London: Joseph Johnson, 1795.

Gidal, Eric. *Poetic Exhibitions: Romantic Aesthetics and the Pleasures of the British Museum*. Bucknell UP, 2001.

Gill, Christopher. 'Introduction'. *Discourses, Fragments, Handbook*, by Epictetus, edited by Christopher Gill, translated by Robin Hard, Oxford UP, 2014, pp. vii–xvii.

Gilroy, Paul. *After Empire: Melancholia or Convivial Culture?* Routledge, 2004.

Girard, René. 'The Plague in Literature and Myth'. *Texas Studies in Literature and Language*, vol. 15, no. 5, 1974, pp. 833–50.

Glanvill, Joseph. *Orientalis, or An Enquiry into the Opinion of the Eastern Sages Concerning the Praexistence of the Souls*. London: J. Collins and S. Lowndes, 1682.

Gleadle, Kathryn, and Ryan Hanley. 'Children against Slavery: Juvenile Agency and the Sugar Boycotts in Britain'. *Transactions of the Royal Historical Society*, vol. 30, 2020, pp. 97–117.

Godwin, William (pseud. Edward Baldwin). *Fables, Ancient and Modern*. 1807. Philadelphia: Benjamin Warner, 1811.

———. *The Political and Philosophical Writings of William Godwin*. Edited by Mark Philp et al., Routledge, 1993.

Goldsmith, Oliver. *The Collected Works of Oliver Goldsmith*. Edited by Arthur Friedman, Clarendon P, 1966. 5 vols.

———. *A History of the Earth, and Animated Nature*. London: J. Nourse, 1774.

———. Review of *The Orphan of China, a Tragedy*. *Critical Review*, vol. 7, May 1759, pp. 434–40.

Gray, Patrick. *Shakespeare and the Fall of the Roman Republic: Selfhood, Stoicism and Civil War*. Edinburgh UP, 2019.

Grenby, Matthew. 'Politicizing the Nursery: British Children's Literature and the French Revolution'. *The Lion and the Unicorn*, vol. 27, no. 1, 2003, pp. 1–26.

Gronniosaw, Ukawsaw. *A Narrative of the Most Remarkable Particulars in the Life of James Albert Ukawsaw Gronniosaw*. Bath: W. Gye, 1772.

Haakonssen, Knud. 'Introduction'. *Theory of Moral Sentiments* by Adam Smith, edited by Knud Haakonssen, Cambridge UP, 2002, pp. vii–xxiv.

Habermas, Jürgen. 'Bewusstmachen oder rettende Kritik – Die Aktualität Walter Benjamins'. *Zur Aktualität Walter Benjamins*, edited by Siegfried Unseld, Suhrkamp, 1972, pp. 173–224.

———. 'Remarks of Legitimation'. *Philosophy and Social Criticism*, vol. 24, nos. 2–3, 1998, pp. 157–71.

'The Haitian Declaration of Independence, January 1, 1804'. *Slave Revolution in the Caribbean, 1789–1804: A Brief History with Documents*, edited by Laurent Dubois and John D. Garrigus, Bedford / St Martin's, 2006, pp. 188–91.

The Happy Family: or, Winter Evenings' Employment. York: T. Wilson and R. Spence, 1801.

Hargraves, Neil. 'The "Progress of Ambition": Character, Narrative, and Philosophy in the Works of William Robertson'. *Journal of the History of Ideas*, vol. 63, no. 2, 2002, pp. 261–82.

Harrison, Thomas. 'Through British Eyes: The Athenian Empire and Modern Historiography'. *Classics and Colonialism*, edited by Barbara Goff, Duckworth, 2005, pp. 25–73.

Hartman, Saidiya. *Lose Your Mother: A Journey along the Atlantic Slave Route*. Serpent's Tail: 2007.

Hayman, John G. 'Notions of National Character in the Eighteenth Century'. *Huntington Library Quarterly*, vol. 35, no. 1, 1971, pp. 1–17.

Hazlitt, William. *Lectures on Comic Writers*, 3rd ed, John Templeman, 1841.

Heater, Derek. *Citizenship in Britain: A History*. Edinburgh UP, 2006.

Heise, Ursula. *Sense of Place and Sense of Planet: The Environmental Imagination of the Global*. Oxford UP, 2008.

Hemans, Felicia. *Modern Greece*. London: John Murray, 1817.

Hill, Lisa, and Eden Blazejak. *Stoicism in Western Political Thought*. Palgrave, 2021.

Hillman, James. 'Cosmology for Soul: From Universe to Cosmos'. *Philosophical Intimations*, edited by Edward S. Casey, Spring Publications, 2016, pp. 85–100.

Hingley, Richard. *The Recovery of Roman Britain: A Colony so Fertile*. Oxford UP, 2008.

Hirschman, Nancy. 'Sympathy, Empathy and Obligation: A Feminist Rereading'. *Feminist Interpretations of David Hume*, edited by Anne Jaap Jacobson, Pennsylvania State UP, 2000, pp. 174–93.

Holton, Richard. *Cosmopolitanisms: New Thinking and New Directions*. Palgrave Macmillan, 2009.

Houghton, John. 'A Collection for Improvement of Husbandry and Trade'. *Husbandry and Trade Improved*, edited by Richard Bradley, vol. 3, London: Woodman and Lyon, 1727.

Howse, Ernest Marshall. *The Saints in Politics: The 'Clapham Sect' and the Growth of Freedom*. 1953. Allen and Unwin, 1971.

Hume, David. *An Enquiry Concerning Human Understanding*. 1748. Edited by Peter Millican, Oxford UP, 2007.

———. 'Of National Characters'. *Political Essays*, edited by Knud Haakonssen, Cambridge UP, 1994, pp. 77–92.

Hunt, Eileen. *The First Last Man: Mary Shelley and the Postapocalyptic Imagination*. U of Pennsylvania P, 2024.

Hunt, Lynn. *Inventing Human Rights: A History*. W. W. Norton, 2007.

Hutcheson, Francis. *An Essay on the Nature and Conduct of the Passions and Affections* 1742, edited by Aaron Garrett, Liberty Fund, 2002.

Hutton, James. *Theory of the Earth: From the Transactions of the Royal Society of Edinburg*. Edinburgh: Royal Society of Edinburgh, 1785.

Hutton, Sarah. 'Virtue, God, and Stoicism in the Thought of Elizabeth Carter and Catharine Macaulay'. *Virtue, Liberty, and Toleration: Political Ideas of European Women, 1400–1800*, edited by J. Broad and K. Green, Springer, 2007, pp. 137–48.

Inglis, David, and Roland Robertson. 'From Cosmos to Globe: Globalization and Globality'. *The Ashgate Research Companion to Cosmopolitanism*, edited by Maria Rovisco and Magdalena Nowicka, Routledge, 2018, pp. 295–311.

———. 'From Republican Virtue to Global Imaginary: Changing Visions of the Historian Polybius'. *History of the Human Sciences*, vol. 19, no. 1, 2006, pp. 1–18.

Intorcetta, Prosperi, et al. *Confucius sinarum philosophus, sive Scientia sinensis.* Paris: Patrum Societatis Jesu, 1687.

Ivanhoe, Philip. 'Confucian Cosmopolitanism'. *The Journal of Religious Ethics*, vol. 42, no. 1, 2014, pp. 22–44.

Jacobs, Margaret C. *Strangers Nowhere in the World: The Rise of Cosmopolitanism in Early Modern Europe.* U of Pennsylvania P, 2006.

Janowitz, Anne. 'Amiable and Radical Sociability: Anna Laetitia Barbauld's "Free Familiar Conversation"'. *Romantic Sociability: Social Networks and Literary Culture in Britain, 1770–1840*, edited by Gillian Russell and Clara Tuite, Cambridge UP, 2002, pp. 62–81.

Johns, Alessa. 'Jane Austen the Stoic: Channeling Elizabeth Carter and the Bluestocking Ethos'. *Women's Writing*, vol. 21, no. 4, 2014, pp. 444–63.

Johnson, Barbara. '*The Last Man*.' *The Other Mary Shelley: Beyond Frankenstein*, edited by A. A. Fisch, A. K. Mellor and E. H. Schor, Oxford UP, 1993, pp. 258–66.

Johnson, Samuel. *The Dictionary of the English Language.* London: Rivington et al., 1755.

———. *The Yale Edition of the Works of Samuel Johnson.* Edited by E. L. McAdam Jr et al., Yale UP, 1958–2018. 23 vols.

Johnston, Patricia. 'Juno's Anger and the Sibyl at Cumae'. *Vergilius*, vol. 44, 1998, pp. 13–23.

Jonnès, Moreau de. *Rapport au conseil supérieur de santé sur le choléra-morbus pestilentiel.* Paris: Cosson, 1831.

Jordheim, Helge. 'Keeping the "Ism" in "Cosmopolitanism" – Wieland and the Origins of Cosmopolitan Discourse'. *Journal of Political Ideologies*, vol. 23, no. 3, 2028, pp. 299–319.

Juengel, Scott J. 'Mary Wollstonecraft's Perpetual Disaster'. *Romantic Circles*, 2012.

Kant, Immanuel. 'Idea for a Universal History from a Cosmopolitan Perspective'. *Toward Perpetual Peace and Other Writings on Politics, Peace, and History*, edited by Pauline Kleingeld, translated by David Colclasure, Yale UP, 2006, pp. 3–16.

———. 'M. Immanuel Kant's Announcement of the Programme of his Lectures for the Winter Semester 1765–1766'. *Theoretical Philosophy 1755–1770*, edited and translated by David Walford, Cambridge UP, 1992, pp. 298–99.

———. *Observations on the Feeling of the Sublime and Beautiful.* Edited and translated by Patrick Frierson and Paul Guyer, Cambridge UP, 2011.

———. 'Toward Perpetual Peace: A Philosophical Sketch'. *Toward Perpetual*

Peace and Other Writings on Politics, Peace, and History, edited by Pauline Kleingeld, translated by David Colclasure, Yale UP, 2006, pp. 67–110.

Kantzios, Ippokratis. 'Fénelon's Subversive Uses of *Aeneid* 6'. *The Comparatist*, vol. 40, 2016, pp. 190–204.

Karsh, Ephraim, and Inari Karsh. *Empires of the Sand: The Struggle for Mastery in the Middle East, 1789–1923*. Harvard UP, 2001.

Khan, Abu Talib. *The Travels of Mirza Abu Taleb Khan in Asia, Africa, Europe, during the Years 1799, 1800, 1801, 1802, and 1803*. Translated by Charles Stewart, edited by Daniel O'Quinn, Broadview, 2009.

———. *Les Voyages de Mirza Abu Taleb Khan, en Asie, en Afrique et en Europe*. Paris: Treutel and Würtz, 1811.

Khan, Gulfishan. *Indian Muslim Perceptions of the West during the Eighteenth Century*. Oxford UP, 1993.

Kia, Mana. '*Adab* as Literary Form and Social Conduct: Reading the Gulistan in Late Mughal India'. *No Tapping Around Philology: A Festschrift in Celebration and Honor of Wheeler McIntosh Thackston Jr.'s 70th Birthday*, edited by Alireza Korangy and Daniel J. Sheffield, Harrassowitz, 2014, pp. 281–308.

Kim, Minchul. 'Volney and the French Revolution'. *Journal of the History of Ideas*, vol. 79, no. 2, 2018, pp. 221–42.

Kirkley, Laura. '"Bound in Amity to All": Euthanasia's Cosmopolitan Ethic of Caring'. *The Keats–Shelley Review*, vol. 37, no. 2 2023, pp. 108–22.

———. *Mary Wollstonecraft: Cosmopolitan*. Edinburgh UP, 2022.

Kitching, Megan. 'The Solitary Animal: Professional Authorship and Persona in Goldsmith's *The Citizen of the World*'. *Eighteenth-Century Fiction*, vol. 25, no. 1, 2012, pp. 175–98.

Kleingeld, Pauline. 'Kant's Changing Cosmopolitanism'. *Kant's Idea for a Universal History with a Cosmopolitan Aim: A Critical Guide*, edited by Amélie Rorty and James Schmidt, Cambridge UP, 2009, pp. 171–86.

———. 'Kant's Moral and Political Cosmopolitanism'. *Philosophy Compass*, vol. 11, no. 1, 2016, pp. 14–23.

———. 'Six Varieties of Cosmopolitanism in Late Eighteenth-Century Germany'. *Journal of the History of Ideas*, vol. 60, no. 3, 1999, pp. 505–24.

———, and Eric Brown. 'Cosmopolitanism'. *The Stanford Encyclopedia of Philosophy*, edited by Edward N. Zalta. 2019.

Koselleck, Reinhart. 'Einleitung'. *Geschichtliche Grundbegriffe. Historisches Lexikon zur politisch-sozialen Sprache in Deutschland*, edited by O. Brunner et al., vol. 1, Klett-Cotta, 1972, pp. xiii–xxviii.

Krikler, Jeremy. 'A Chain of Murder in the Slave Trade: A Wider Context of the Zong Massacre'. *International Review of Social History*, vol. 57, no. 3, 2012, pp. 393–415.

Kumar, Krishan. 'Greece and Rome in the British Empire: Contrasting Role Models'. *Journal of British Studies*, vol. 51, no. 1, 2012, pp. 76–101.

Landry-Deron, Isabelle. *La Preuve par la Chine: la description de J.-B. Du Halde, Jésuite*. Editions de l'École des Hautes Études en Science Sociales, 2002.

Leask, Nigel. '"Travelling the Other Way": *The Travels of Mirza Abu Taleb Khan* and Romantic Orientalism'. *Romantic Representations of British India*, edited by Michael J. Franklin, Routledge, 2006, pp. 220–37.

Le Cosmopolite: Aix-les-Bains la Gazette, vol. 2, 19–21 June 1889.

Lee, Debbie. 'Yellow Fever and the Slave Trade: Coleridge's *The Rime of the Ancient Mariner*'. *ELH*, vol. 65, no. 3, 1998, pp. 675–700.

Lee, Thomas H. C. 'Christianity and Chinese Intellectuals: From the Chinese Point of View'. *China and Europe: Images and Influences in Sixteenth to Eighteenth Centuries*, edited by Thomas H. C. Lee, Chinese UP, 1991, pp. 1–28.

Leopold, Anita. 'The Architecture of Syncretism: A Methodological Illustration of the Dynamics of Syncretism'. *Retrofitting Syncretism*, special issue of *Historical Reflections / Réflexions historiques*, vol. 27, no. 3, 2001, pp. 401–23.

Lesses, Glenn. 'Austere Friends: The Stoics and Friendship'. *Apeiron*, vol. 26, 1993, pp 57–75.

Lettevall, Rebecka. 'The Idea of Kosmopolis: Two Kinds of Cosmopolitanism'. *The Idea of Kosmopolis: History, Philosophy and Politics of World Citizenship*, edited by Rebecka Letteval and My Klockar Linder, Södertörns Högskola, 2008, pp. 13–30.

Levander, Caroline. 'Witness and Participant: Frederick Douglass's Child'. *Study in American Fiction*, vol. 33, no. 2, 2005, pp. 183–92.

Levy, David, and Natan Sznaider. 'Cosmopolitan Memory and Human Rights'. *The Ashgate Research Companion to Cosmopolitanism*, edited by Maria Rovisco and Magdalena Nowicka, Routledge, 2018, pp. 195–210.

Lewis, Bernard. *The Muslim Discovery of Europe*. Norton, 1982.

Lloyd, Genevieve. 'Providence as Progress: Kant's Variations on a Tale of Origins'. *Kant's Idea for a Universal History with a Cosmopolitan Aim: A Critical Guide*, edited by Amélie Rorty and James Schmidt, Cambridge UP, 2009, pp. 200–15.

Locke, John. *An Essay Concerning Human Understanding*. London: Tegg and Son, 1836.

Long, A. A., and D. N Sedley, translators. *The Hellenistic Philosophers*. Cambridge UP, 1987. 2 vols.

Lundbaek, Knud. 'The First European Translations of Chinese Historical and Philosophical Works'. *China and Europe: Images and Influences in Sixteenth to Eighteenth Centuries*, edited by Thomas H. C. Lee, Chinese UP, 1991. pp. 29–43.

Macaulay, Catharine. *Letters on Education, with Observations on Religious and Metaphysical Subjects*. Cambridge UP, 2014.

Macaulay, Thomas Babington. *Archives of Empire: From the East India Company to the Suez Canal*. Edited by Mia Carter and Barbara Harlow, vol. 1, Duke UP, 2003.

Macauley, David. *Elemental Philosophy: Earth, Air, Fire, and Water as Environmental Ideas*. New York: SUNY P, 2010.

Machiavelli, Niccolò. *The Discourses II*. 1531. Edited by Bernard Crick, translated by Leslie J. Walker, Penguin, 1970.

Maclean, Charles. *Results of an Investigation, Respecting Epidemic and Pestilential Diseases*. London: Thomas and George Underwood, 1817–18.

Mair, Lucille Mathurin. *A Historical Study of Women in Jamaica, 1655–1844*. U of the West Indies P, 2006.

Malthus, Thomas. *An Essay on the Principle of Population*. London: J. Johnson, 1798.

Marotta, Vince P. 'The Cosmopolitan Stranger'. *Questioning Cosmopolitanism*, edited by Stan van Hooft and Wim Vandekerckhove, Springer, 2010, pp. 105–20.

Martin, Luther H. 'Syncretism, Historicism, and Cognition: A Response to Michael Pye'. *Method & Theory in the Study of Religion*, vol. 8, 1996, pp. 215–24.

McClean, David. *Richard Rorty, Liberalism and Cosmopolitanism*. Routledge, 2015.

McGrew, R. E. 'The First Cholera Epidemic and Social History'. *Bulletin of the History of Medicine*, vol. 34, no. 1, 1960, pp. 61–73.

McMurran, Mary Helen. 'The New Cosmopolitanism and the Eighteenth Century'. *Eighteenth-Century Studies*, vol. 47, no. 1, 2013, pp. 19–38.

McWhir, Anne. 'Mary Shelley's Anti-Contagionism: *The Last Man* as "Fatal Narrative"'. *Mosaic*, vol. 35, no. 2, 2002, pp. 23–38.

Mehta, Pratap Banu. 'Cosmopolitanism and Reason'. *Political Theory*, vol. 28, no. 5, 2000, pp. 619–39.

Mellor, Anne K. 'Blake, the Apocalypse, and the Romantic Women Writers'. *Romanticism and Millenarism*, edited by Tim Fulford, Palgrave, 2002, pp. 139–52.

———. 'Embodied Cosmopolitanism and the British Romantic Woman Writer'. *European Romantic Review*, vol. 17, no. 3, 2006, pp. 289–300.

Melville, Peter. 'The Problem of Immunity in *The Last Man*'. *Studies in English Literature 1500–1900*, vol. 47, no. 4, 2007, pp. 825–46.

———. *Romantic Hospitality and the Resistance to Accommodation*. Wilfrid Laurier UP, 2007.

Mignolo, Walter. 'Delinking, Decoloniality & Dewesternization: Interview with Walter Mignolo (Part II)'. criticallegalthinking.com, 2 May 2012.

———. 'Many Faces of Cosmo-Polis: Border Thinking and Critical Cosmopolitanism'. *Public Culture*, vol. 12, no. 3, 2000, pp. 721–48.

Mignolo, Walter, and Rubén Gastambide-Fernandez. 'Decolonial Options and Artistic/AestheSic Entanglements'. *Decolonization: Indigeneity, Education & Society*, vol. 3, no. 1, 2014, pp. 196–212.

Mill, James. *The History of British India*, 3rd ed. London: Baldwin, Cradock and Joy, 1826.

Miller, Nicholas. *John Millar and the Scottish Enlightenment: Family Life and World History*. Oxford UP, 2017.

Milton, John. *Paradise Lost*. 1674. Edited by Stephen Orgel and Jonathan Goldberg, Oxford UP, 2008.

Moles, John L. 'Cynic Cosmopolitanism'. *The Cynics: The Cynic Movement in Antiquity and Its Legacy*, edited by R. Bracht Branham and Marie-Odile Goulet-Cazé, California UP, 1996, pp. 105–20.

Monbron, Charles Fougeret de. *Le cosmopolite, ou le citoyen du monde*. London, 1753.

Montagu, Lady Mary Wortley. *The Works of the Right Honourable Lady Mary Wortley Montagu*. Edited by J. Dallawy, Richard Phillips, London: 1803. 5 vols.

Montes, Leonidas. 'Adam Smith as an Eclectic Stoic'. *The Adam Smith Review*, edited by Vivienne Brown, vol. 4, 2008, pp. 30–56.

Moore, J., and M. Silverthorne. 'Introduction'. *The Meditations of the Emperor*

Marcus Aurelius, translated by F. Hutcheson and J. Moor, edited by J. Moore and M. Silverthorne, Liberty Fund, 2008, pp. ix–xxviii.
The Morals of Confucius. London: Randal Taylor, 1691.
Morrison, Lucy, and Staci L. Stone. *A Mary Shelley Encyclopedia*. Greenwood P, 2003.
Morrison, Robert. *Horæ Sinicæ: Translations from the Popular Literature of the Chinese*. London: Black and Parry, 1812.
Morrison, Toni. *Playing in the Dark: Whiteness and the Literary Imagination*. Vintage Books, 1992.
Mortley, Raoul. *The Idea of Universal History from Hellenistic Philosophy to Early Christian Historiography*. Mellen, 1996.
Mungello, D. E. 'Confucianism in the Enlightenment: Antagonism and Collaboration between the Jesuits and the Philosophes'. *China and Europe: Images and Influences in Sixteenth to Eighteenth Centuries*, edited by Thomas H. C. Lee, Chinese UP, 1991, pp. 99–128.
Muñoz, José Esteban. *Disidentifications: Queers of Color and the Performance of Politics*. U of Minnesota P, 1999.
Muthu, Sankar. '"A Cosmopolitanism of Countervailing Powers": Resistance against Global Domination in the Political Thought of Immanuel Kant and Quobna Ottobah Cuguano'. *Cosmopolitanism and the Enlightenment*, edited by Joan-Pau Rubiés and Neil Safier, Cambridge UP, 2023, pp. 239–62.
Newmyer, Stephen T. 'Plutarch on Justice toward Animals: Ancient Insights on a Modern Debate'. *Scholia*, vol. 1, 1992, pp. 38–54.
———. 'Speaking of Beasts: The Stoics and Plutarch on Animal Reason and the Modern Case against Animals'. *Quaderni urbinatti di cultura classica*, vol. 63, no. 3, 1999, pp. 99–110.
Nussbaum, Martha. *The Cosmopolitan Tradition: A Noble but Flawed Ideal*. Belknap P of Harvard UP, 2019.
———. *For Love of Country: Debating the Limits of Patriotism*. Beacon P, 1996.
O'Brien, Karen. *Narratives of the Enlightenment: Cosmopolitan History from Voltaire to Gibbon*. Cambridge UP, 1997.
Oldfield, J. R. 'Anti-Slavery Sentiment in Children's Literature, 1750–1850'. *Slavery & Abolition*, vol. 10, no. 1, 1989, pp. 44–59.
O'Neill, Daniel. *The Burke–Wollstonecraft Debate: Savagery, Civilization, and Democracy*. Pennsylvania State UP, 2007.
Opie, Amelia. *Adeline Mowbray*. 1804. Pandora P, 1986.
O'Quinn, Daniel. 'Introduction'. *The Travels of Mirza Abu Taleb Khan in Asia, Africa, Europe, during the Years 1799, 1800, 1801, 1802, and 1803*, translated by Charles Stewart, edited by Daniel O'Quinn, Broadview, 2009, pp. 9–48.
Pandolfo, Stefania. *Impasse of the Angels: Scenes from a Moroccan Space of Memory*. U of Chicago P, 1997.
Penn, William. *Select Works of William Penn*. London: James Phillips, 1782.
Pensky, Max. 'Two Cheers for Cosmopolitanism: Cosmopolitan Solidarity as Second-Order Inclusion'. *Journal of Social Philosophy*, vol. 38, no. 1, 2007, pp. 165–84.
Pickstone, John V. 'Fever Epidemics and British "Public Health", 1780–1850'. *Epidemic and Ideas: Essay on the Historical Perception of*

Pestilence, edited by Terence Ranger and Paul Slack, Cambridge UP, 1992, pp. 125–48.

Plumwood, Val. *Environmental Culture: The Ecological Crisis of Reason*. Routledge, 2022.

———. *The Eye of the Crocodile*. ANU P, 2012.

———. 'Integrating Ethical Frameworks for Animals, Humans, and Nature: A Critical Feminist Eco-Socialist Analysis'. *Ethics and Environment*, vol. 5, no. 2, 2000, pp. 285–322.

Plutarch, Lucius. *Moralia*. Translated by Harold Cherniss and W. C. Helmbold, vol. 12, Loeb Classical Library, Harvard UP, 1957.

———. *Morals: Translated from Greek by Several Hands*, London: W. Taylor, 1718.

Pollock, S., H. K. Bhabha, C. A. Beckenridge and D. Chakrabarty. 'Cosmopolitanisms'. *Public Culture*, vol. 12, 2000, pp. 577–89.

Pope, Alexander. *Poetry and Prose of Alexander Pope*. Edited by Aubrey Williams. Houghton Mifflin, 1969.

Price, Richard. *A Discourse on the Love of Our Country*. London: T. Cadell, 1790.

Pringle, Sir John. *Observations on the Diseases of the Army*, 2nd ed. 1752. London: A. Millar, 1753.

Pullin, Naomi. *Female Friends and the Making of Transatlantic Quakerism, 1650–1750*. Cambridge UP, 2018.

Ramelli, Ilaria. *Hierocles the Stoic: Elements of Ethics, Fragments, and Excerpts*. Society of Biblical Literature, 2009.

Raschke, Carl. *Force of God: Political Theology and the Crisis of Liberal Democracy*. Columbia UP, 2015.

Reese, Alan M. 'English Friends and the Abolition of the British Slave Trade'. *Bulletin of Friends Historical Association*, vol. 44, no. 2, 1955, pp. 74–87.

'Reflections on National Prejudices'. *British Magazine*, Aug. 1760, pp. 460–62.

Reinhardt, Tobias. 'Introduction'. *Dialogues and Essays* by Lucius Annaeus Seneca, translated by John Davie, edited by Tobias Reinhardt, Oxford UP, 2007, pp. vii–xxvii.

Reisman, David C. 'Al-Farabi and the Philosophical Curriculum'. *The Cambridge Companion to Arabic Philosophy*, edited by Peter Adamson and Richard Taylor, Cambridge UP, 2005, pp. 52–71.

Rendall, Jane. '"The Grand Causes which Combine to Carry Mankind Forward": Wollstonecraft, History and Revolution'. *Women's Writing*, vol. 4, no. 2, 1997, pp. 155–72.

Report of the Committee of the Society for the Mitigation and Gradual Abolition of Slavery throughout the British Dominions, Read at the General Meeting of the Society, Held on the 25th Day of June 1824. Together with an Account of the Proceedings which Took Place at that Meeting. London: Richard Taylor, 1824, pp. 70–79.

Review of *The Travels of Abu Taleb Khan*, by Abu Taleb Khan. *Quarterly Review*, Aug. 1810, pp. 80–95.

Review of *The Travels of Mirza Abu Taleb Khan*, by Abu Taleb Khan. *The British Critic*, vol. 36, Sept. 1810, p. 274.

Reynolds, Matthew. 'Principles and Norms'. *The Oxford History of Literary*

Translation in English, 1790–1900, edited by Peter France and Kenneth Haynes, vol. 4, Oxford UP, 2006, pp. 61–82. 5 vols.

Richter, Daniel. *Cosmopolis: Imagining Community in Late Classical Athens and the Early Roman Empire*. Oxford UP, 2011.

Risinger, Jacob. *Stoic Romanticism and the Ethics of Emotion*. Princeton UP, 2021.

Robbins, Bruce. *Feeling Global: Internationalism in Distress*. New York UP, 1999.

———. *Perpetual War: Cosmopolitanism from the Viewpoint of Violence*. Duke UP, 2012.

Rose, Jenny. *The Image of Zoroaster: The Persian Mage through European Eyes*. Bibliotheca Persica P, 2000.

Rousseau, Jean-Jacques. *Discourse on Inequality*. Edited by Patrick Coleman, translated by Franklin Philip, Oxford UP, 2009.

———. *Discourse on Political Economy; The Social Contract*. Translated by Christopher Betts, Oxford UP, 1999.

———. *Emile, or on Education*. Translated by Allan Bloom, Basic Books, 1979.

———. *Letter to Beaumont, Letters Written from the Mountain, and Related Writings*. Edited by C. Kelly and E. Grace, translated by C. Kelly and J. R. Bush, UP of New England, 2001.

Rubiés, Joan-Pau. 'The Cosmopolitan Paradox: Travel, Anthropology, and the Problem of Cultural Diversity in Early Modern Thought'. *Cosmopolitanism and the Enlightenment*, edited by Neil Safier and Joan-Pau Rubiés, Cambridge UP, 2023, pp. 55–90.

———, and Neil Safier, editors. *Cosmopolitanism and the Enlightenment*. Cambridge UP, 2023.

Rudwick, Martin J. *Earth's Deep History: How It Was Discovered and Why It Matters*. U of Chicago P, 2014.

Ruppert, Timothy. 'Time and the Sibyl in Mary Shelley's *The Last Man*'. *Studies in the Novel*, vol. 41, no. 2, 2009, pp. 141–56.

Ryden, David Beck. *West Indian Slavery and British Abolition, 1783–1807*. Cambridge UP, 2009.

Sacks, Peter. *The English Elegy: Studies in the Genre from Spenser to Yeats*. Johns Hopkins UP, 1985.

Said, Edward. *Culture and Orientalism*. 1993. Random House, 1994.

Sanjabi, Maryam. 'Zoroaster's French Moment'. *The Allure of the Ancient: Receptions of the Ancient Middle East, circa 1600–1800*, edited by Margaret Geoga and John Steele, Brill, 2022, pp. 167–84.

Schlereth, Thomas. *The Cosmopolitan Ideal in Enlightenment Thought*. U of Notre Dame P, 1977.

Schneewind, J. B. 'Good Out of Evil: Kant and the Idea of Unsociable Sociability'. *Kant's Idea for a Universal History with a Cosmopolitan Aim: A Critical Guide*, edited by Amélie Rorty and James Schmidt, Cambridge UP, 2009, pp. 94–111.

Schwarz, Suzanne, editor. *Slave Captain: The Career of James Irving in the Liverpool Slave Trade*. Liverpool UP, 2008.

Scott, John T. 'Rousseau's Paradoxical Cosmopolitan Anti-Cosmopolitanism'. *Cosmopolitanism and Its Discontents*, edited by Lee Ward, Lexington Books, 2020, pp. 53–66.

Scott, Walter. *Biographical and Critical Notices of Eminent Novelists.* Edinburgh: Cadell & Company, 1827.

Sebastiani, Silvia. 'Beyond Ancient Virtues: Civil Society and Passions in the Scottish Englightenment'. *Passions and Virtues in Early Modern Europe*, special issue of *History of Political Thought*, vol. 32, no. 5, 2011, pp. 821–40.

———. 'National Character and Race'. *Character, Self, and Sociability in the Scottish Enlightenment*, edited by Thomas Ahnert and Susan Manning, Palgrave, 2012, pp. 187–206.

Seiler-Smith, Rachel. 'Bearing/Barren Life: The Conditions of Wollstonecraft's Morbid Maternity'. *European Romantic Review*, vol 28, no. 2, 2017, pp. 163–83.

Sellars, John. 'Introduction'. *The Routledge Handbook of the Stoic Tradition*, edited by John Sellars, Routledge, 2016, pp. 1–13.

Seneca, Lucius Annaeus. *Anger, Mercy, Revenge.* Translated by Robert A. Kaster and Martha Nussbaum, Chicago UP, 2010.

———. *Dialogues and Essays.* Translated by John Davie, edited by Tobias Reinhardt, Oxford UP, 2007.

Shea, Louisa. *The Cynic Enlightenment: Diogenes in the Salon.* Johns Hopkins UP, 2010.

Shelley, Mary. *Frankenstein.* Edited by D. L. Macdonald and K Scherf. Broadview, 2001.

———. *The Last Man.* Edited by Anne McWhir, Broadview, 1996.

———. *Lives of the Most Eminent Literary and Scientific Men of France*, vol 1, London: Longman et al., 1838.

Shelley, Percy Bysshe. *Alastor; or The Spirit of Solitude.* 1816. London: Reeves and Turner, 1885.

Simond, Louis. *Journal of a Tour and Residence in Great Britain during the Years 1810 and 1811.* Edinburgh: George Ramsay, 1815.

'Slave Holder'. *The Slave's Friend*, vol. 3, no. 10, 1837, p. 2.

The Slave's Friend. New York: American Anti-Slavery Society, 1836–38.

Smith, Adam. *An Inquiry into the Nature and Causes of the Wealth of the Nations.* 1776. Edited and introduction by Edwin Cannan, Random House, 1937.

———. *Theory of Moral Sentiments*, 2nd ed. 1759. Edinburgh: A. Millar, 1761.

Smith, Felipe. *American Body Politics: Race, Gender, and Black Literary Renaissance.* U of Georgia P, 1998.

Smith, Nigel. 'Hidden Things Brought to Light: Enthusiasm and Quaker Discourse'. *The Emergence of Quaker Writing: Dissenting Literature in Seventeenth-Century England*, edited by Thomas N. Corns and David Loewenstein, Frank Cass, 1995, pp. 57–69.

Smith, Thomas Southwood. *A Treatise on Fever.* London: Longman, 1830.

Snowden, Frank. *Epidemics and Society: From the Black Death to the Present.* Yale UP, 2019.

Snyder, Robert Lance. 'Apocalypse and Indeterminacy in Mary Shelley's *The Last Man*'. *Studies in Romanticism*, vol. 17, no. 4, 1978, pp. 435–52.

Soderlund, Jean R. 'The Lenape Origins of Delaware Valley Peace and Freedom'. *Quakers and Native Americans*, edited by Gallup-Diaz Ignacio, and Geoffrey Plank, Brill, 2019, pp. 15–29.

The Spectator, vol. 1. London: S. Buckley and J. Tonson, 1712.

Spencer, Colin. *The Heretic's Feast: A History of Vegetarianism.* UP of New England, 1995.

Spenser, Edmund. *The Faerie Queene.* 1596. Edited by J. C. Smith, Oxford UP, 1963.

Spivak, Gayatri C. *Death of a Discipline.* Columbia UP, 2003.

———. *Outside in the Teaching Machine.* 1993. Routledge, 2009.

———. 'Reply'. *PMLA*, vol. 123, no. 1, 2008, p. 247.

———. 'World Systems & the Creole'. *Narrative*, vol. 14, no. 1, 2006, pp. 102–12.

Sredanovic, Djordje. 'Was Citizenship born with the Enlightenment? Developments of Citizenship between Britain and France and "Everyday Citizenship" Implications'. *Miranda: Multidisciplinary Journal of the English-Speaking World*, vol. 15, 2017.

Staël, Germaine de. *Corinne, or Italy.* Introduction by John Isbell, translated by Sylvia Raphael, Oxford UP, 1998.

———. *The Influence of the Passions on the Happiness of Individuals and of Nations.* 1796. London: Henry Colburn, 1813.

Stafford, Fiona. *The Last of the Race: The Growth of a Myth from Milton to Darwin.* Clarendon P, 1994.

Stagl, Justin. *A History of Curiosity: The Theory of Travel 1550–1800.* 1995. Routledge, 2004.

Standaert, Nicholas. 'The Transmission of Renaissance Culture in Seventeenth-Century China'. *Asian Travel in the Renaissance*, special issue of *Renaissance Studies*, vol. 17, no. 3, 2003, pp. 367–91.

Stausberg, Michael. *Faszination Zarathushtra: Zoroaster und die Europäische Religionsgeschichte der frühen Neuzeit.* De Gruyter, 1998.

Steiner, Enit Karafili. 'Cultures of Sensibility'. *The Cambridge History of European Romantic Literature*, edited by Patrick Vincent, Cambridge UP, 2024, pp. 135–61.

———. 'Lessons of Skin: Cosmopolitan Solidarity in *The Woman of Colour*'. *Women's Writing*, vol. 27, no. 1, 2020, pp. 46–62.

———. 'Mood, Provisionality, and Planetarity in Mary Wollstonecraft's *A Short Residence in Sweden, Norway, and Denmark*'. *Criticism*, vol. 61, no. 1, 2019, pp. 27–50.

Sterne, Lawrence. *A Sentimental Journey through France and Italy.* Edited by Katherine Turner, Broadview, 2010.

Stewart, Charles. 'Advertisement to this Edition'. *The Travels of Mirza Abu Taleb Khan in Asia, Africa, Europe, during the Years 1799, 1800, 1801, 1802, and 1803*, translated by Charles Stewart, edited by Daniel O'Quinn, Broadview, 2009, p. 58.

———. 'To the Most Noble the Marchioness of Hertford'. *The Travels of Mirza Abu Taleb Khan in Asia, Africa, Europe, during the Years 1799, 1800, 1801, 1802, and 1803*, translated by Charles Stewart, edited by Daniel O'Quinn, Broadview, 2009, p. 56.

———. 'Translator's Preface'. *The Travels of Mirza Abu Taleb Khan in Asia, Africa, Europe, during the Years 1799, 1800, 1801, 1802, and 1803*, London: Longman, Hurst, Rees and Orme, 1810, pp. v–viii.

———. 'Translator's Preface'. *The Travels of Mirza Abu Taleb Khan in Asia, Africa, Europe, during the Years 1799, 1800, 1801, 1802, and 1803*, trans-

lated by Charles Stewart, edited by Daniel O'Quinn, Broadview, 2009, pp. 57–58.
Stock, Paul. *The Shelley–Byron Circle and the Idea of Europe*. Palgrave Macmillan, 2010.
Subrahmanyam, Sanjay. 'Connected Histories: Notes towards a Reconfiguration of Early Modern Eurasia'. *Modern Asian Studies*, vol. 31, no. 3, 1997, pp. 735–62.
The Substance of the Debates on the Bill for Abolishing the Slave Trade, which was Brought into the House of Lords on the 2d January, 1807, and into the House of Commons on the 10th of February, 1807, and which was Finally Passed into a Law on the 25th March, 1807. London: W. Phillips, 1808.
The Substance of the Report Delivered by the Court of Directors of the Sierra Leone Company: To the General Court of Proprietors, on Thursday, the 27th March 1794. London: James Phillips, 1794.
Sussman, Charlotte. *Consuming Anxieties: Consumer Protest, Gender, and British Slavery, 1713–1833*. Stanford UP, 2000.
Sweet, Rosemary. *Antiquaries: The Discovery of the Past in Eighteenth-Century Britain*. Bloomsbury, 2004.
Swift, Simon. 'Stoicism and Romantic Literature'. *The Routledge Handbook of the Stoic Tradition*, edited by John Sellars, Routledge, 2016, pp. 303–18.
Tague, Ingrid. *Animal Companions: Pets and Social Change in Eighteenth-Century Britain*. Pennsylvania State UP, 2015.
Tavakoli-Targhi, Mohamad. *Refashioning Iran: Orientalism, Occidentalism and Historiography*. Palgrave, 2001.
Taylor, Barbara. 'For the Love of God: Religion and the Erotic Imagination in Wollstonecraft's Feminism'. *Mary Wollstonecraft and 200 Years of Feminism*, edited by Eileen Jane Yeo, Rivers Oram P, 1997, pp. 15–35.
Taylor, Natalie F. '"Mistaken Notions of Female Excellence": Mary Wollstonecraft's Vindication of Virtue'. *Called to Civil Existence*, edited by Enit Karafili Steiner, Brill, 2014, pp. 93–112.
Taylor, Richard C. *Goldsmith as Journalist*. Associated UP, 1993.
Telescope, Tom. *The Newtonian System of Philosophy Adapted to the Capacities of young Gentlemen and Ladies*. London: John Newbery, 1761.
Teltscher, Kate. *India Inscribed: European and British Writing on India 1600–1800*. Oxford UP, 1995.
Thiong'o, Ngugi wa. *Decolonising the Mind: The Politics of Language in African Literature*. James Curray, 1981.
Thomas, Claudia. '"Th'Instructive Moral, and Important Thought": Elizabeth Carter Reads Pope, Johnson, and Epictetus'. *The Age of Johnson: A Scholarly Annual*, vol. 4, 1991, pp. 137–69.
Tihanov, Galin. 'Cosmopolitanism in the Discursive Landscape of Modernity: Two Enlightenment Articulations'. *Enlightenment Cosmopolitanism*, edited by Galin Tihanov and David Adams, Legenda, 2011, pp. 133–52.
Tilly, Charles. 'The Emergence of Citizenship in France and Elsewhere'. *International Review of Social History*, vol. 40, no. 3, 1995, pp. 223–36.
Todorov, Tzvetan. *On Human Diversity: Nationalism, Racism and Exoticism in French Thought*. Translated by Catherine Porter, Harvard UP, 1993.

'To Juvenile Anti-Slavery Societies'. *Slave's Friend*, vol. 3, no. 2, 1837, p. 8.
Trénard, Louis. 'Images de la Russie dans l'œuvre de Voltaire'. *Revue des études slaves*, vol. 57, no. 4, 1985, pp. 577–89.
Turner, Bryan. 'Cosmopolitan Virtue, Globalization, and Patriotism'. *Theory, Culture & Society*, vol. 19, no. 17/2, 2002, pp. 45–63.
Tutrone, Fabio. '*Commune ius animantium* (*Clem.* 1.18.2): Seneca's Naturalism and the Problem of Animal Rights'. *Phasis: Greek and Roman Studies*, vol. 15/16, 2012–13, pp. 511–50.
Tytler, Alexander Fraser. *Essay on the Principles of Translation.* London: J. M. Dent & Co., 1791.
'Valence'. *Encyclopédie ou Dictionnaire raisonné des sciences, des arts, et des métiers*, edited by Denis Diderot and Jean le Rond d'Alembert, Paris: Briasson, David, Le Breton, Durand, 1752–72.
Vance, Norman. *The Victorians, and the Ancient Rome.* Blackwell, 1997.
Vargo, Lisa. 'The Aikins and the Godwins: Notions of Conflict and Stoicism in Anna Barbauld and Mary Shelley.' *Romanticism*, vol. 11, no. 1, 2005, pp. 84–98.
———. 'Mary Shelley, *Corinne*, and "the Mantle of Enthusiasm"'. *European Romantic Review*, vol. 19, no. 2, 2008, pp. 171–77.
Vasunia, Phiroze. 'Greater Rome and Greater Britain'. *Classics and Colonialism*, edited by Barbara Goff, Duckworth, 2005, pp. 38–64.
Vernon, James. *Distant Strangers: How Britain Became Modern.* U of California P, 2014.
Vertovec, Steven, and Robin Cohen. 'Introduction'. *Conceiving Cosmopolitanism: Theory, Context and Practice*, edited by Steven Vertovec and Robin Cohen, Oxford UP, 2002, pp. 1–22.
Vice, Sue. *Introducing Bakhtin.* Manchester UP, 1997.
Vila, Anne. *Enlightenment and Pathology: Sensibility in the Literature and Medicine of Eighteenth-Century France.* Johns Hopkins UP, 1998.
Virgil. *The Aeneid.* Introduction by Bernard Knox, translated by Robert Fagles, Penguin, 2006.
Visram, Rozina. *Ayahs, Lascars and Princes: The Story of Indians in Britain 1700–1947.* Routledge, 1986.
Vlassopoulos, Kosta. 'Imperial Encounters: Discourse on Empire and the Uses of Ancient History during the Eighteenth Century'. *Classics and Imperialism in the British Empire*, edited by Mark Bradley, Oxford UP, 2010, pp. 29–53.
Volney, Comte de. *The Ruins, or A Survey of the Revolutions of Empire.* London: J. Johnson, 1795.
Wakefield, Priscilla. *Excursions in North America.* London: Danton and Harvey, 1806.
Walkowitz, Rebecca L. *Cosmopolitan Style: Modernism beyond the Nation.* Columbia UP, 2006.
Walzer, Arthur. 'Quintilian's "*Vir Bonus*" and the Stoic Wise Man'. *Rhetoric Society Quarterly*, vol. 33, no. 4, 2003, pp. 25–41.
Watt, James. 'Goldsmith's Cosmopolitanism'. *Eighteenth-Century Life*, vol. 30, 2005, pp. 56–73.
Weber, Ralph. '"How to Compare?" – On the Methodological State of Comparative Philosophy'. *Philosophy Compass*, vol. 8, no. 7, 2013, pp. 593–603.

Weiss, Deborah. 'Suffering, Sentiment, and Civilization: Pain and Politics in Mary Wollstonecraft's *Short Residence*'. *Studies in Romanticism*, vol. 45, no. 2, 2006, pp. 199–221.

Weiss, Robin. 'Stoic Utopia: The Use of Friendship in Creating the Ideal Society'. *Apeiron*, vol. 49, no. 2, 2016, pp. 193–228.

Werbner, Pnina. 'Anthropology and the New Ethical Cosmopolitanism'. *Routledge Handbook of Cosmopolitan Studies*, Routledge, 2012, pp. 153–65.

Werkmeister, Lucyle. *The London Daily Press, 1772–1792*, U of Nebraska P, 1963.

'What is Abolition?' *The Slave's Friend*, vol. 3, no. 2, 1837, p. 3.

Wheeler, Roxann. *The Complexion of Race: Categories of Difference in Eighteenth-Century British Culture*. Philadelphia: U of Pennsylvania P, 2000.

Williams, Cynric R. *Hamel, the Obeah Man*, edited by Tim Watson and Candace Ward, Broadview, 2010.

Wilson, Kathleen. 'Citizenship, Empire in the English Provinces, c. 1720–1790'. *Eighteenth-Century Studies*, vol. 29, no. 1, 1995, pp. 69–96.

Wohlgemut, Esther. *Romantic Cosmopolitanism*. Palgrave Macmillan, 2009.

Wollstonecraft, Mary. Review of *A Discourse on the Love of our Country*, by R. Price. *Analytical Review*, vol. 5, 1789, pp. 471–72.

———. Review of *Travels in the United States of North America*, by J. P. Brissot. *Analytical Review*, vol. 11, no. 72, 1791, pp. 37–43.

———. *A Short Residence in Sweden, Norway and Denmark*, edited by Richard Holmes, Penguin, 1987.

———. *A Vindication of the Rights of Men; A Vindication of the Rights of Woman; A Historical View of the French Revolution*. Edited by Janet Todd, Oxford UP, 1994.

———. *A Vindication of the Rights of Woman and The Wrongs of Woman, or Maria*. Edited by Anne K. Mellor and Noelle Chao, Longman Cultural Editions, 2007.

———. *The Works of Mary Wollstonecraft*. Edited by Janet Todd and Marilyn Butler, vol. 7, New York UP 1989.

The Woman of Colour. 1808. Edited by Lyndon J. Dominique, Broadview, 2008.

Woolman, John. *The Works of John Woolman*. New York: Johnson and Wood, 1807.

Wordsworth, William. 'Preface to Lyrical Ballads'. *Wordsworth's Poetry and Prose*, edited by Nicholas Halmi, Norton, 2014, pp. 149–86.

Yang, Chi-Ming. *Performing China: Virtue, Commerce, and Orientalism in Eighteenth-Century England, 1660–1760*. Johns Hopkins UP, 2011.

Yao, Sijia. 'Pessimistic Chinese Cosmopolitanism and Jia Zhangke's *The World*'. *The Comparatist*, vol. 43, 2019, pp. 147–58.

Yates, Francis. *Astraea*. Routledge, 1975.

Zerubavel, E. 'Lumping and Splitting: Notes on Social Classification'. *Sociological Forum*, vol. 11, 1996, pp. 421–33.

Zonana, Joyce. '"They Will Prove the Truth of My Tale": Safie's Letters as the Feminist Core of Mary Shelley's *Frankenstein*'. *The Journal of Narrative Technique*, vol. 21, no. 2 1991, pp. 170–84.

Index

EU Authorised Representative:
Easy Access System Europe Mustamäe tee 50, 10621 Tallinn, Estonia
gpsr.requests@easproject.com

Printed and bound by CPI Group (UK) Ltd, Croydon, CR0 4YY
29/09/2026
02224981-0011